# CAGE!

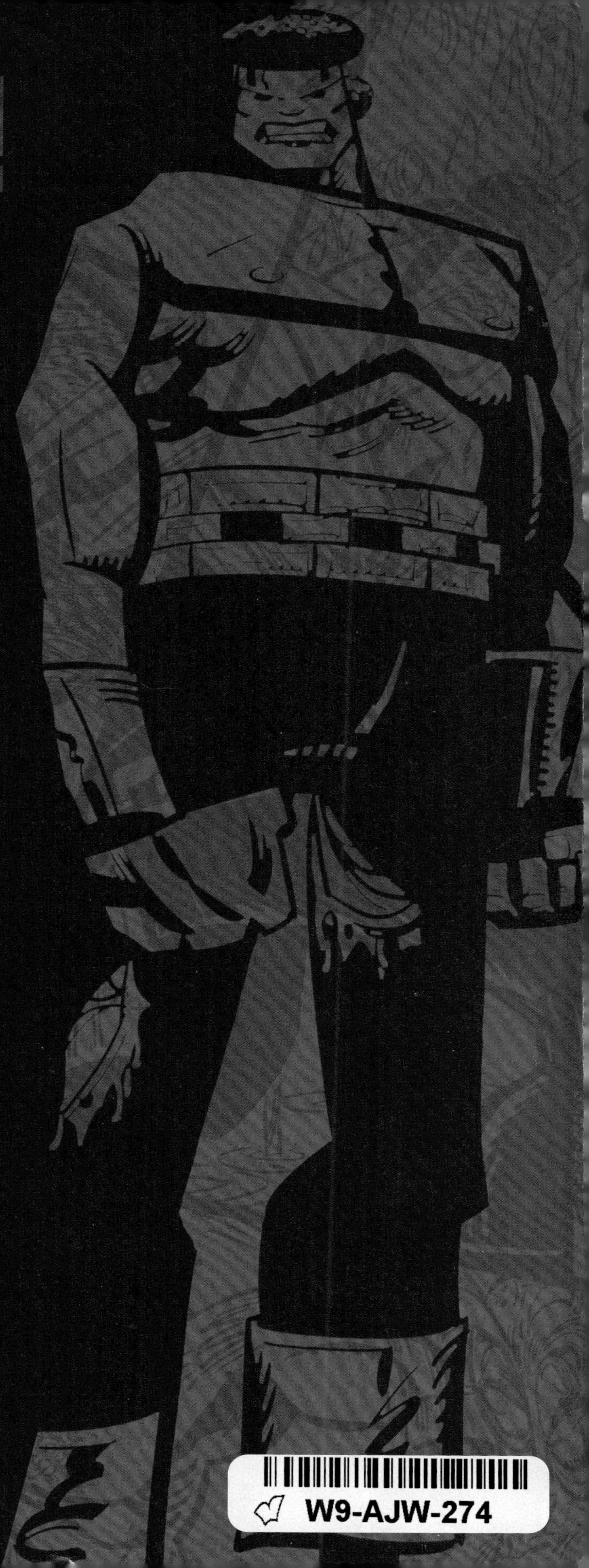

**GENNDY TARTAKOVSKY**
Writer/Penciler

**STEPHEN DeSTEFANO**
Inker

**SCOTT WILLS (#1, #3-4) & BILL WRAY (#2) WITH GENNDY TARTAKOVSKY (#2)**
Colorists

**VC's CLAYTON COWLES**
Letterer

**GENNDY TARTAKOVSKY, STEPHEN DeSTEFANO & SCOTT WILLS**
Cover Art

**ALANNA SMITH**
Assistant Editor

**AUBREY SITTERSON WITH TOM BREVOORT**
Editors

Special Thanks to
Alejandro Arbona & Michael Horwitz

Collection Editor: **Jennifer Grünwald**
Assistant Editor: **Caitlin O'Connell**
Associate Managing Editor: **Kateri Woody**
Editor, Special Projects: **Mark D. Beazley**
VP Production & Special Projects: **Jeff Youngquist**
SVP Print, Sales & Marketing: **David Gabriel**
Book Designer: **Adam Del Re**

Editor in Chief: **Axel Alonso**
Chief Creative Officer: **Joe Quesada**
President: **Dan Buckley**
Executive Producer: **Alan Fine**

E! Contains material originally published in magazine form as CAGE! #1-4 and ) FOR HIRE #1. First printing 2017. ISBN# 978-0-7851-2786-4. Published by VEL WORLDWIDE, INC., a subsidiary of MARVEL ENTERTAINMENT, LLC. OFFICE OF LICATION: 135 West 50th Street, New York, NY 10020. Copyright © 2017 MARVEL imilarity between any of the names, characters, persons, and/or institutions in magazine with those of any living or dead person or institution is intended, and such similarity which may exist is purely coincidental. **Printed in Canada.** DAN KLEY, President, Marvel Entertainment; JOE QUESADA, Chief Creative Officer; TOM VOORT, SVP of Publishing; DAVID BOGART, SVP of Business Affairs & Operations, shing & Partnership; C.B. CEBULSKI, VP of Brand Management & Development, DAVID GABRIEL, SVP of Sales & Marketing, Publishing; JEFF YOUNGQUIST, VP of uction & Special Projects; DAN CARR, Executive Director of Publishing Technology; MORALES, Director of Publishing Operations; SUSAN CRESPI, Production Manager; LEE, Chairman Emeritus. For information regarding advertising in Marvel Comics Marvel.com, please contact Vit DeBellis, Integrated Sales Manager, at vdebellis@ el.com. For Marvel subscription inquiries, please call 888-511-5480. **Manufactured een 2/24/2017 and 3/28/2017 by SOLISCO PRINTERS, SCOTT, QC, CANADA.**

8 7 6 5 4 3 2 1

DIG IT!

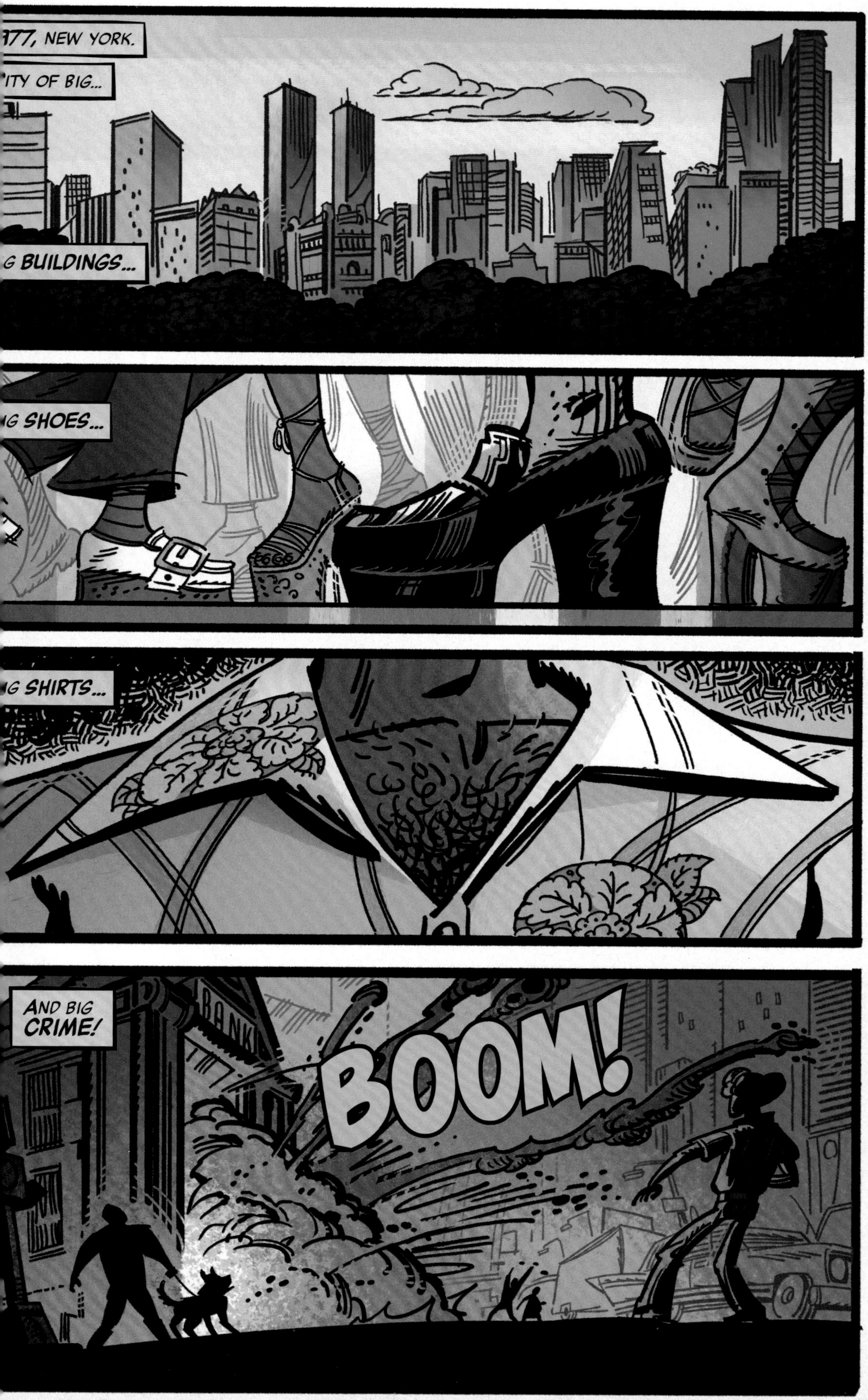

977, NEW YORK.
ITY OF BIG...
G BUILDINGS...
G SHOES...
G SHIRTS...
AND BIG CRIME!
BANK
BOOM!

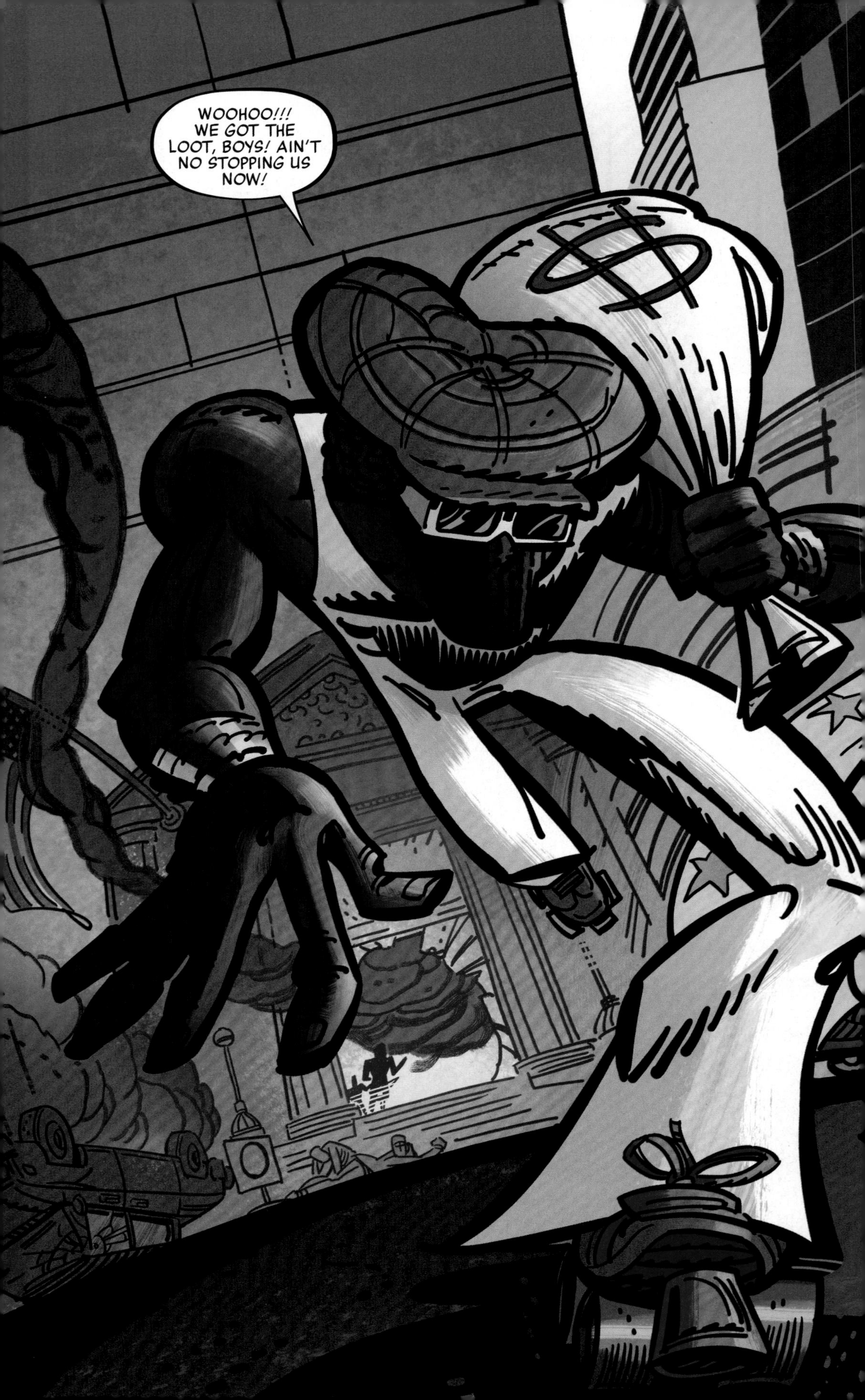
WOOHOO!!! WE GOT THE LOOT, BOYS! AIN'T NO STOPPING US NOW!

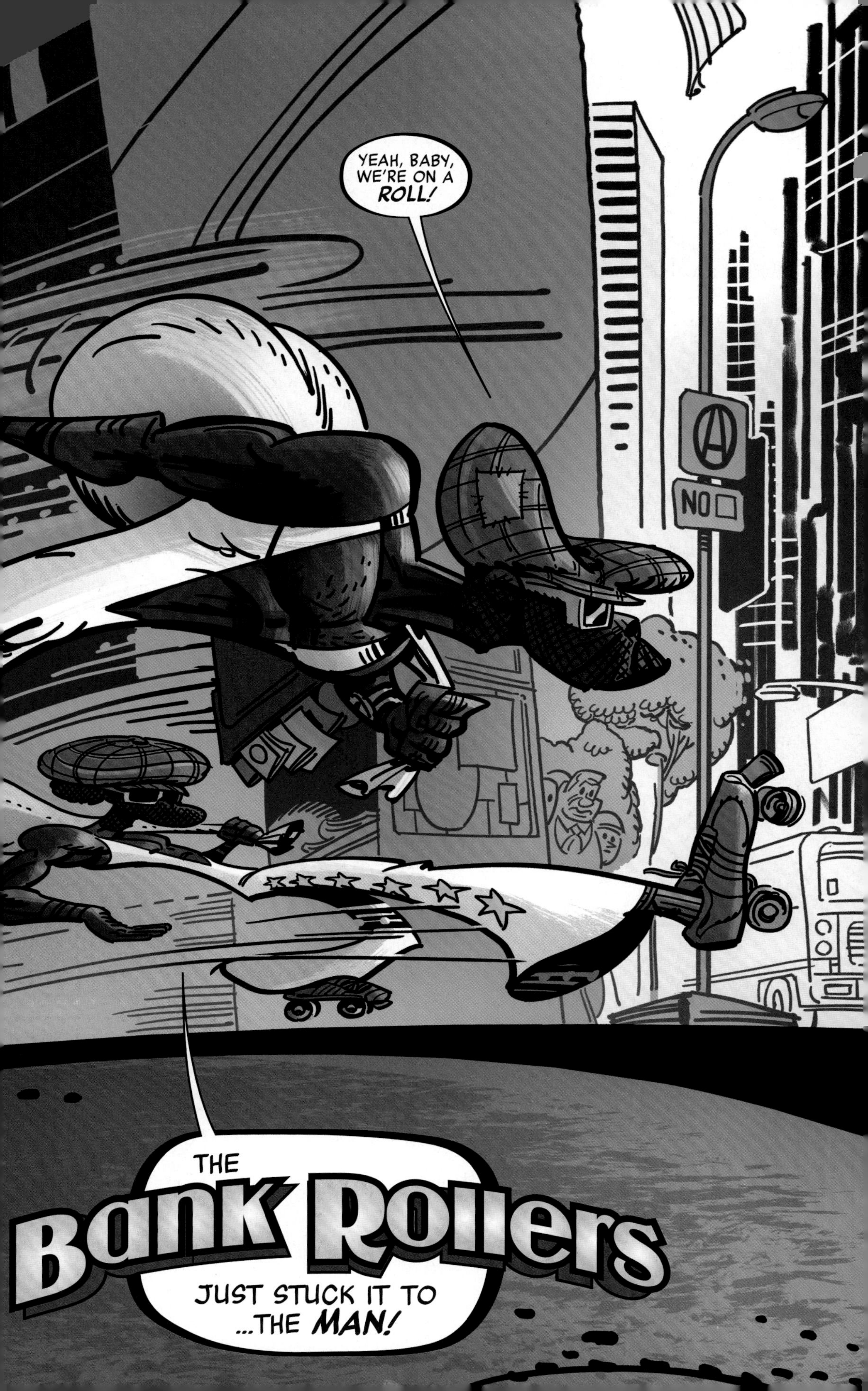
YEAH, BABY, WE'RE ON A ROLL!
NO
THE Bank Rollers JUST STUCK IT TO ...THE MAN!

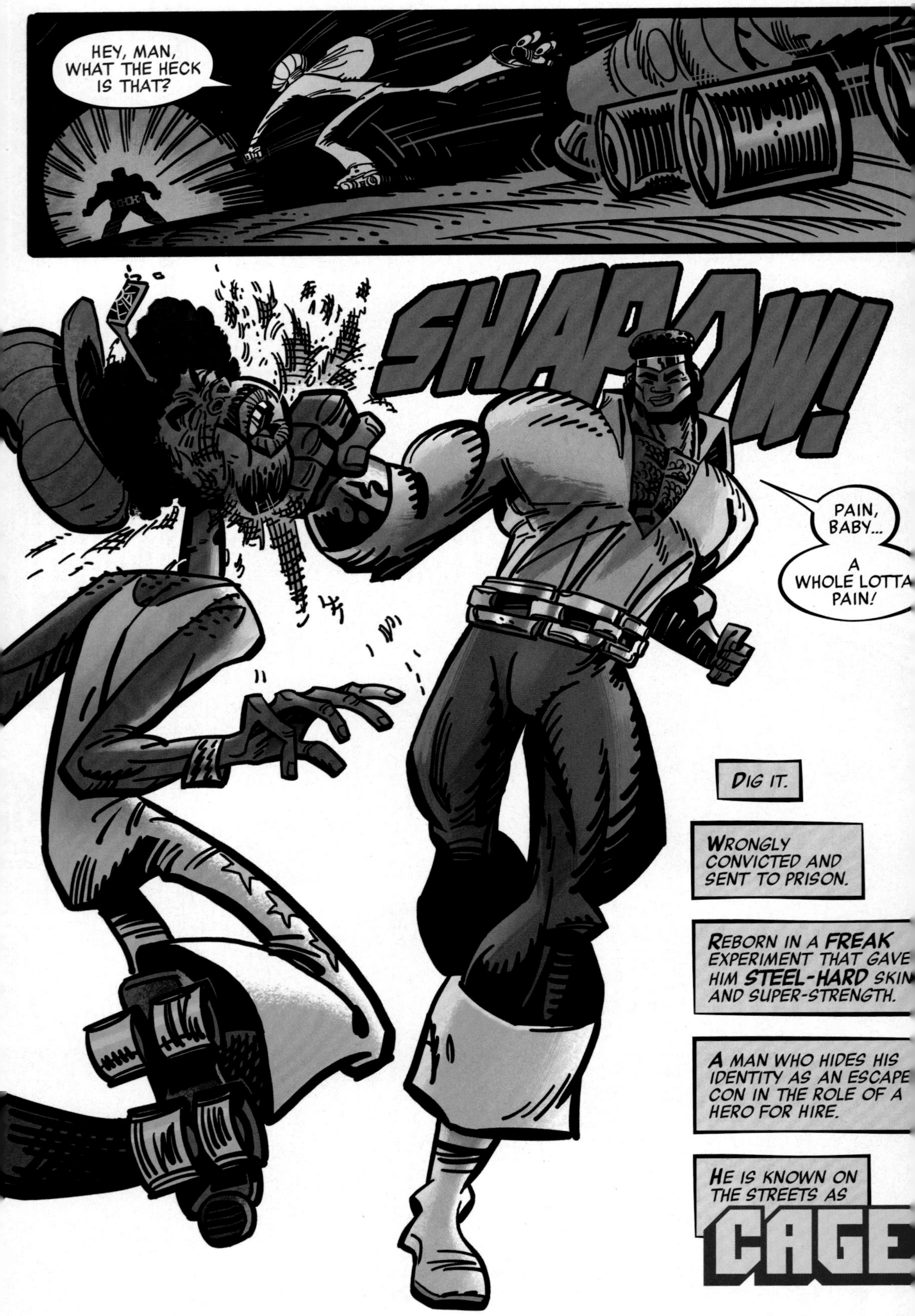
HEY, MAN, WHAT THE HECK IS THAT?
SHABOW!!
PAIN, BABY...
A WHOLE LOTTA PAIN!
DIG IT.
WRONGLY CONVICTED AND SENT TO PRISON.
REBORN IN A FREAK EXPERIMENT THAT GAVE HIM STEEL-HARD SKIN AND SUPER-STRENGTH.
A MAN WHO HIDES HIS IDENTITY AS AN ESCAPED CON IN THE ROLE OF A HERO FOR HIRE.
HE IS KNOWN ON THE STREETS AS
CAGE

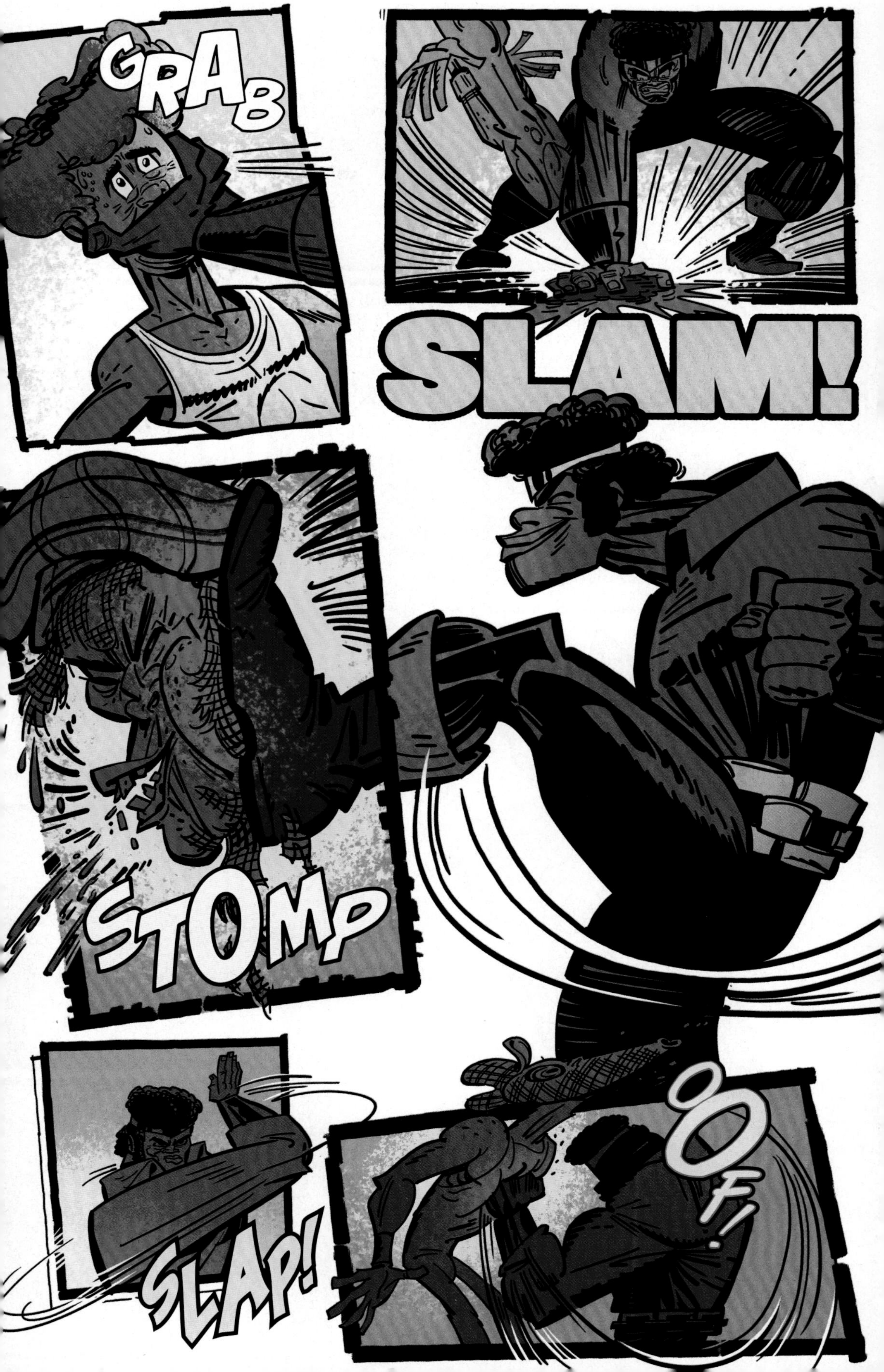
GRAB
SLAM!
STOMP
SLAP!
OOF!

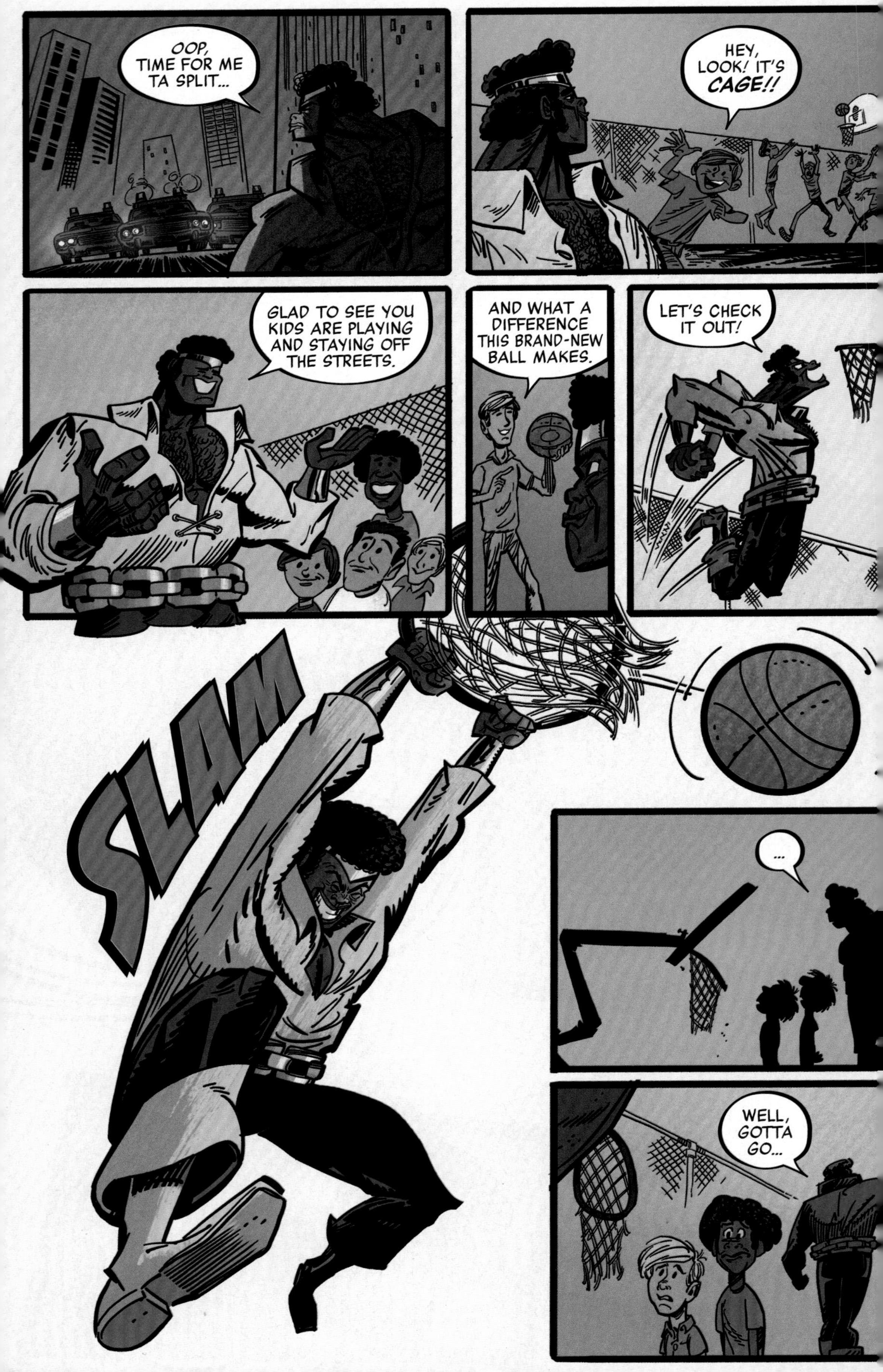
OOP, TIME FOR ME TA SPLIT...
HEY, LOOK! IT'S CAGE!!
GLAD TO SEE YOU KIDS ARE PLAYING AND STAYING OFF THE STREETS.
AND WHAT A DIFFERENCE THIS BRAND-NEW BALL MAKES.
LET'S CHECK IT OUT!
SLAM
...
WELL, GOTTA GO...

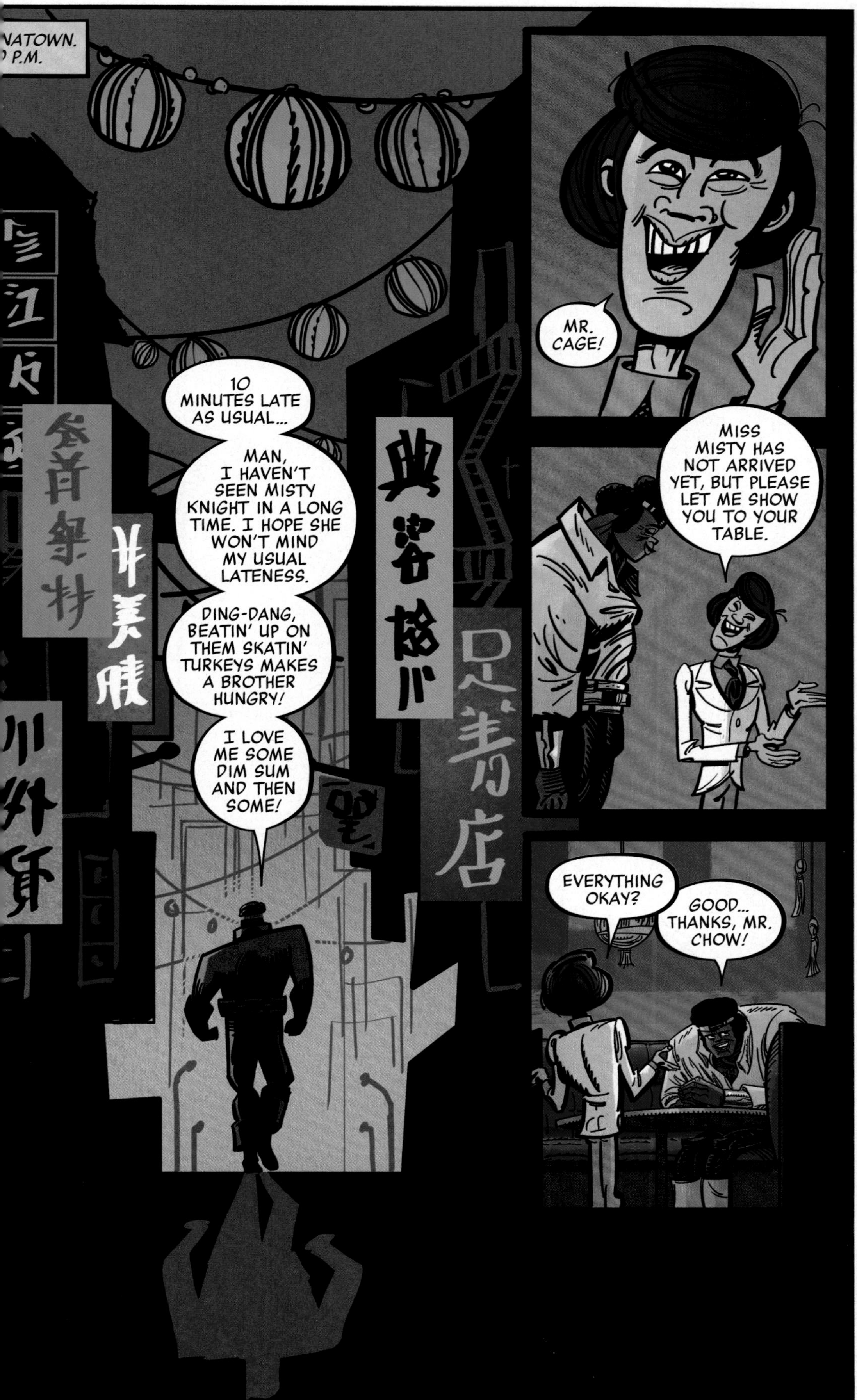
NATOWN.
P.M.
10 MINUTES LATE AS USUAL...
MAN, I HAVEN'T SEEN MISTY KNIGHT IN A LONG TIME. I HOPE SHE WON'T MIND MY USUAL LATENESS.
DING-DANG, BEATIN' UP ON THEM SKATIN' TURKEYS MAKES A BROTHER HUNGRY!
I LOVE ME SOME DIM SUM AND THEN SOME!
MR. CAGE!
MISS MISTY HAS NOT ARRIVED YET, BUT PLEASE LET ME SHOW YOU TO YOUR TABLE.
EVERYTHING OKAY?
GOOD... THANKS, MR. CHOW!

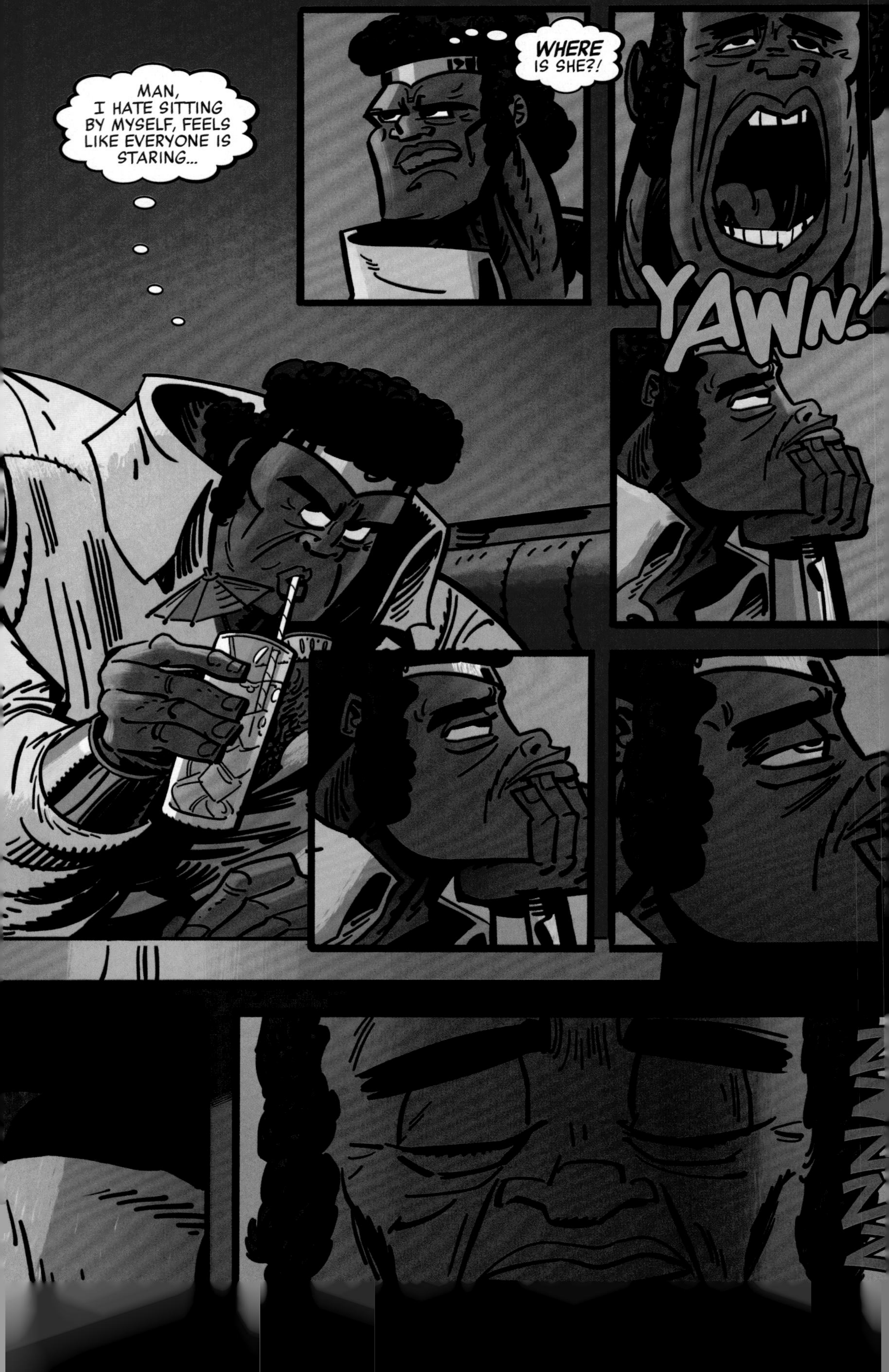

MAN, I HATE SITTING BY MYSELF, FEELS LIKE EVERYONE IS STARING...
WHERE IS SHE?!
YAWN!

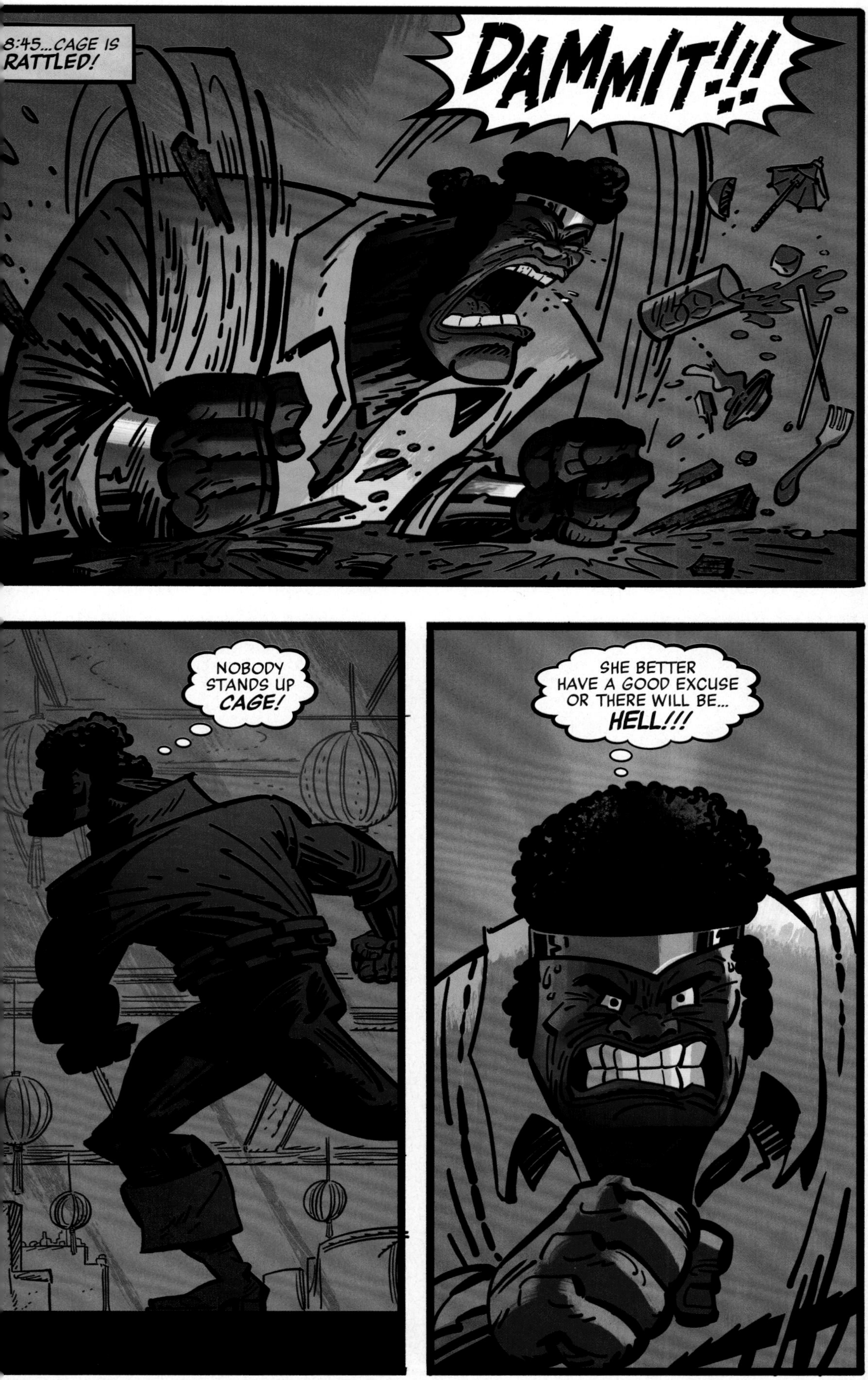
8:45...CAGE IS RATTLED!
DAMMIT!!!
NOBODY STANDS UP CAGE!
SHE BETTER HAVE A GOOD EXCUSE OR THERE WILL BE... HELL!!!

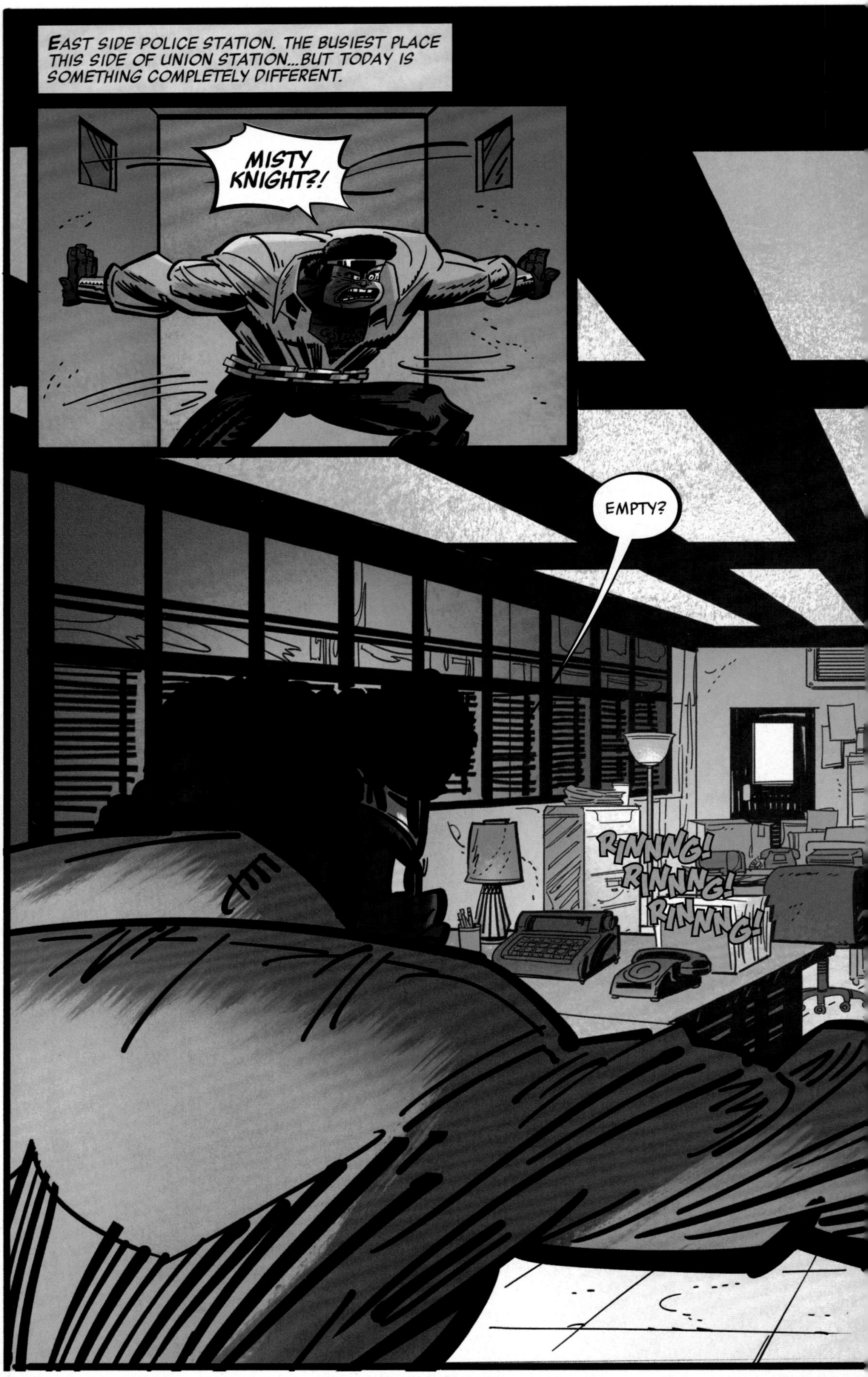
EAST SIDE POLICE STATION. THE BUSIEST PLACE THIS SIDE OF UNION STATION...BUT TODAY IS SOMETHING COMPLETELY DIFFERENT.
MISTY KNIGHT?!
EMPTY?
RINNNG! RINNNG! RINNNG!

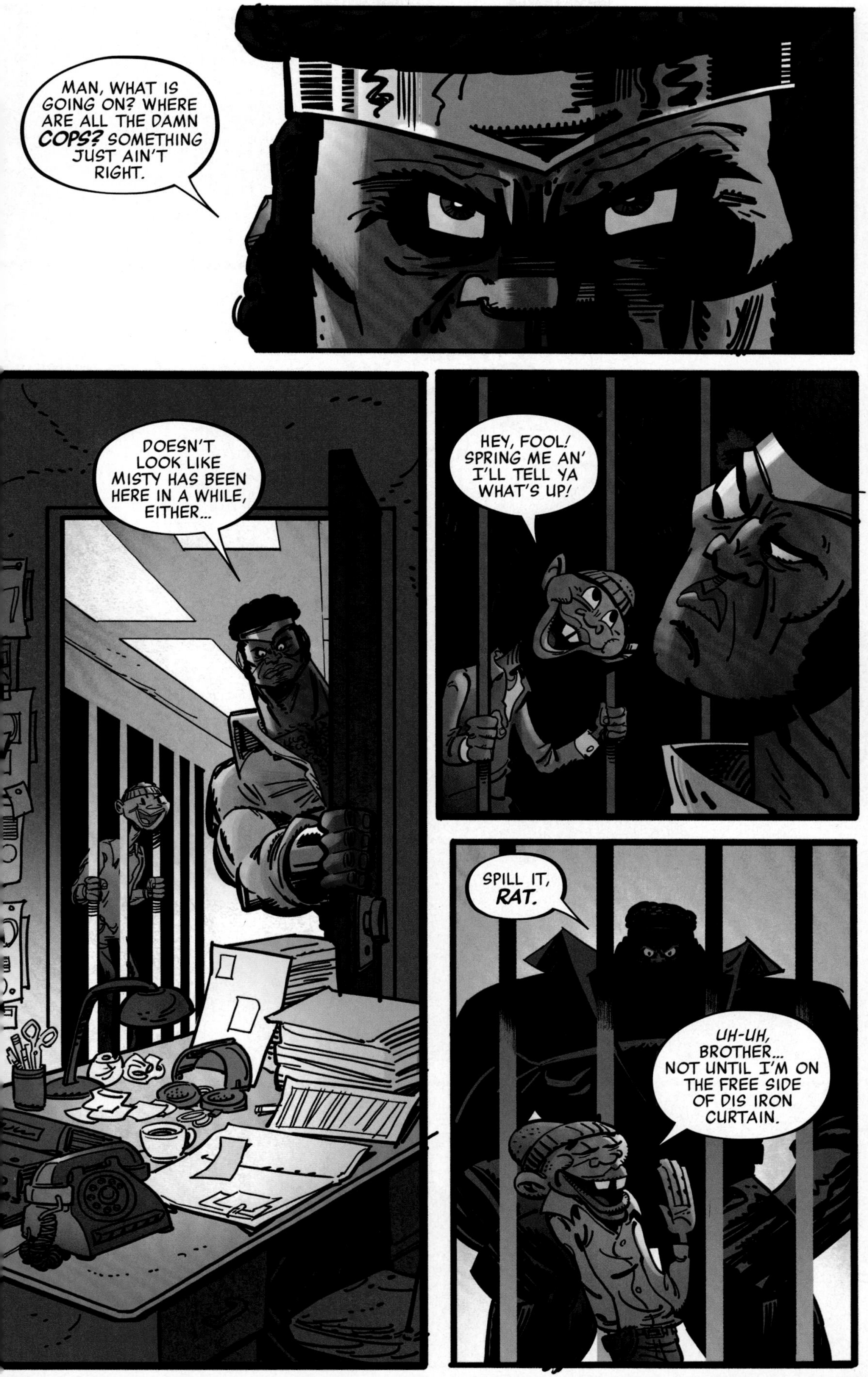
MAN, WHAT IS GOING ON? WHERE ARE ALL THE DAMN COPS? SOMETHING JUST AIN'T RIGHT.
DOESN'T LOOK LIKE MISTY HAS BEEN HERE IN A WHILE, EITHER...
HEY, FOOL! SPRING ME AN' I'LL TELL YA WHAT'S UP!
SPILL IT, RAT.
UH-UH, BROTHER... NOT UNTIL I'M ON THE FREE SIDE OF DIS IRON CURTAIN.

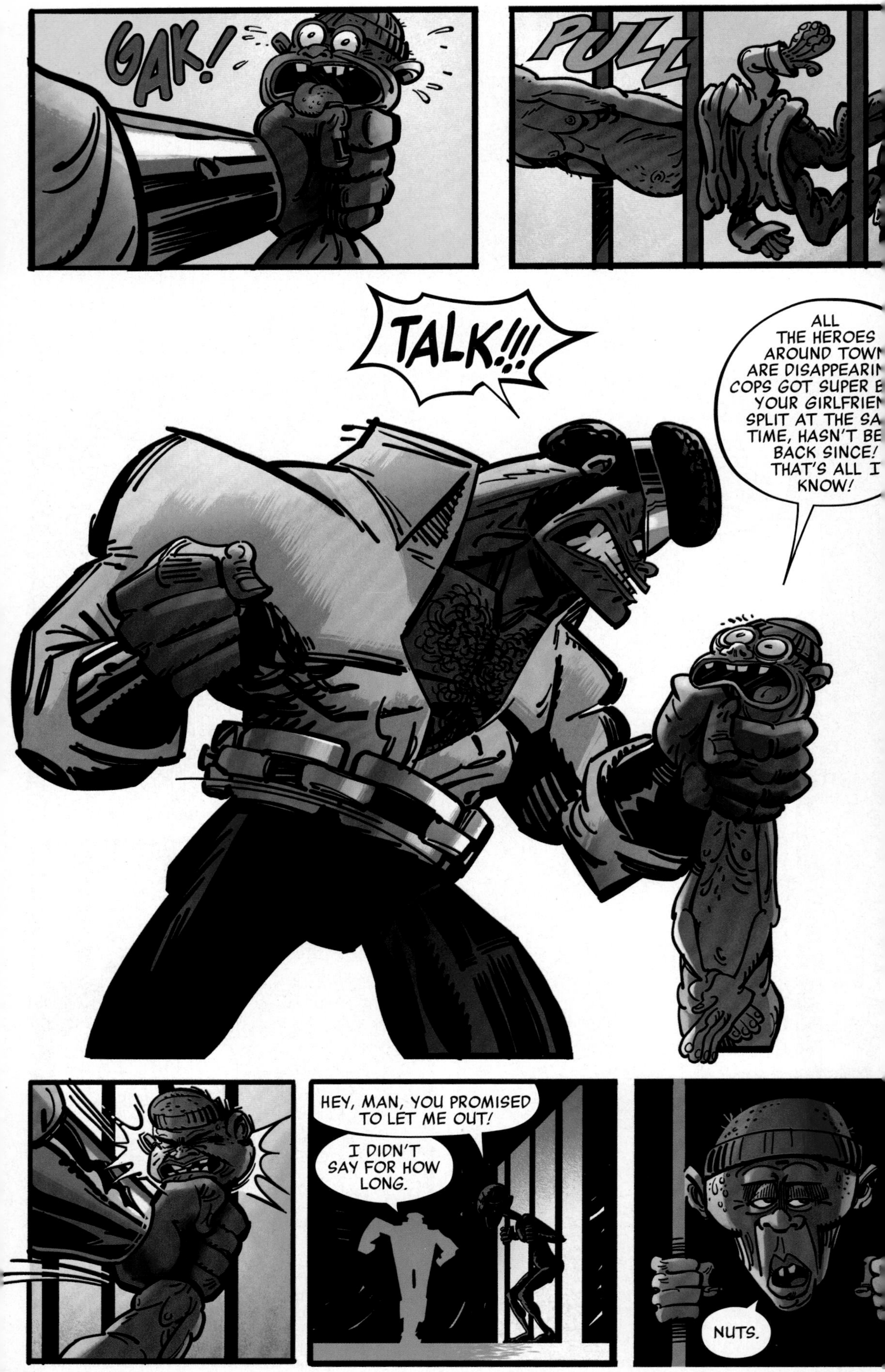
GAK!
PULL
TALK!!!
ALL THE HEROES AROUND TOWN ARE DISAPPEARIN COPS GOT SUPER E YOUR GIRLFRIEN SPLIT AT THE SA TIME, HASN'T BE BACK SINCE! THAT'S ALL I KNOW!
HEY, MAN, YOU PROMISED TO LET ME OUT!
I DIDN'T SAY FOR HOW LONG.
NUTS.

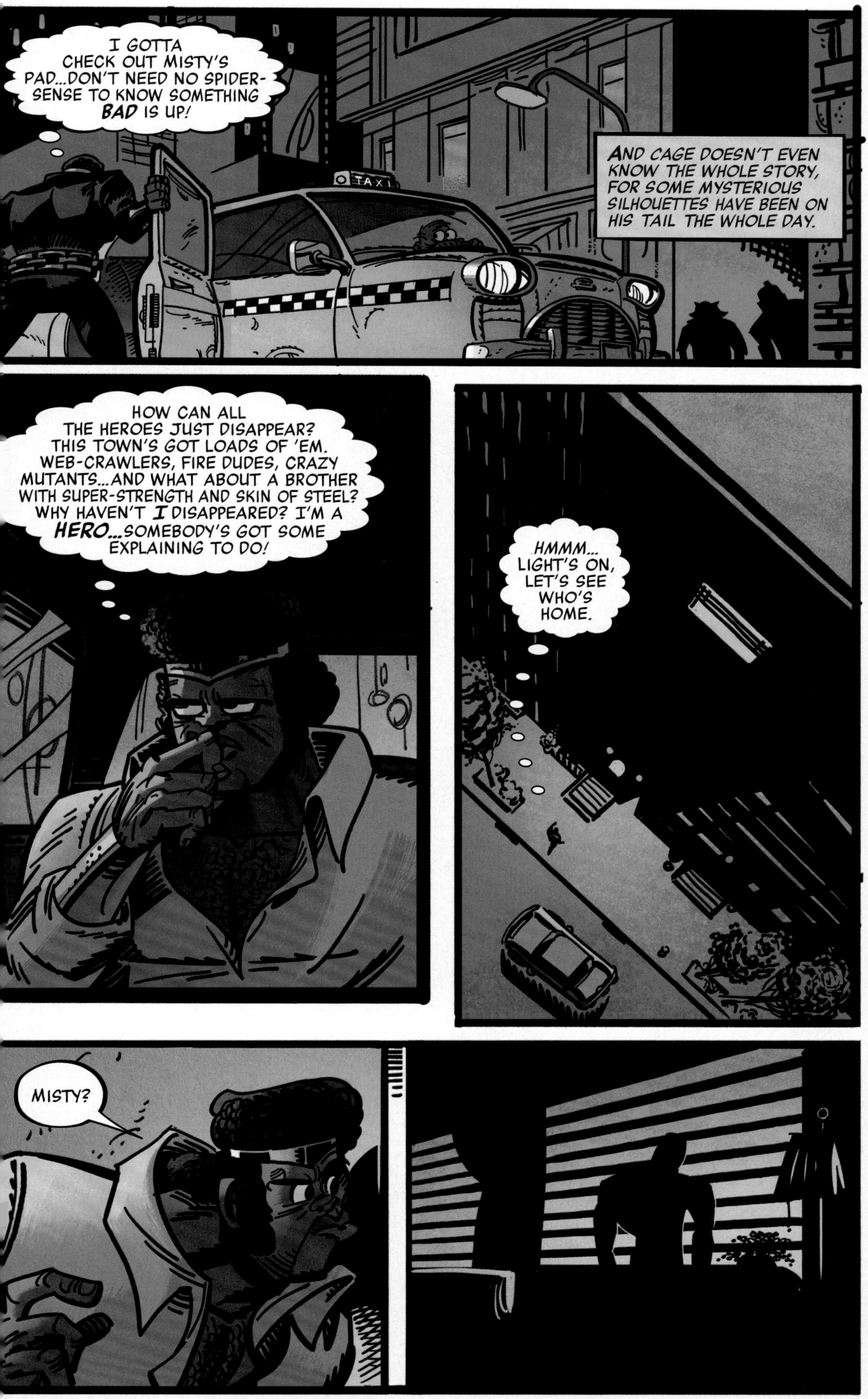
I GOTTA CHECK OUT MISTY'S PAD...DON'T NEED NO SPIDER-SENSE TO KNOW SOMETHING BAD IS UP!
TAXI
AND CAGE DOESN'T EVEN KNOW THE WHOLE STORY, FOR SOME MYSTERIOUS SILHOUETTES HAVE BEEN ON HIS TAIL THE WHOLE DAY.
HOW CAN ALL THE HEROES JUST DISAPPEAR? THIS TOWN'S GOT LOADS OF 'EM. WEB-CRAWLERS, FIRE DUDES, CRAZY MUTANTS...AND WHAT ABOUT A BROTHER WITH SUPER-STRENGTH AND SKIN OF STEEL? WHY HAVEN'T I DISAPPEARED? I'M A HERO...SOMEBODY'S GOT SOME EXPLAINING TO DO!
HMMM... LIGHT'S ON, LET'S SEE WHO'S HOME.
MISTY?

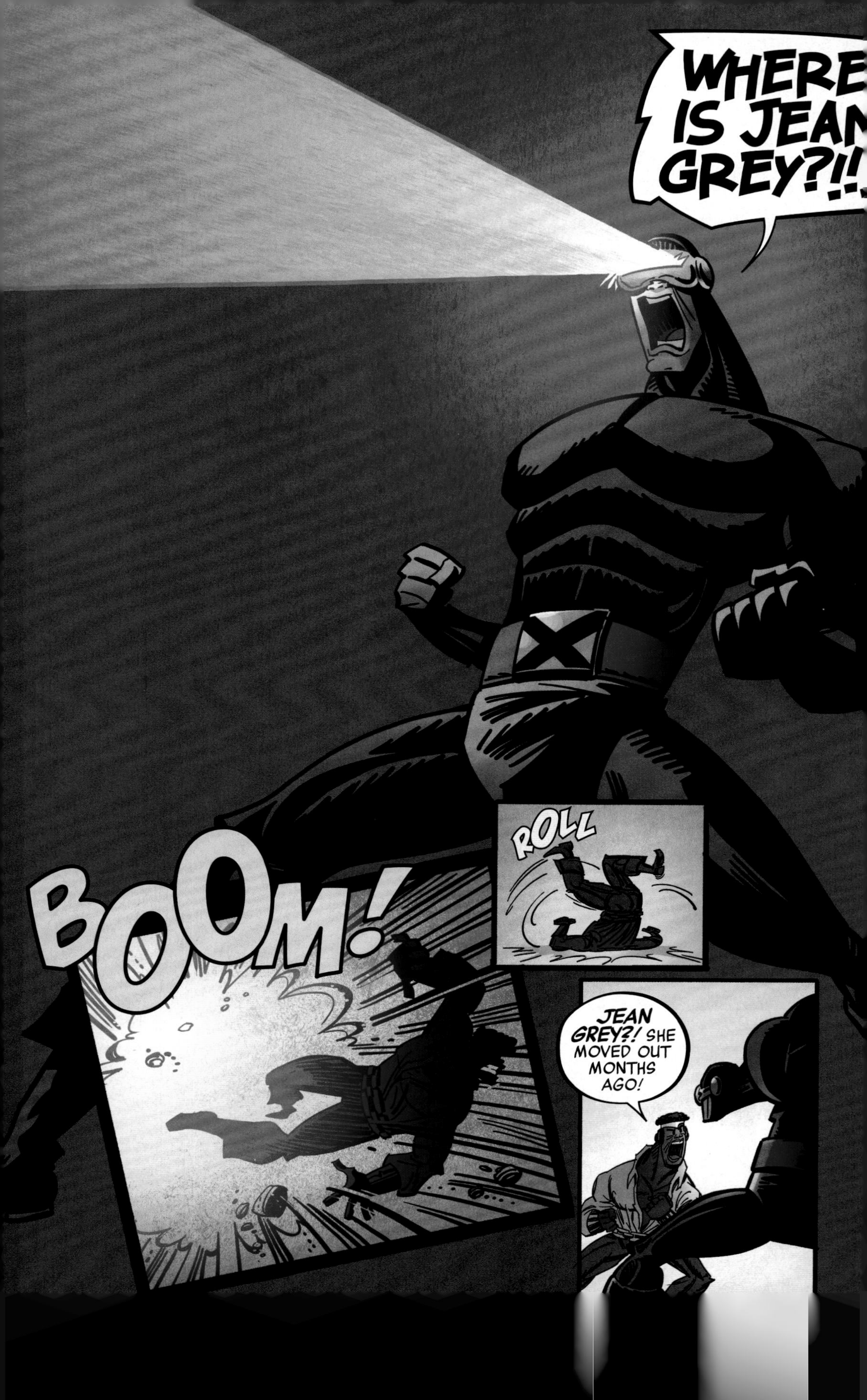
WHERE IS JEAN GREY?!!
BOOM!
ROLL
JEAN GREY?! SHE MOVED OUT MONTHS AGO!

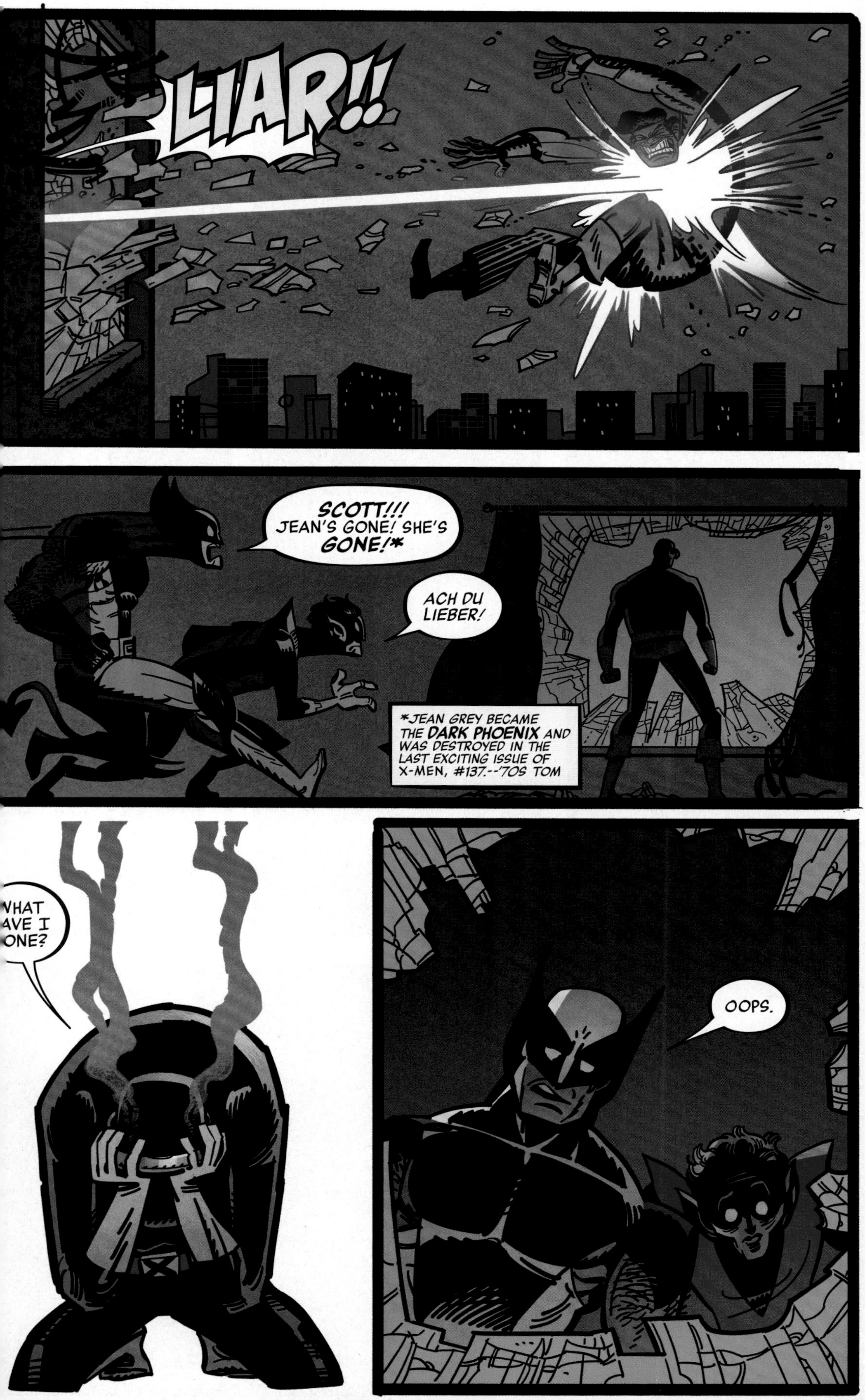
LIAR!!
SCOTT!!! JEAN'S GONE! SHE'S GONE!*
ACH DU LIEBER!
*JEAN GREY BECAME THE DARK PHOENIX AND WAS DESTROYED IN THE LAST EXCITING ISSUE OF X-MEN, #137.--'70S TOM
WHAT AVE I ONE?
OOPS.

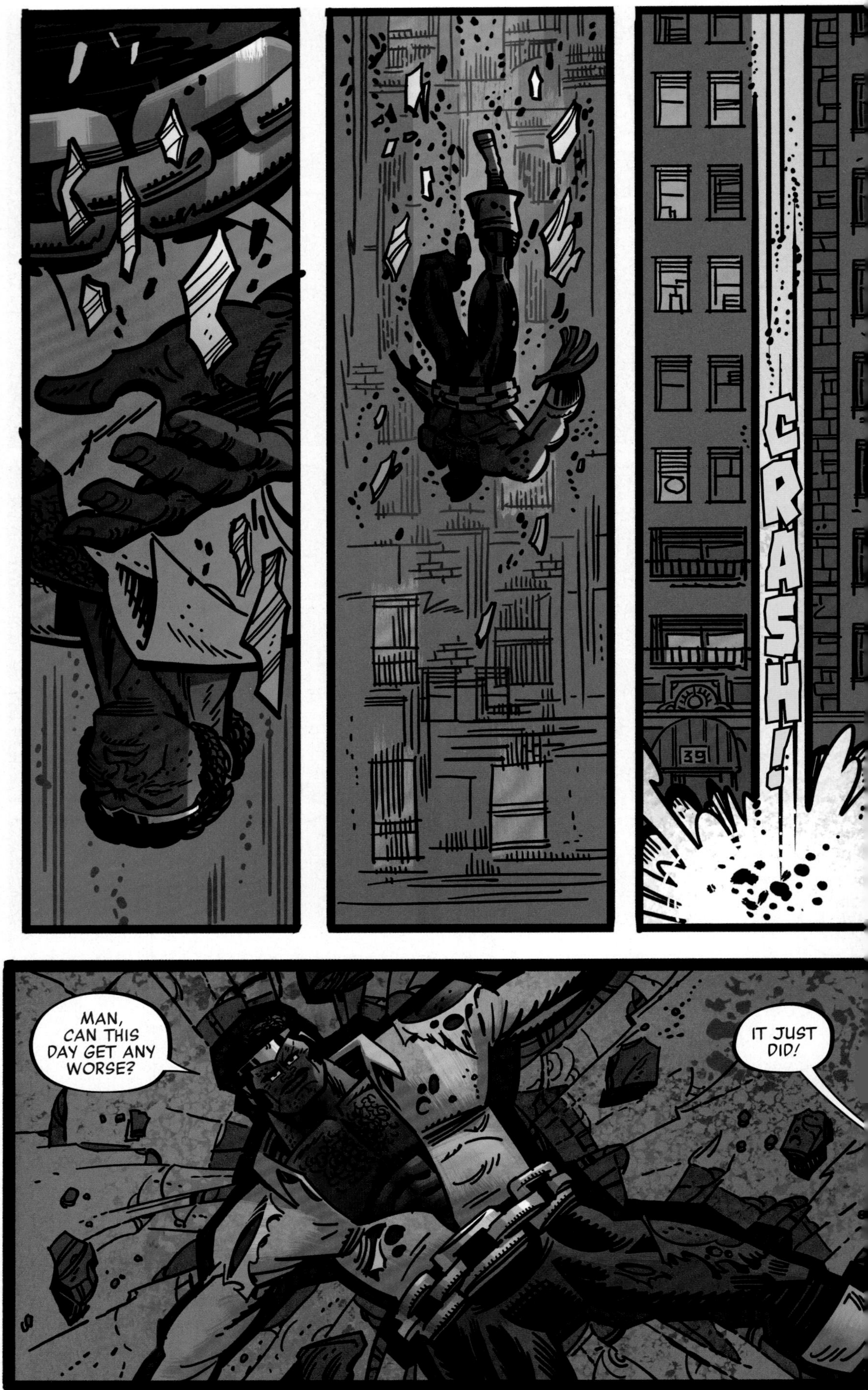
CRASH!
MAN, CAN THIS DAY GET ANY WORSE?
IT JUST DID!

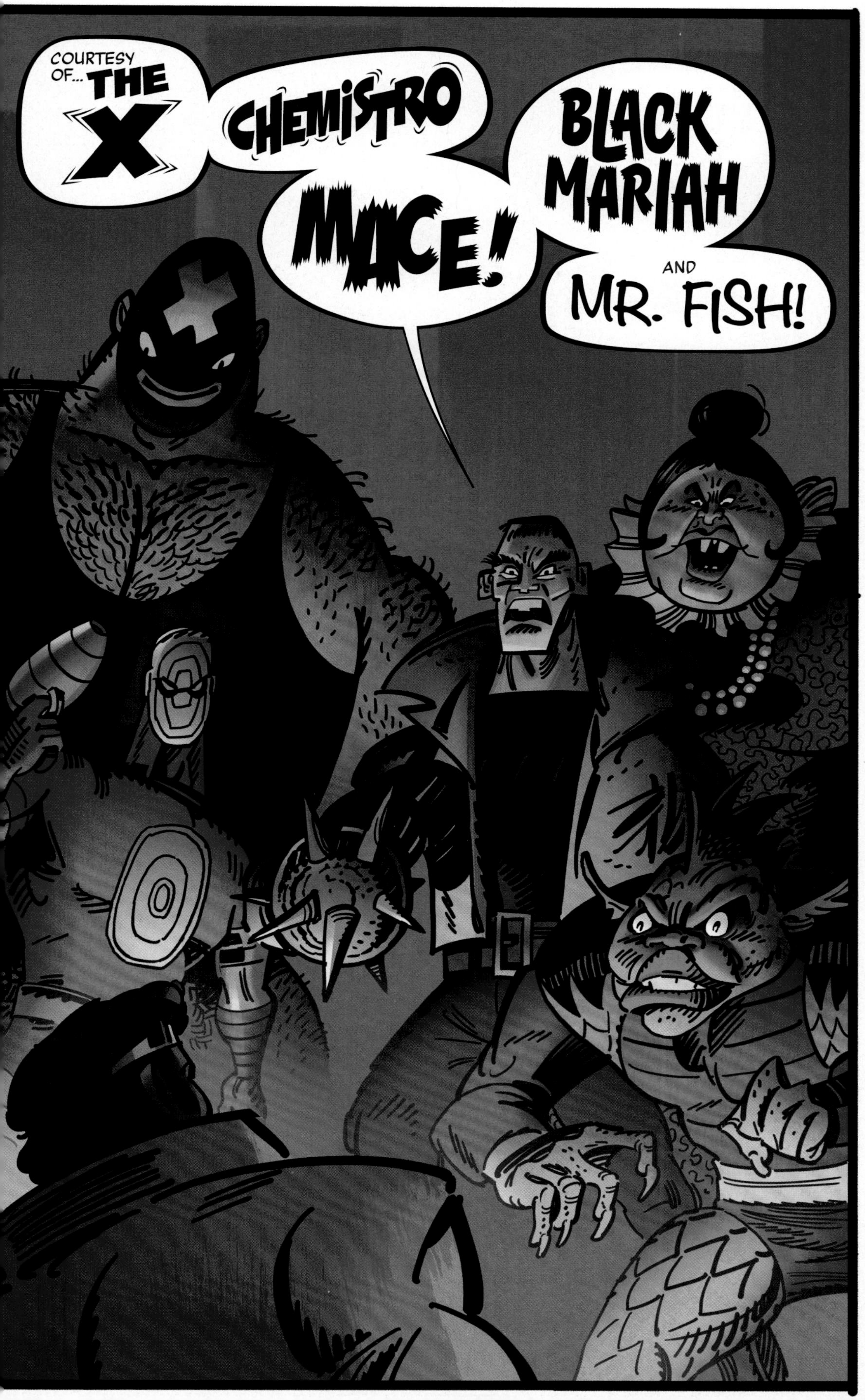
COURTESY OF... THE X
CHEMISTRO
MACE!
BLACK MARIAH
AND MR. FISH!

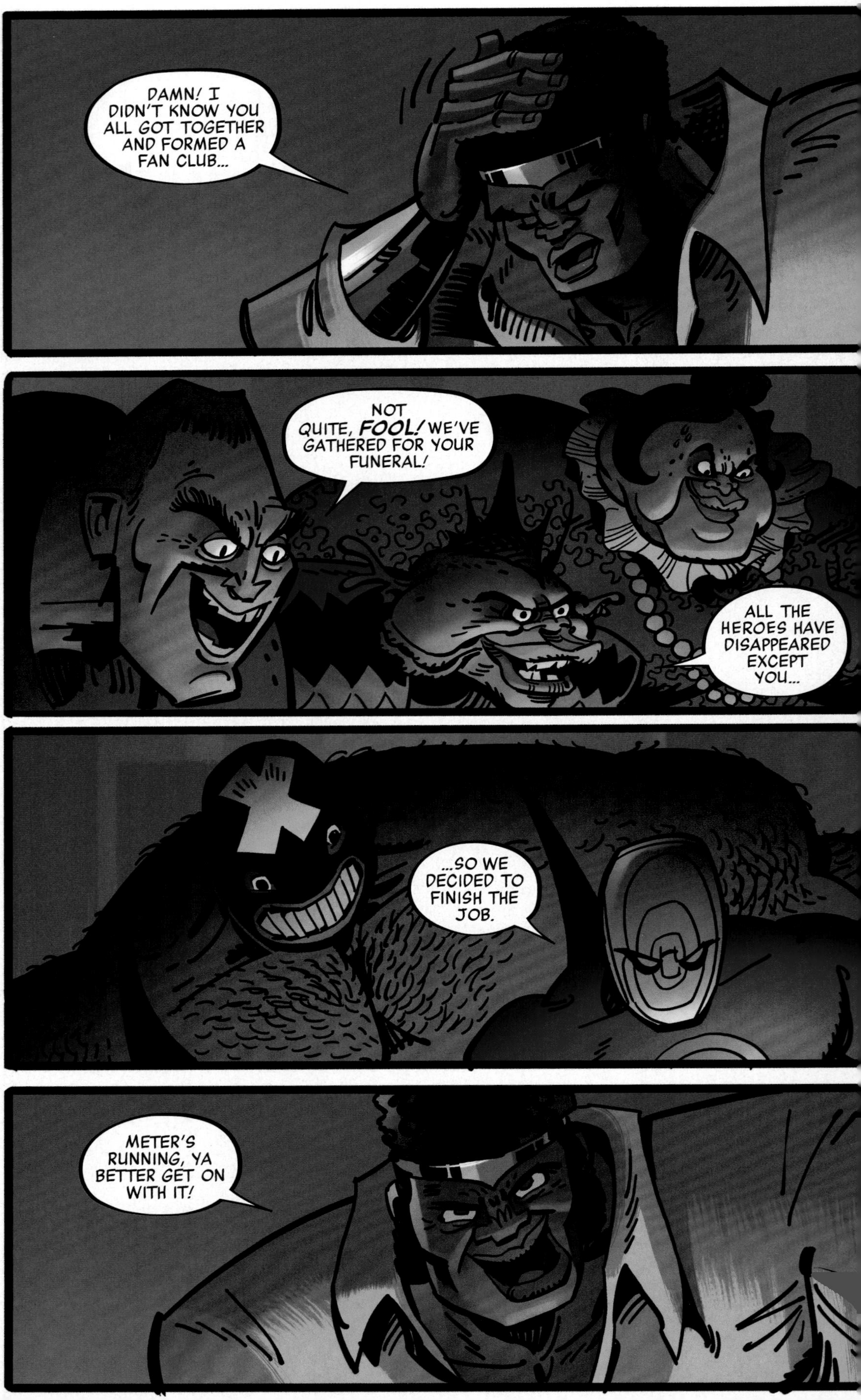
DAMN! I DIDN'T KNOW YOU ALL GOT TOGETHER AND FORMED A FAN CLUB...
NOT QUITE, **FOOL!** WE'VE GATHERED FOR YOUR FUNERAL!
ALL THE HEROES HAVE DISAPPEARED EXCEPT YOU...
...SO WE DECIDED TO FINISH THE JOB.
METER'S RUNNING, YA BETTER GET ON WITH IT!

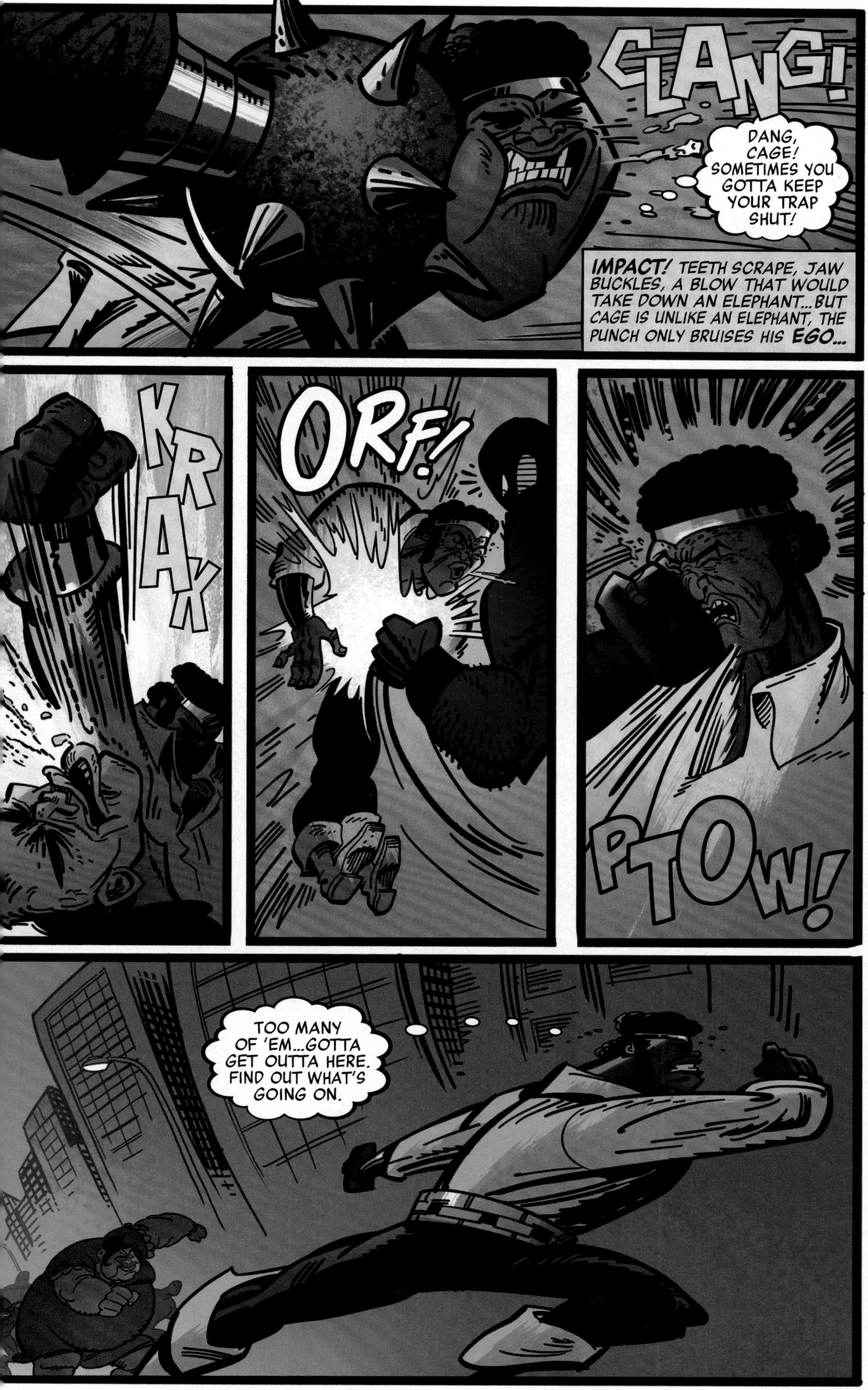
CLANG!
DANG, CAGE! SOMETIMES YOU GOTTA KEEP YOUR TRAP SHUT!
IMPACT! TEETH SCRAPE, JAW BUCKLES, A BLOW THAT WOULD TAKE DOWN AN ELEPHANT...BUT CAGE IS UNLIKE AN ELEPHANT, THE PUNCH ONLY BRUISES HIS EGO...
KRAK
ORF!
PTOW!
TOO MANY OF 'EM...GOTTA GET OUTTA HERE. FIND OUT WHAT'S GOING ON.

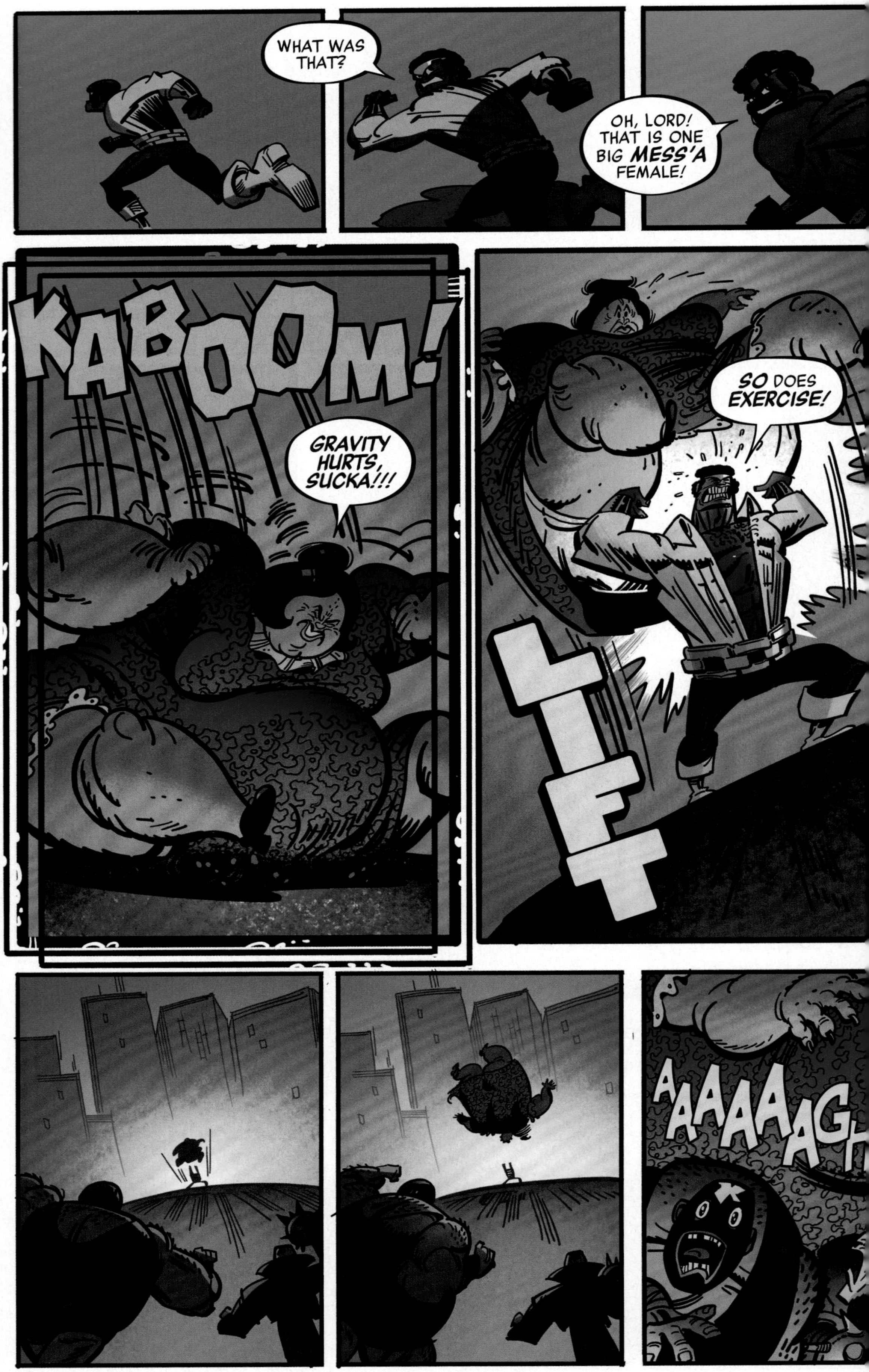
WHAT WAS THAT?
OH, LORD! THAT IS ONE BIG MESS'A FEMALE!
KABOOM!
GRAVITY HURTS, SUCKA!!!
SO DOES EXERCISE!
LIFT
AAAAAAGH

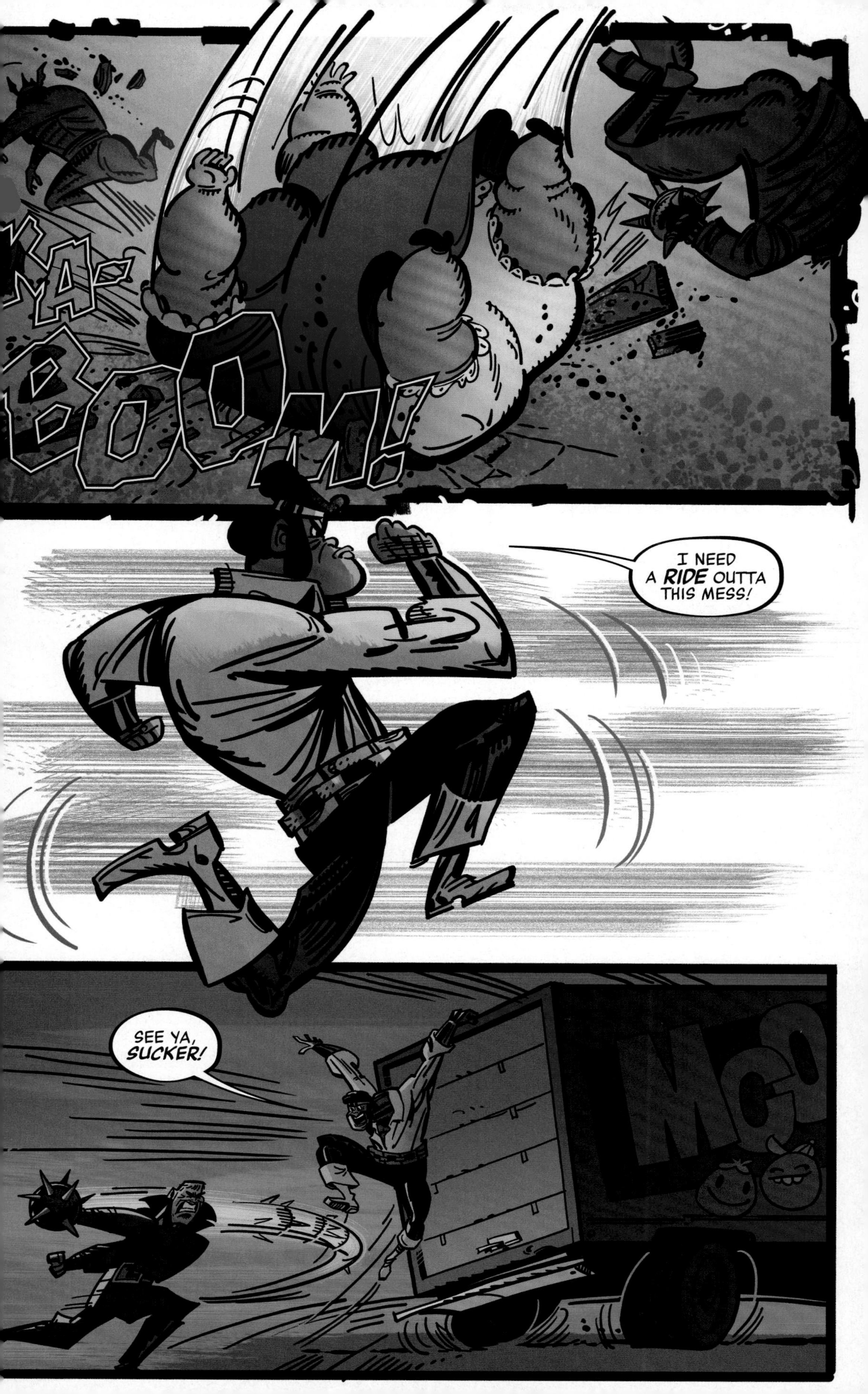
KA-BOOM!
I NEED A RIDE OUTTA THIS MESS!
SEE YA, SUCKER!

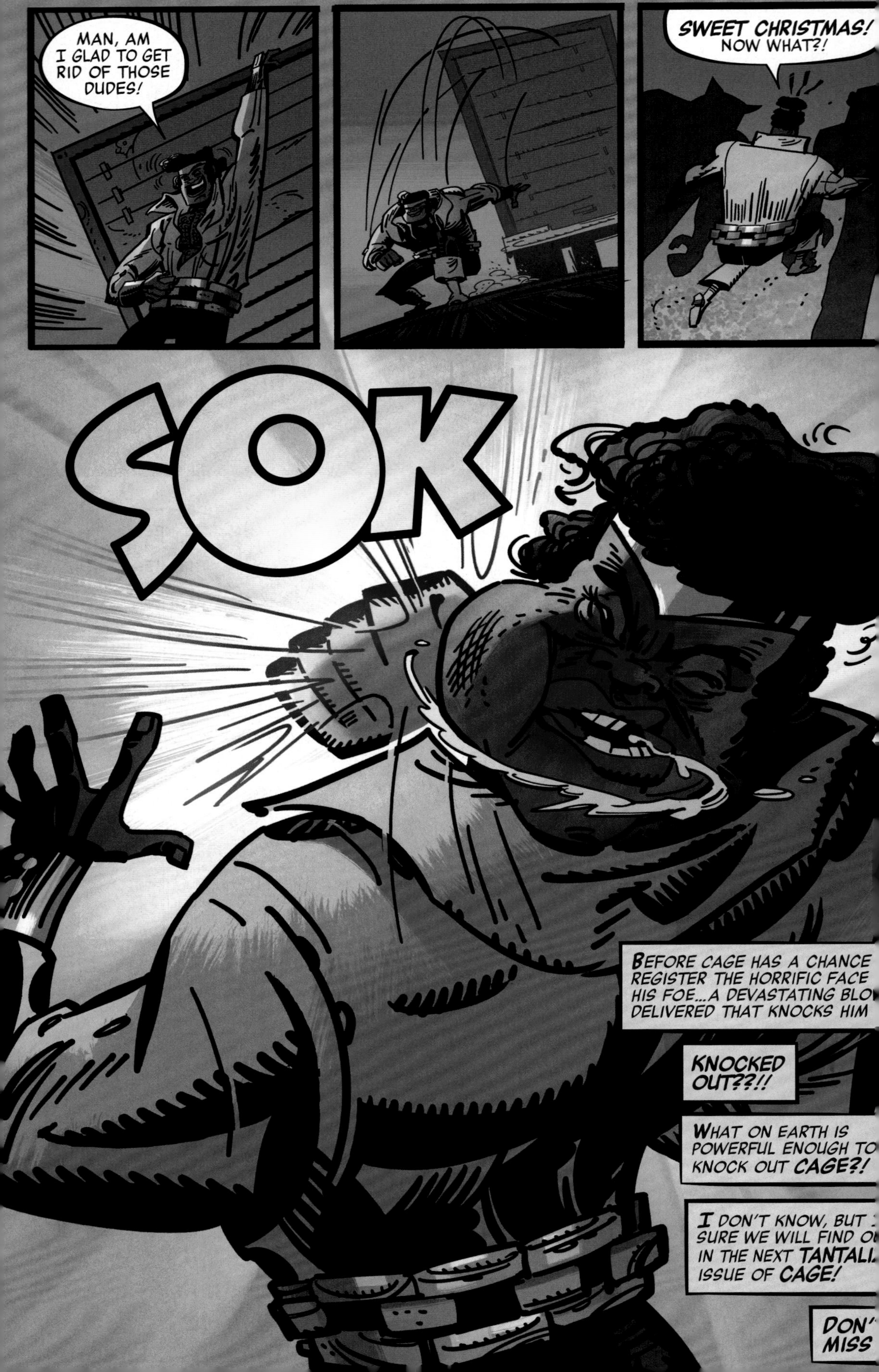
MAN, AM I GLAD TO GET RID OF THOSE DUDES!
SWEET CHRISTMAS! NOW WHAT?!
SOK
BEFORE CAGE HAS A CHANCE REGISTER THE HORRIFIC FACE HIS FOE...A DEVASTATING BLO DELIVERED THAT KNOCKS HIM
KNOCKED OUT??!!
WHAT ON EARTH IS POWERFUL ENOUGH TO KNOCK OUT CAGE?!
I DON'T KNOW, BUT SURE WE WILL FIND O IN THE NEXT TANTALI ISSUE OF CAGE!
DON' MISS

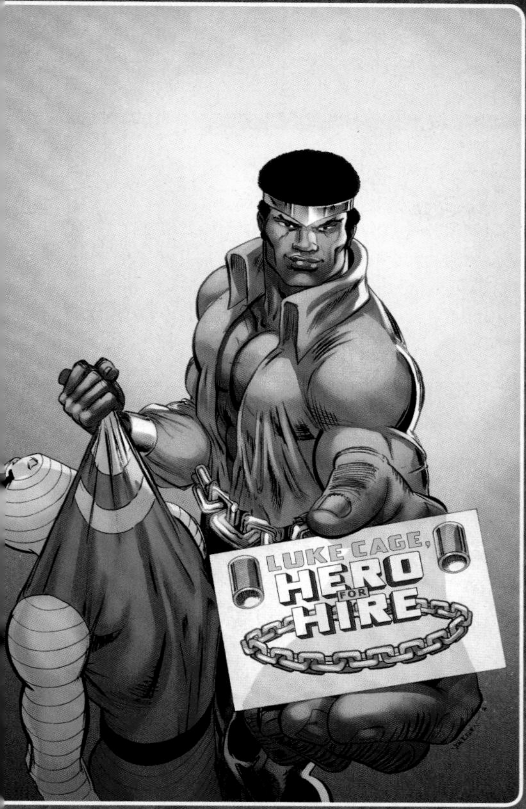
LUKE CAGE,
HERO FOR HIRE

TREVOR VON EEDEN
1 classic variant

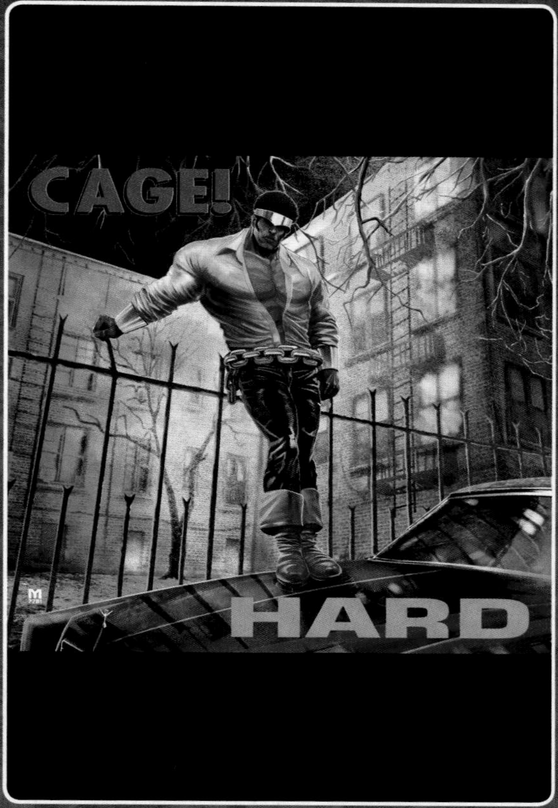
CAGE!
HARD

MARCO D'ALFONSO
1 hip-hop variant

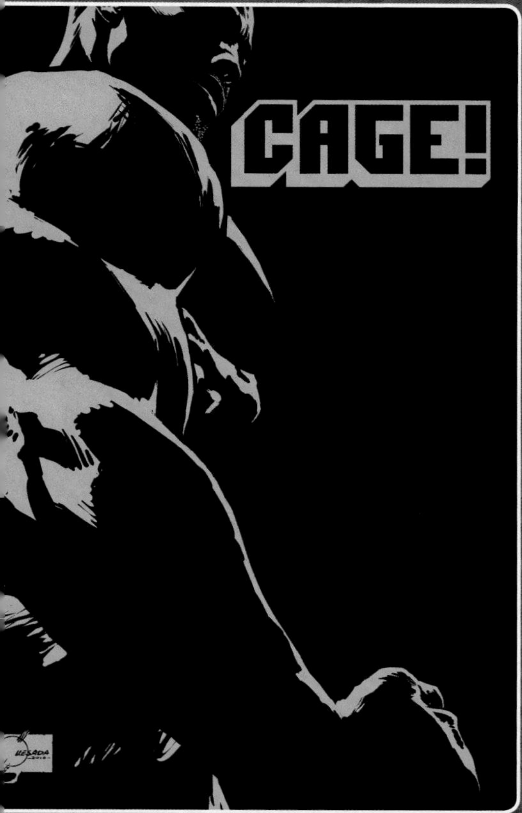
CAGE!

JOE QUESADA
1 variant

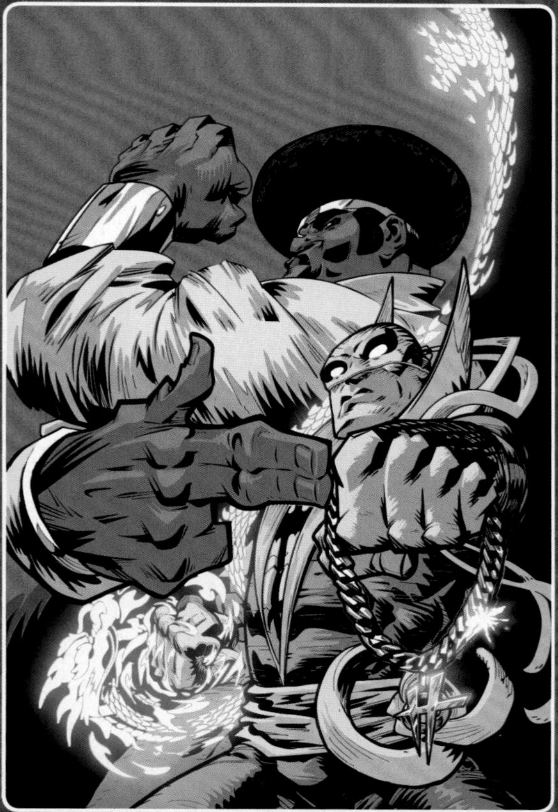

DAMION SCOTT
1 Run the Jewels variant

# CAGE!

## HUNTED

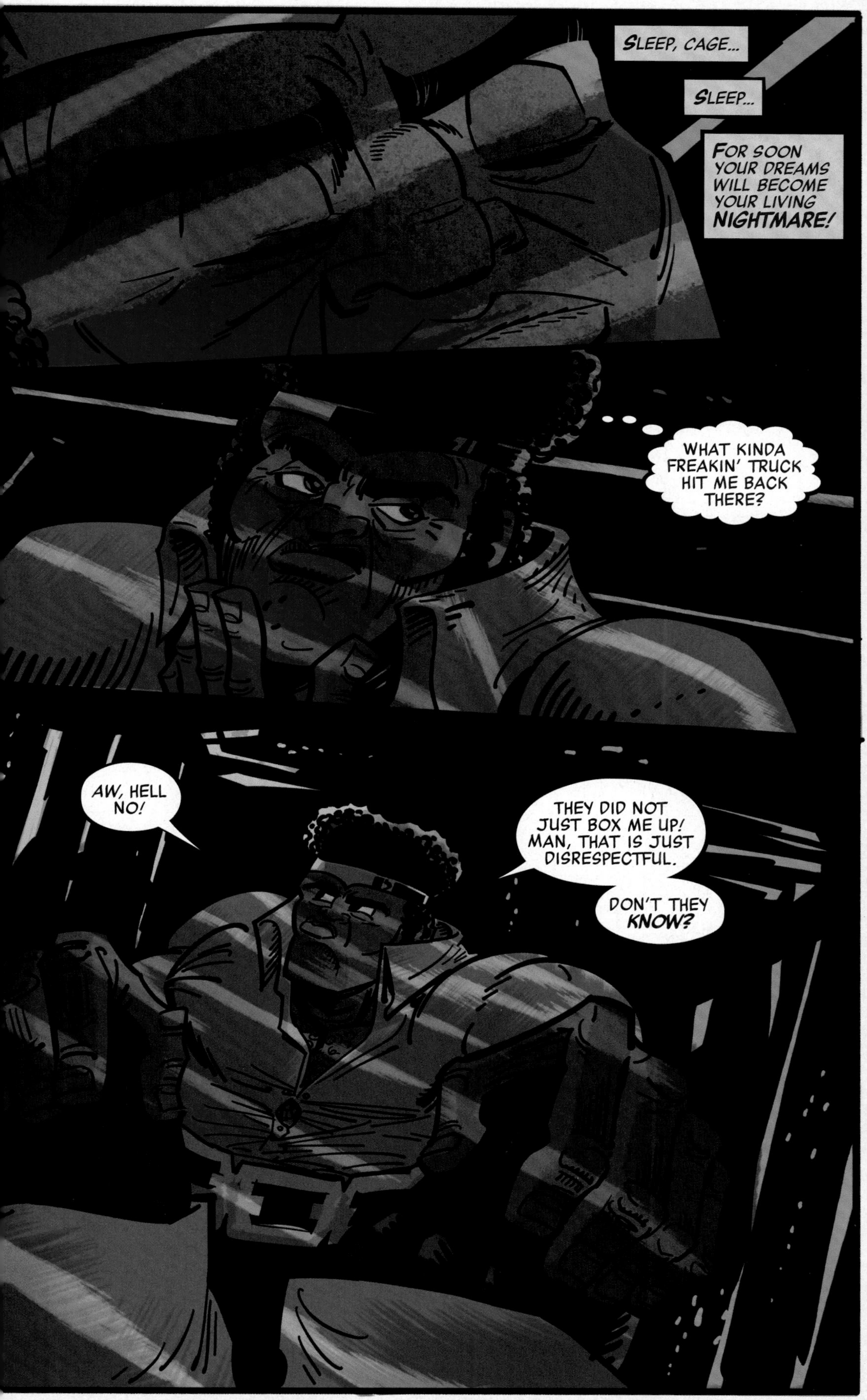
SLEEP, CAGE...
SLEEP...
FOR SOON YOUR DREAMS WILL BECOME YOUR LIVING NIGHTMARE!
WHAT KINDA FREAKIN' TRUCK HIT ME BACK THERE?
AW, HELL NO!
THEY DID NOT JUST BOX ME UP! MAN, THAT IS JUST DISRESPECTFUL.
DON'T THEY KNOW?

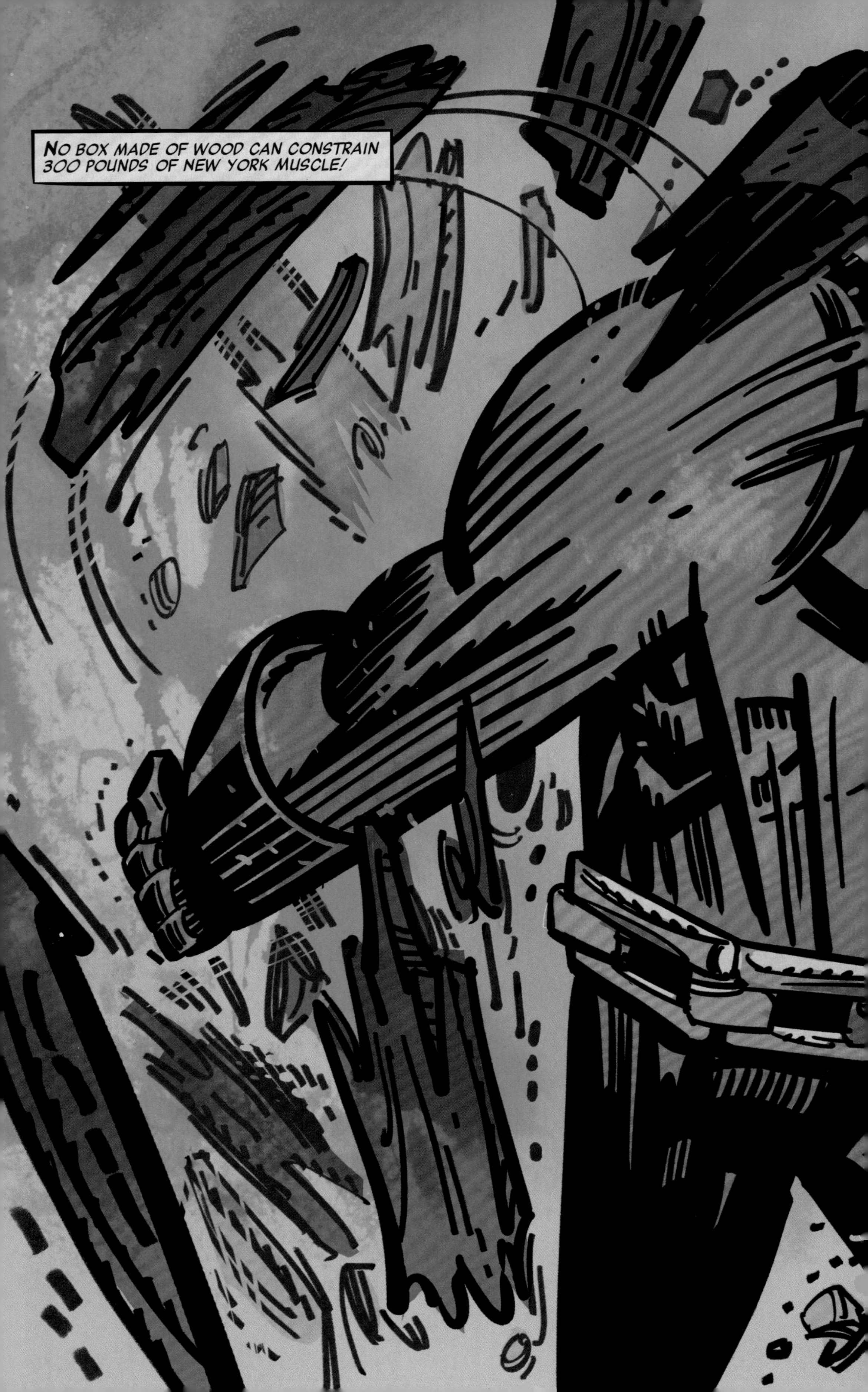
NO BOX MADE OF WOOD CAN CONSTRAIN 300 POUNDS OF NEW YORK MUSCLE!

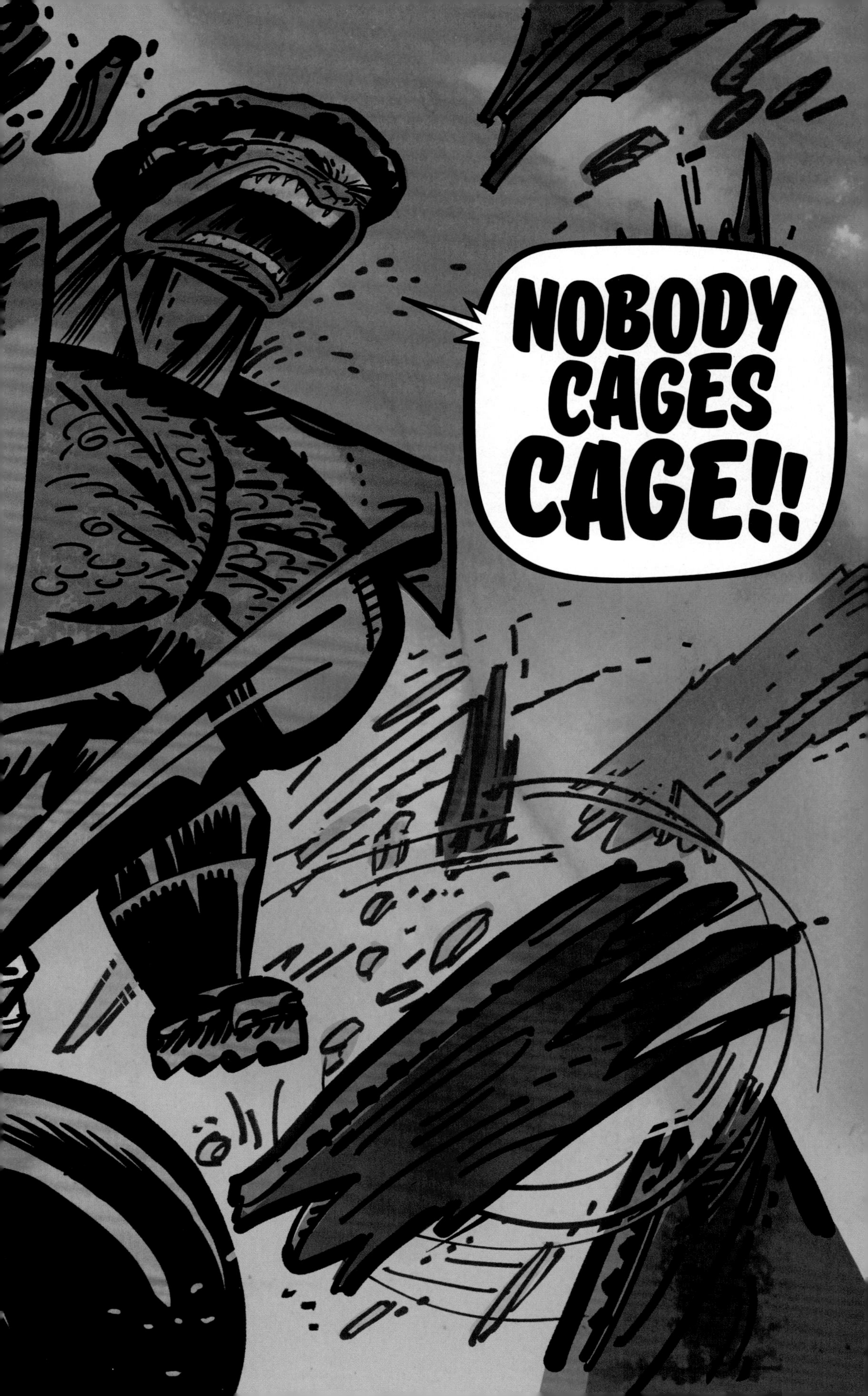
NOBODY CAGES CAGE!!

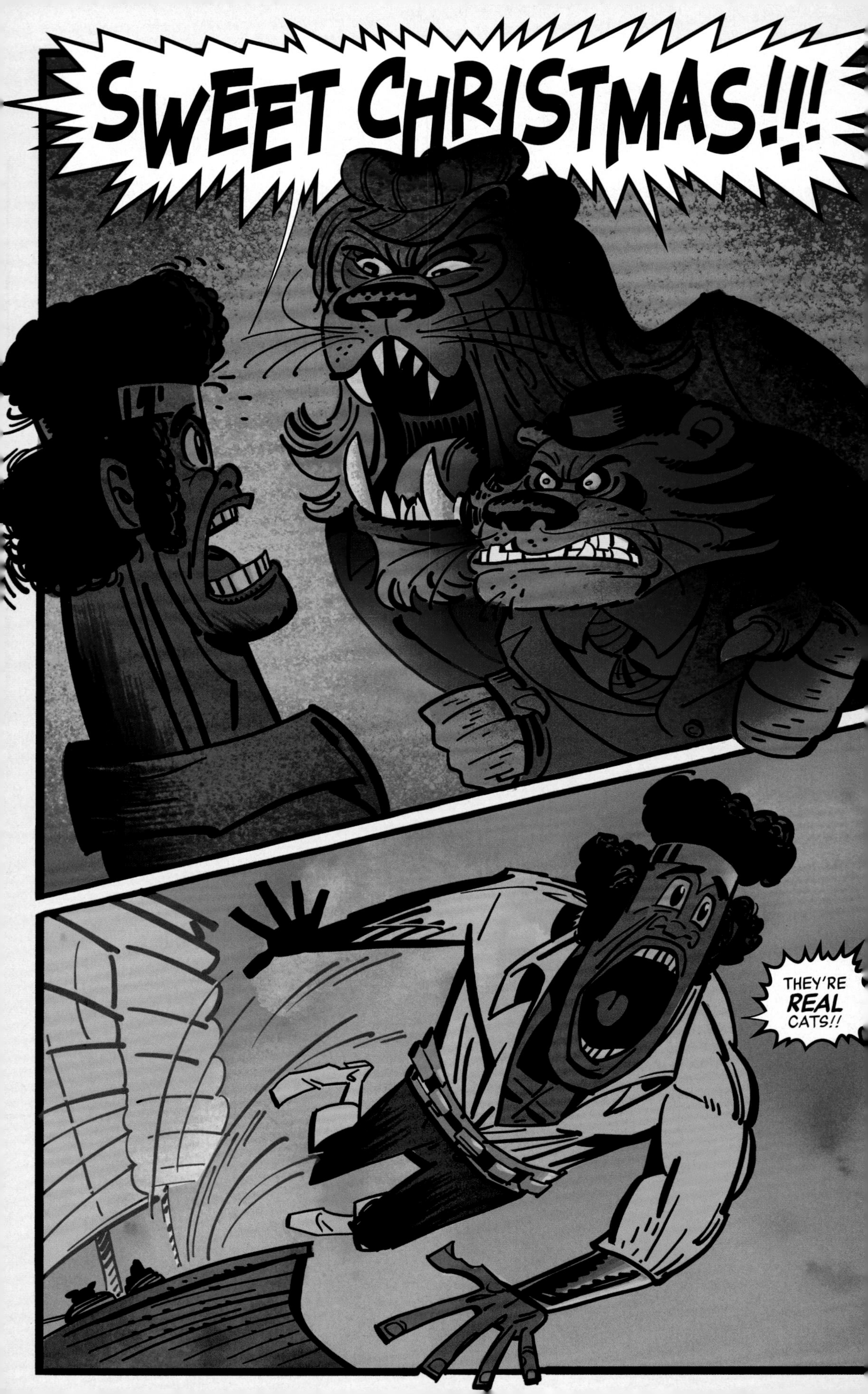
SWEET CHRISTMAS!!!
THEY'RE REAL CATS!!

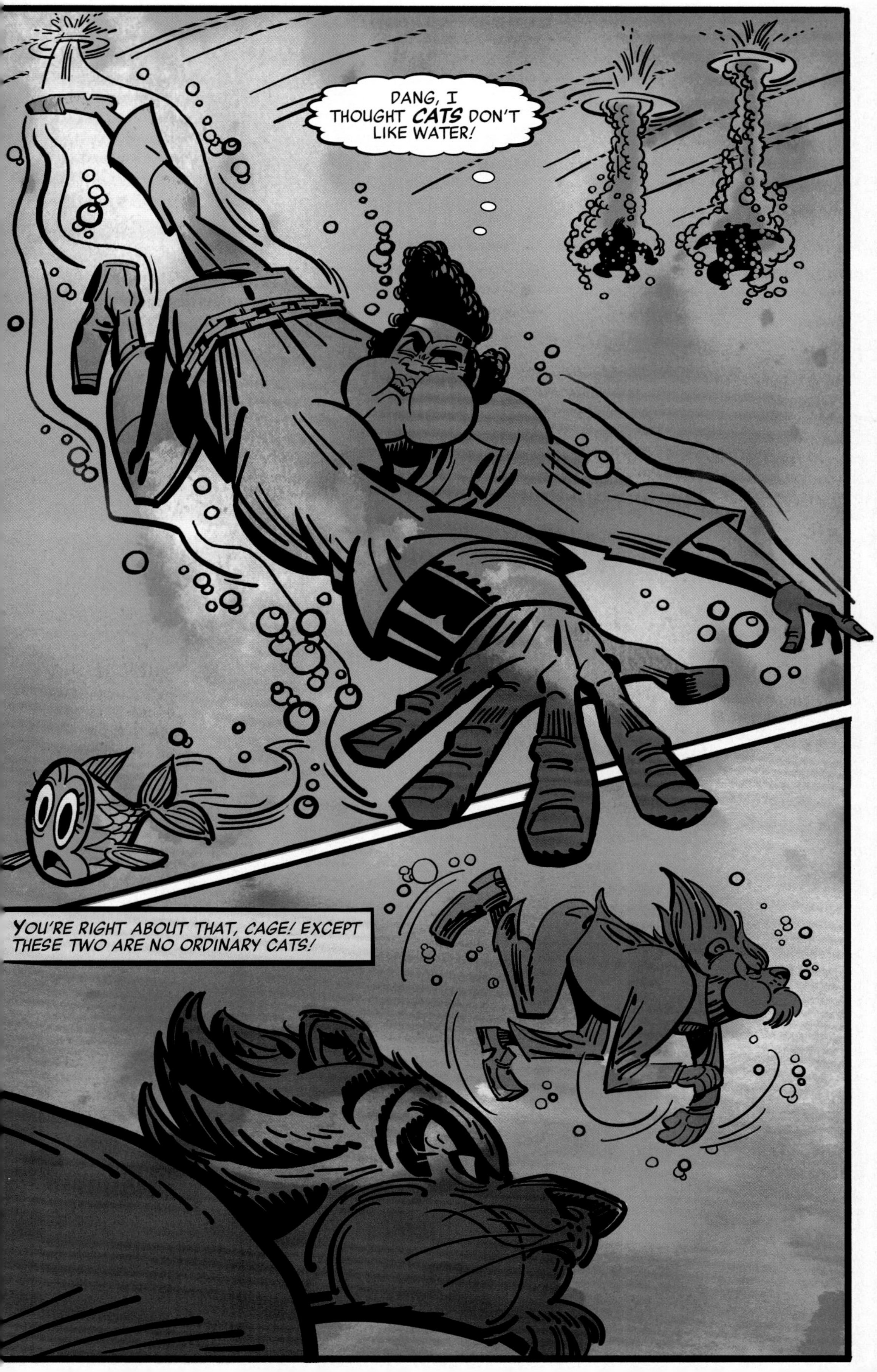
DANG, I THOUGHT CATS DON'T LIKE WATER!
YOU'RE RIGHT ABOUT THAT, CAGE! EXCEPT THESE TWO ARE NO ORDINARY CATS!

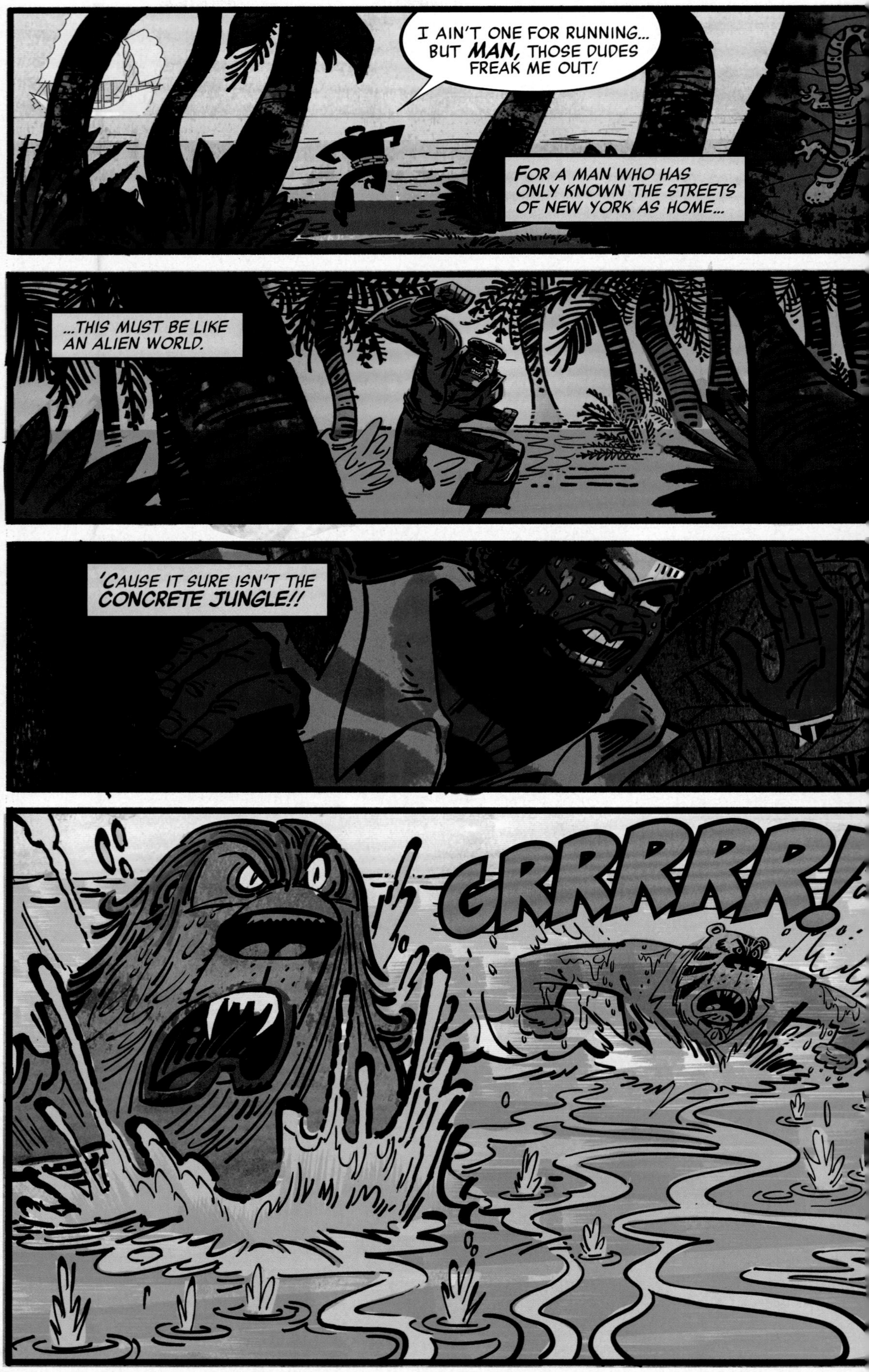
I AIN'T ONE FOR RUNNING... BUT MAN, THOSE DUDES FREAK ME OUT!
FOR A MAN WHO HAS ONLY KNOWN THE STREETS OF NEW YORK AS HOME...
...THIS MUST BE LIKE AN ALIEN WORLD.
'CAUSE IT SURE ISN'T THE CONCRETE JUNGLE!!
GRRRRRR!

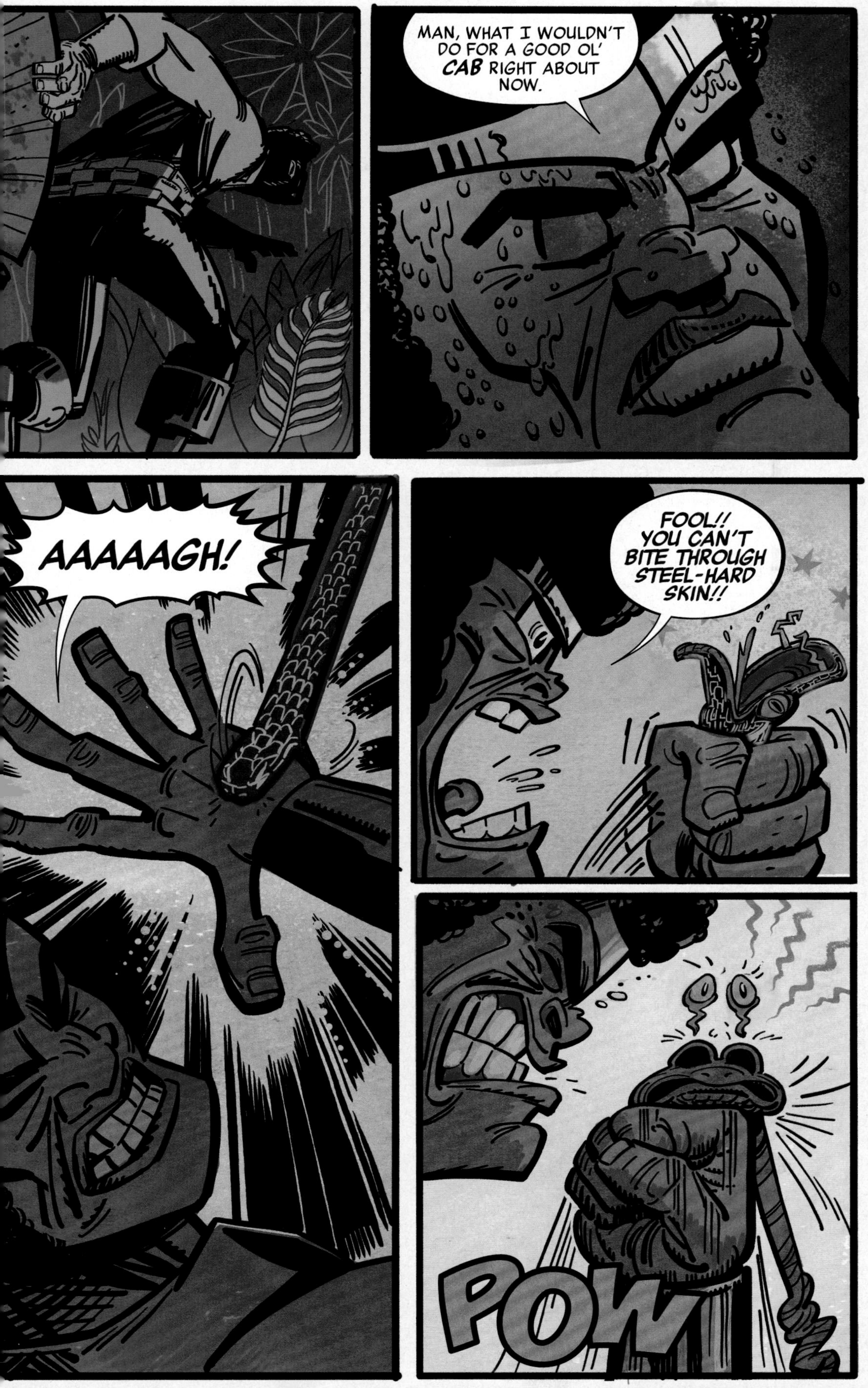
MAN, WHAT I WOULDN'T DO FOR A GOOD OL' CAB RIGHT ABOUT NOW.
AAAAAGH!
FOOL!! YOU CAN'T BITE THROUGH STEEL-HARD SKIN!!
POW

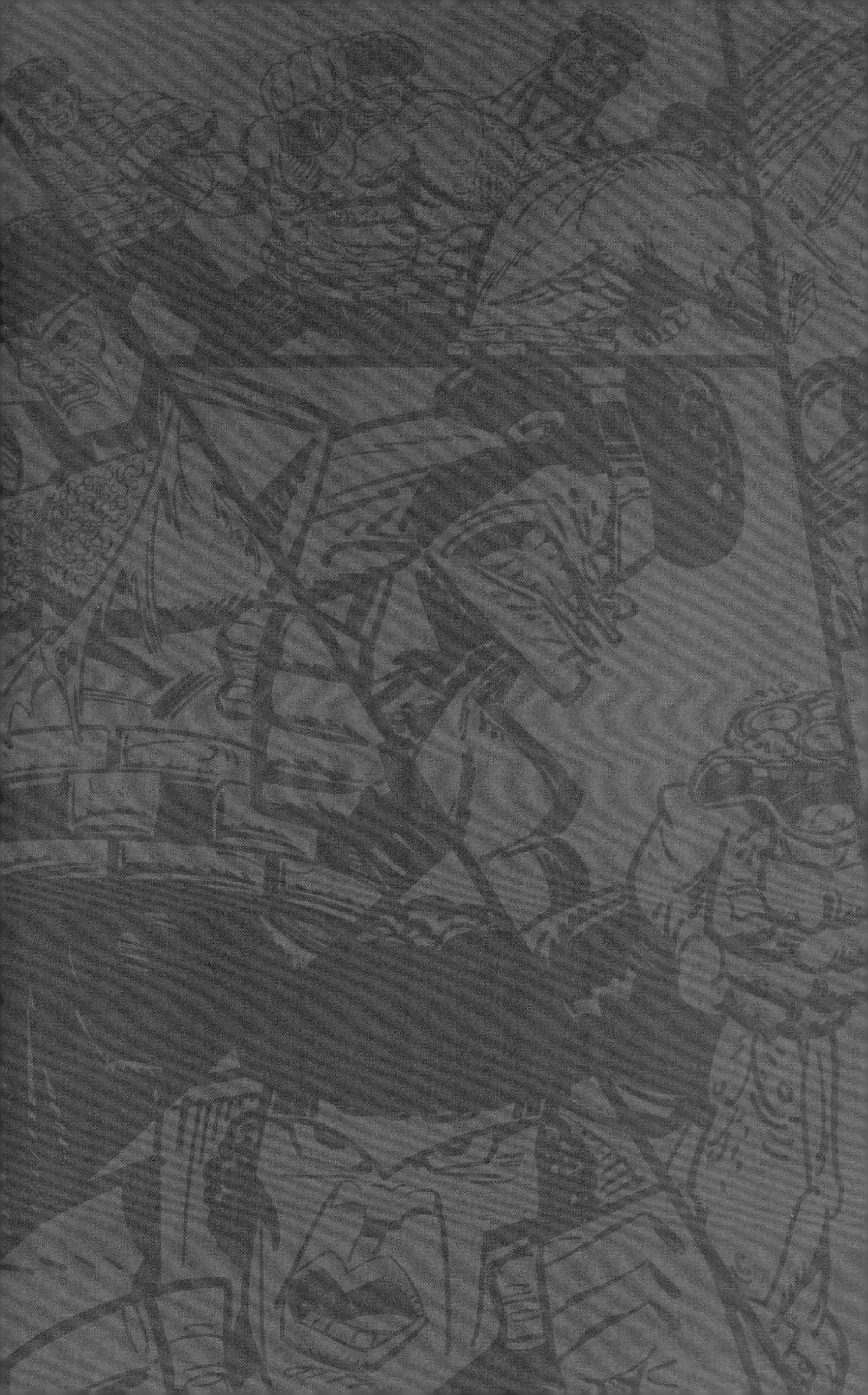

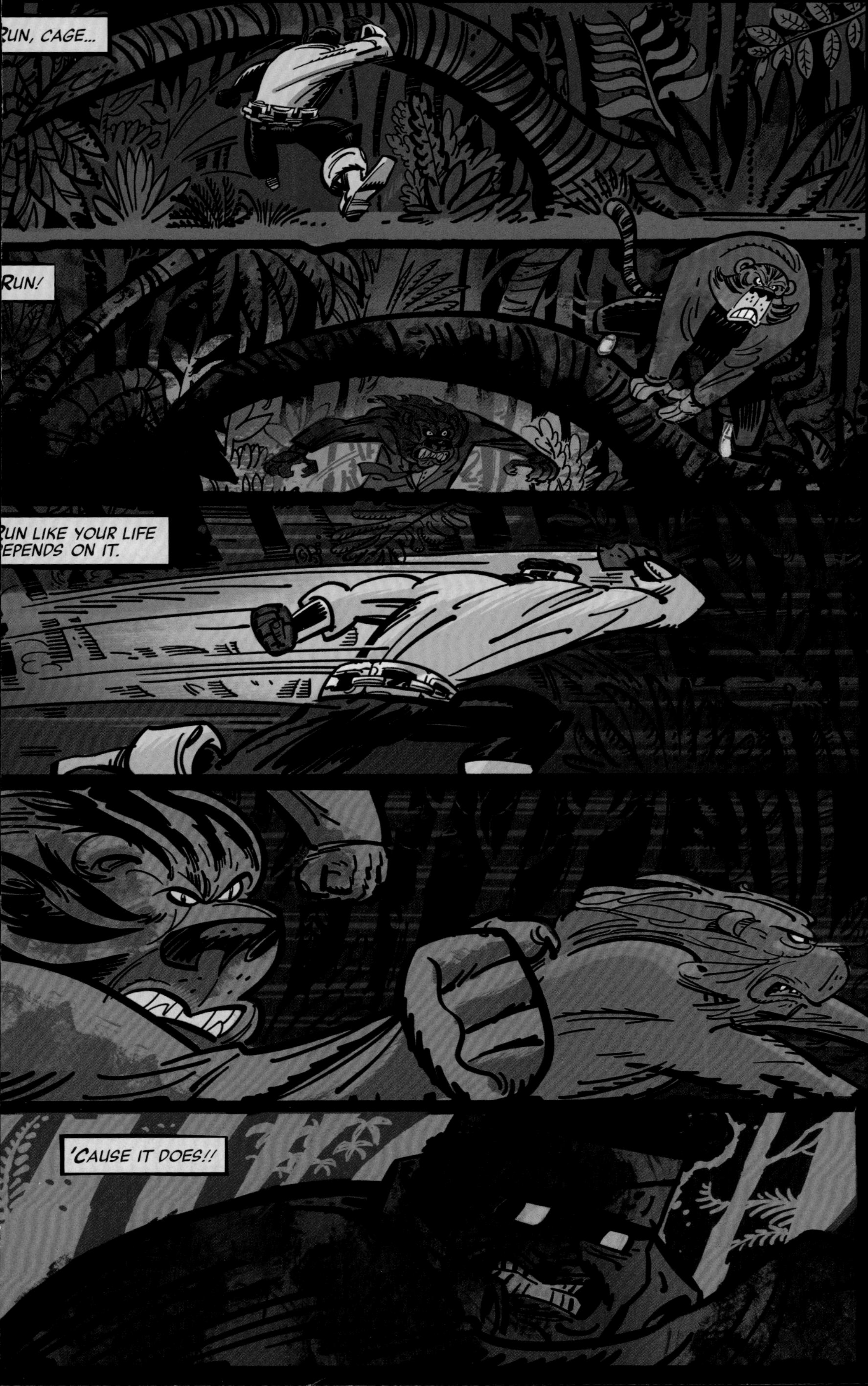
RUN, CAGE...
RUN!
RUN LIKE YOUR LIFE DEPENDS ON IT.
'CAUSE IT DOES!!

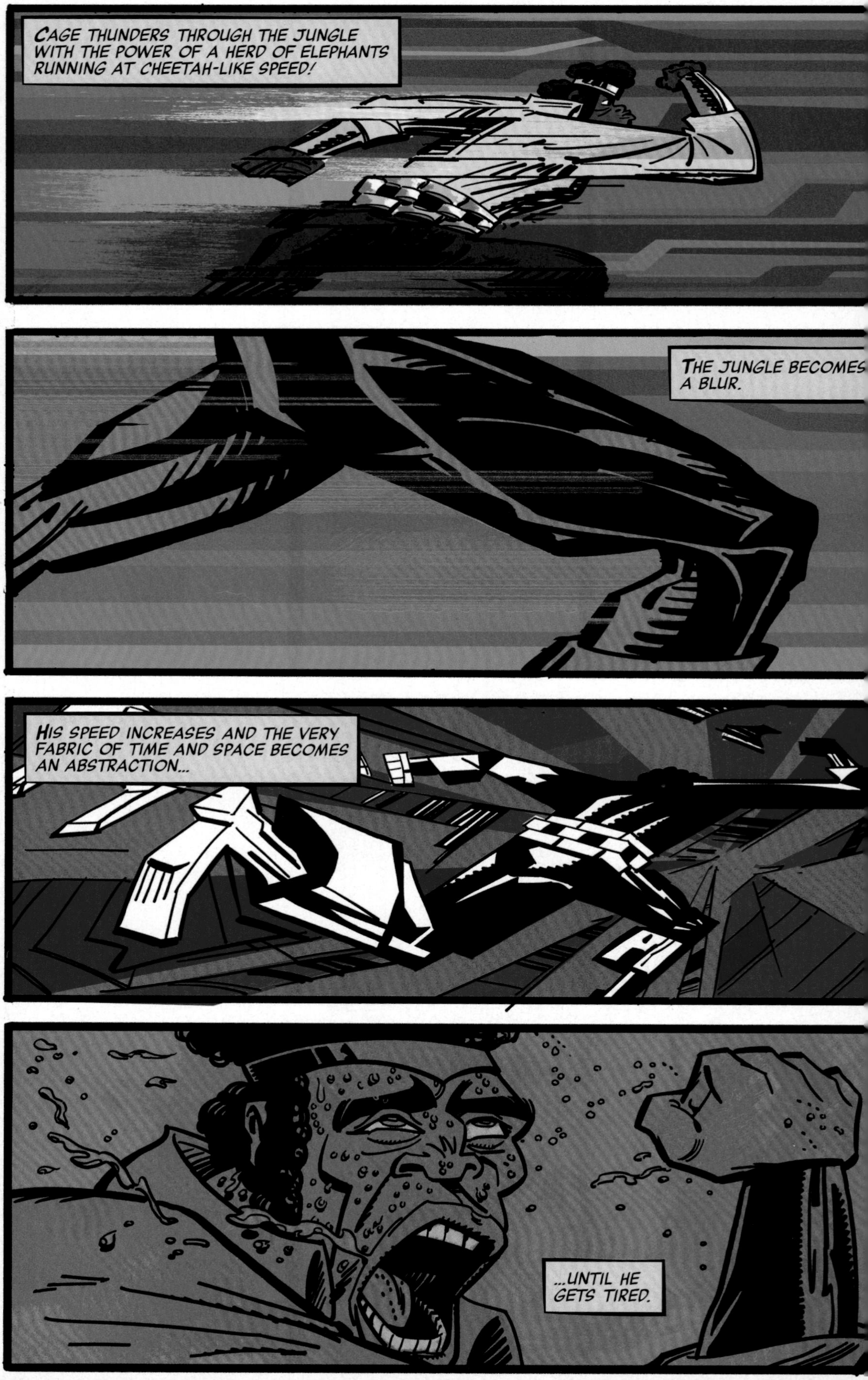
CAGE THUNDERS THROUGH THE JUNGLE WITH THE POWER OF A HERD OF ELEPHANTS RUNNING AT CHEETAH-LIKE SPEED!
THE JUNGLE BECOMES A BLUR.
HIS SPEED INCREASES AND THE VERY FABRIC OF TIME AND SPACE BECOMES AN ABSTRACTION...
...UNTIL HE GETS TIRED.

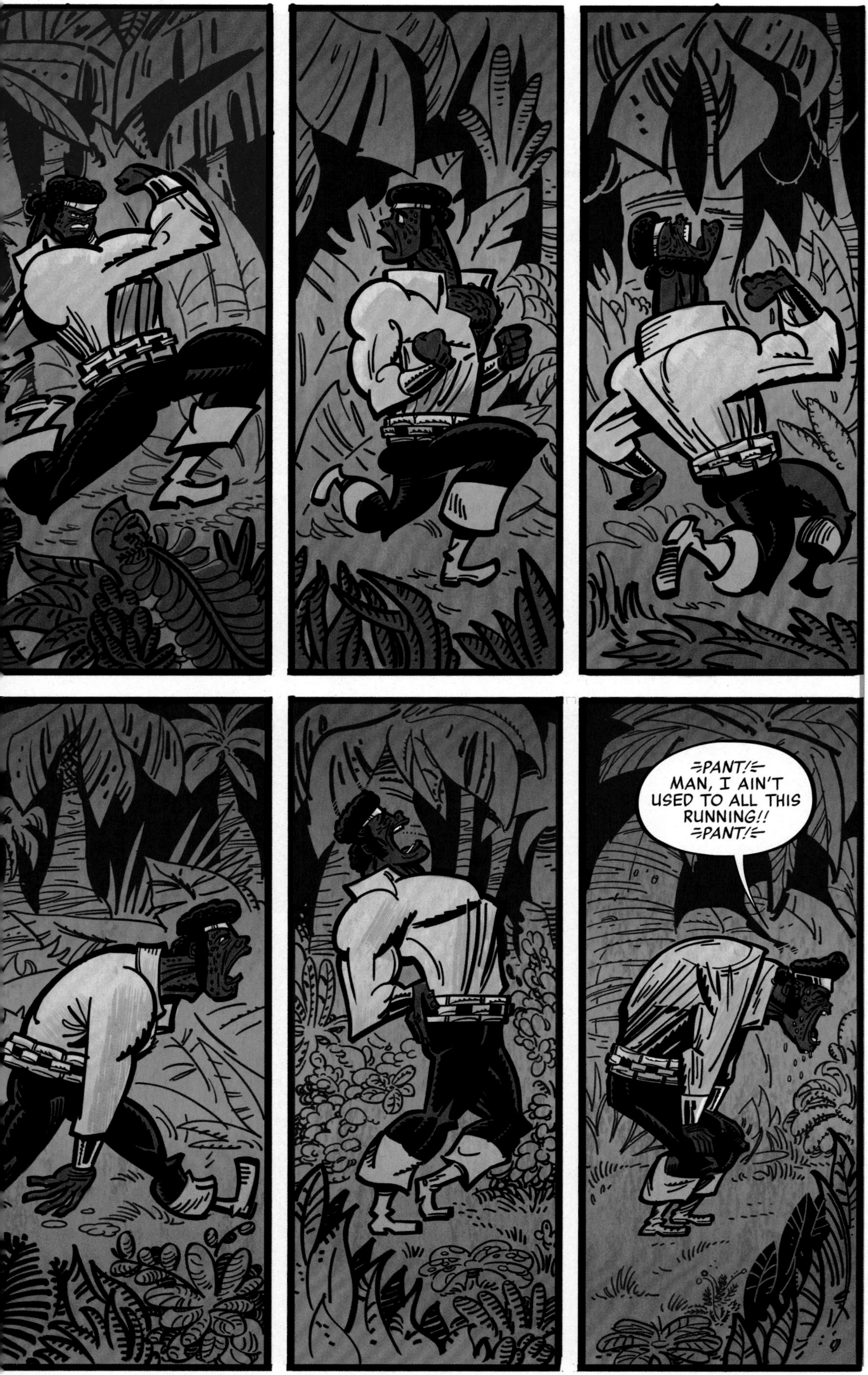
=PANT!= MAN, I AIN'T USED TO ALL THIS RUNNING!! =PANT!=

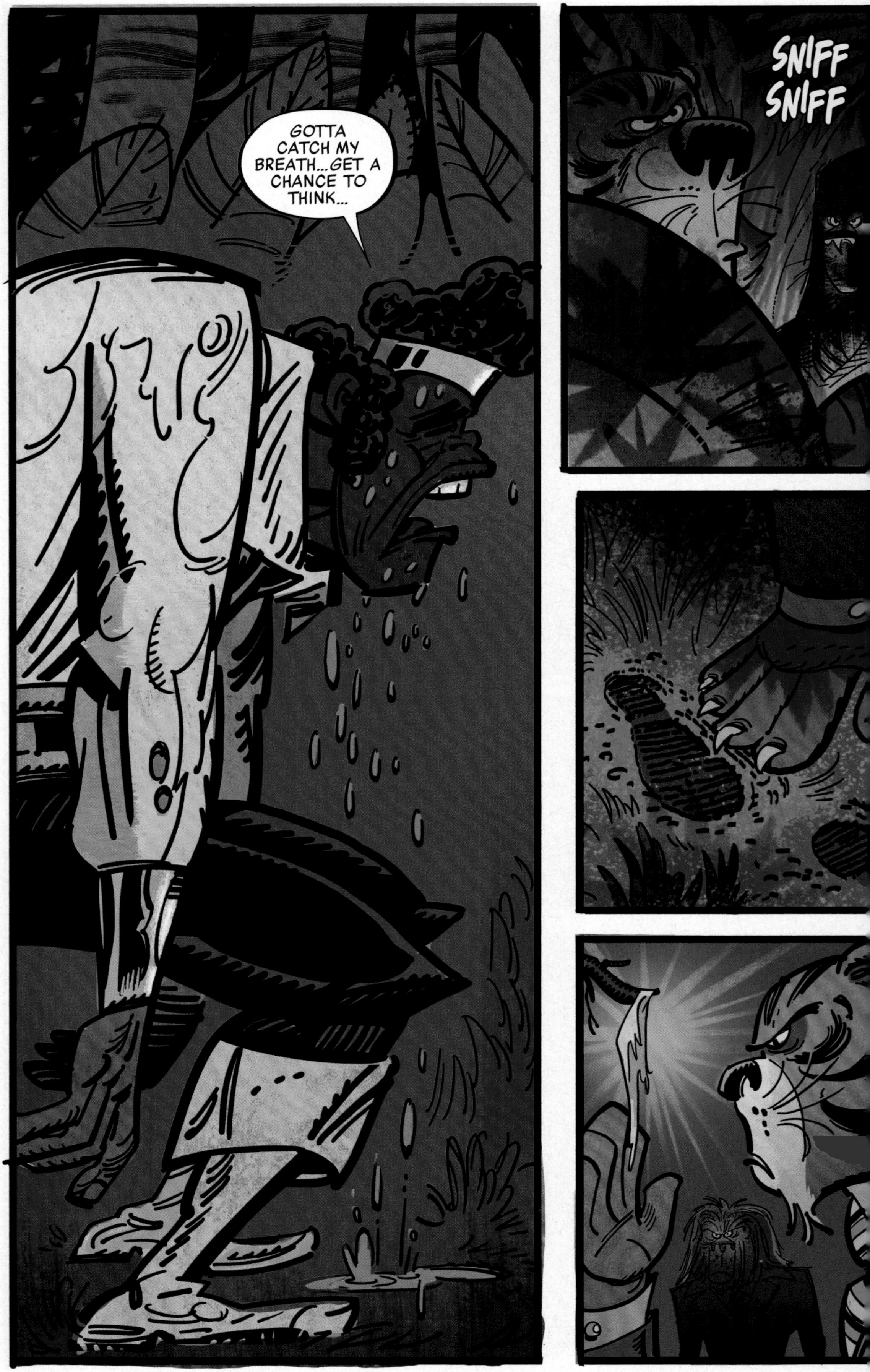
GOTTA CATCH MY BREATH...GET A CHANCE TO THINK...
SNIFF SNIFF

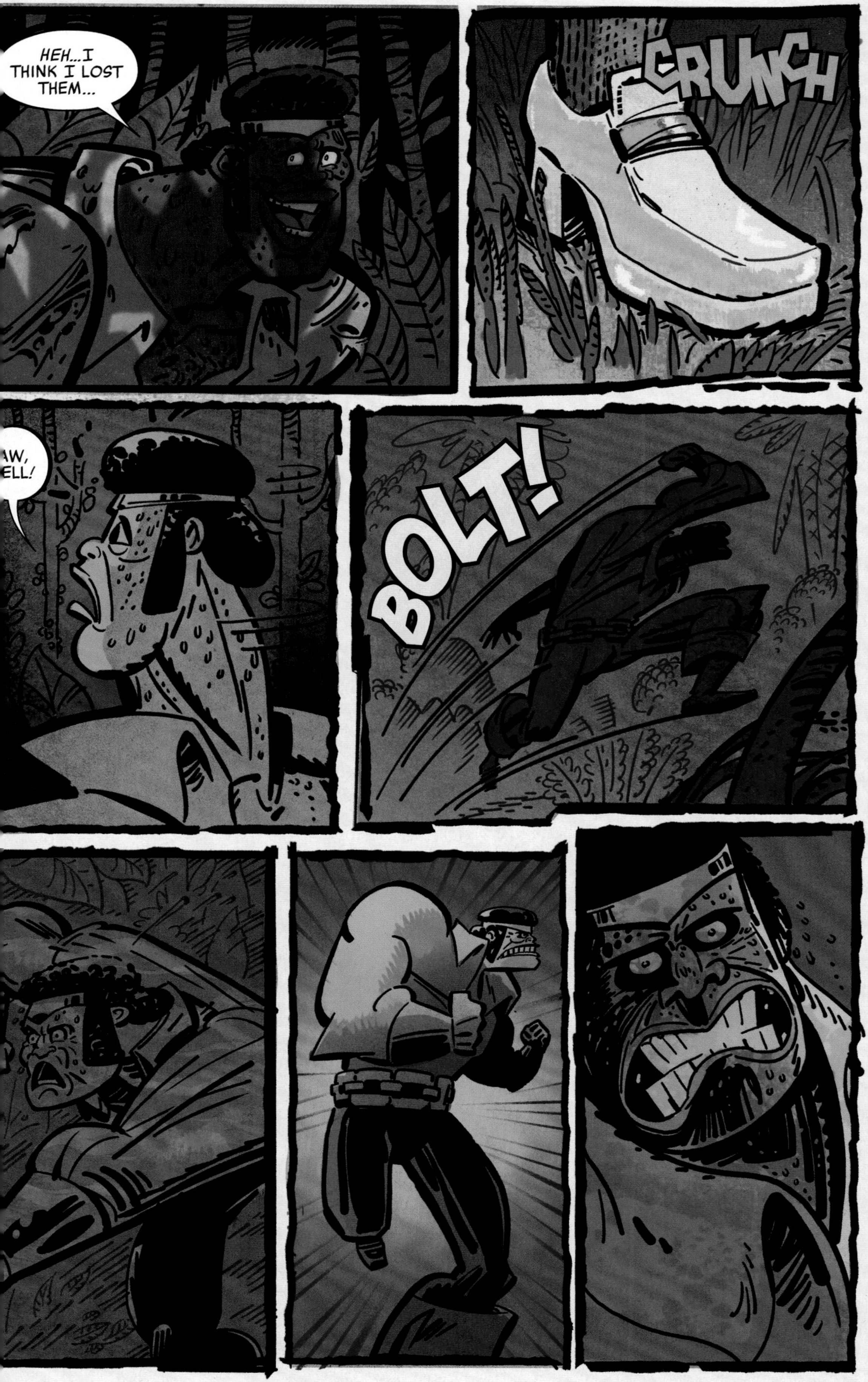
HEH...I THINK I LOST THEM...
CRUNCH
AW, ELL!
BOLT!

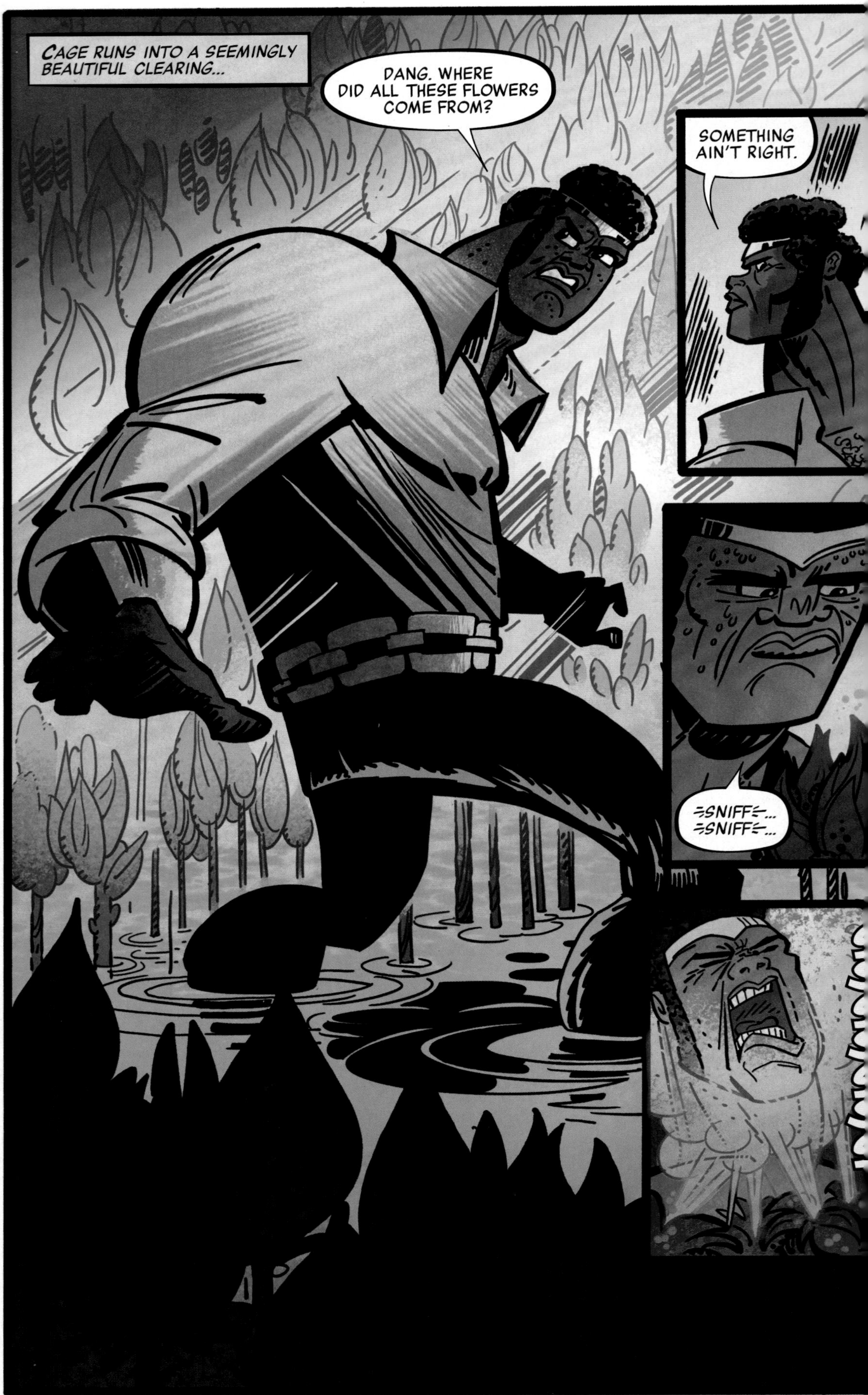
CAGE RUNS INTO A SEEMINGLY BEAUTIFUL CLEARING...
DANG. WHERE DID ALL THESE FLOWERS COME FROM?
SOMETHING AIN'T RIGHT.
=SNIFF=... =SNIFF=...

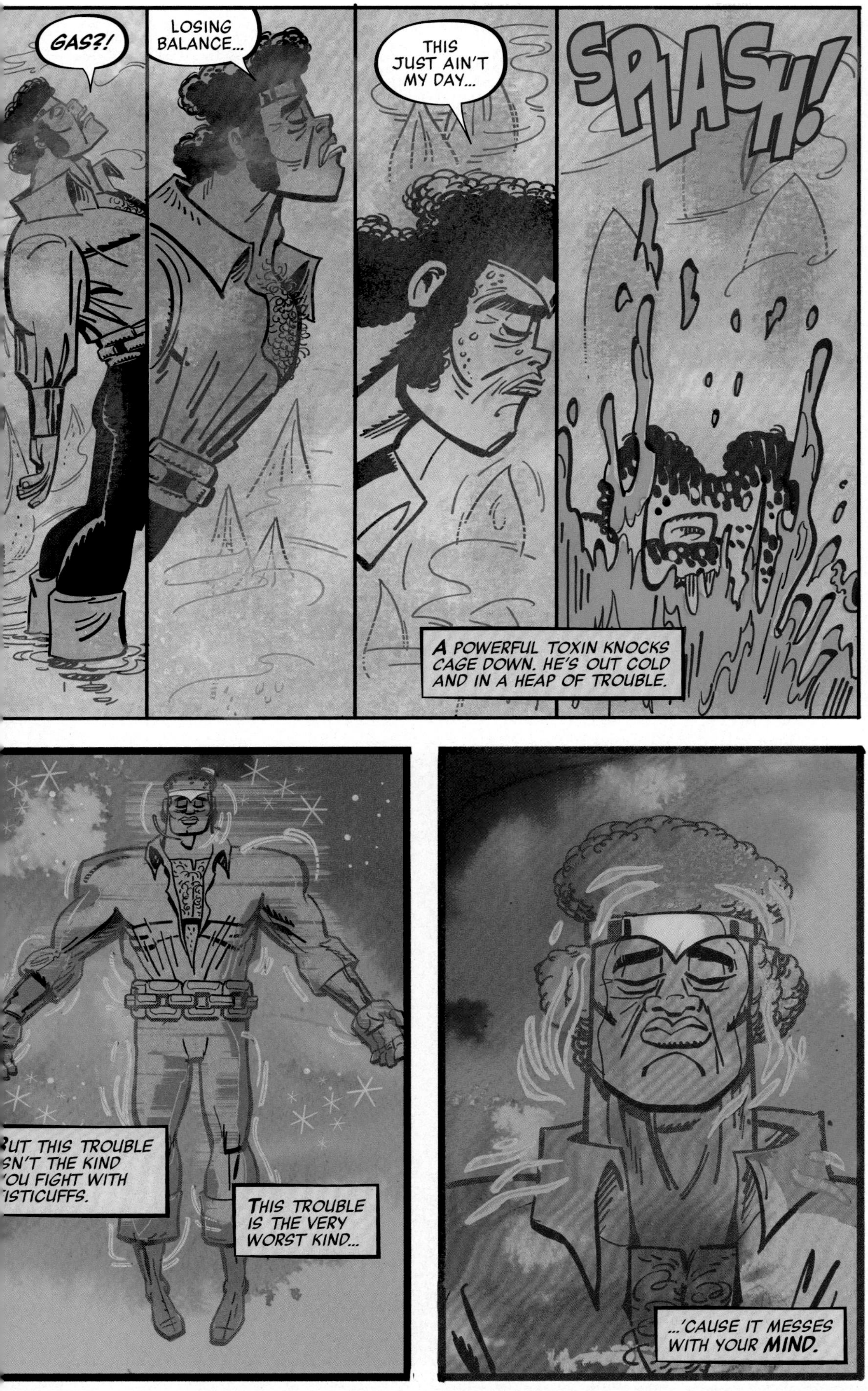
GAS?!
LOSING BALANCE...
THIS JUST AIN'T MY DAY...
SPLASH!
A POWERFUL TOXIN KNOCKS CAGE DOWN. HE'S OUT COLD AND IN A HEAP OF TROUBLE.
UT THIS TROUBLE SN'T THE KIND OU FIGHT WITH ISTICUFFS.
THIS TROUBLE IS THE VERY WORST KIND...
...'CAUSE IT MESSES WITH YOUR MIND.

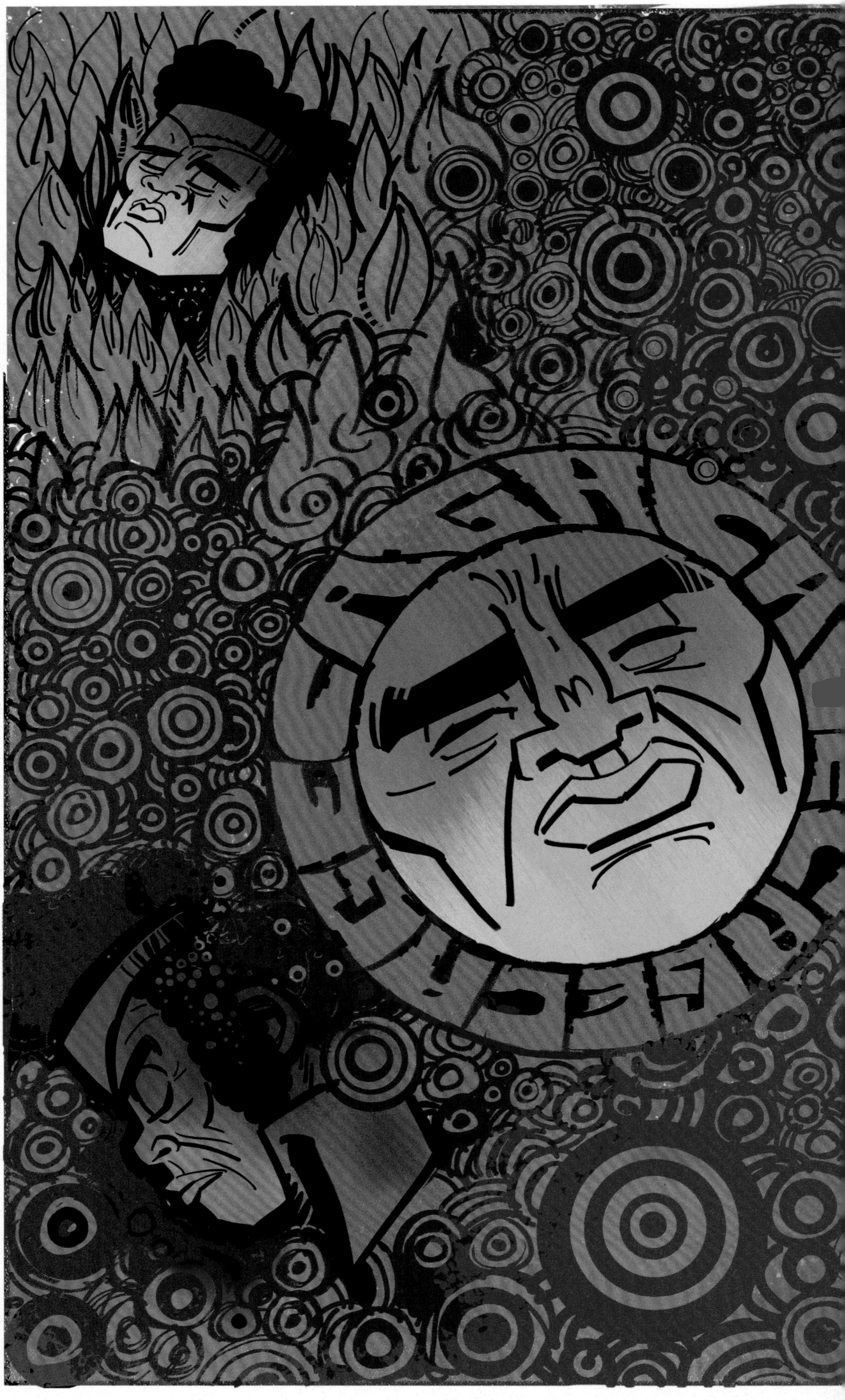

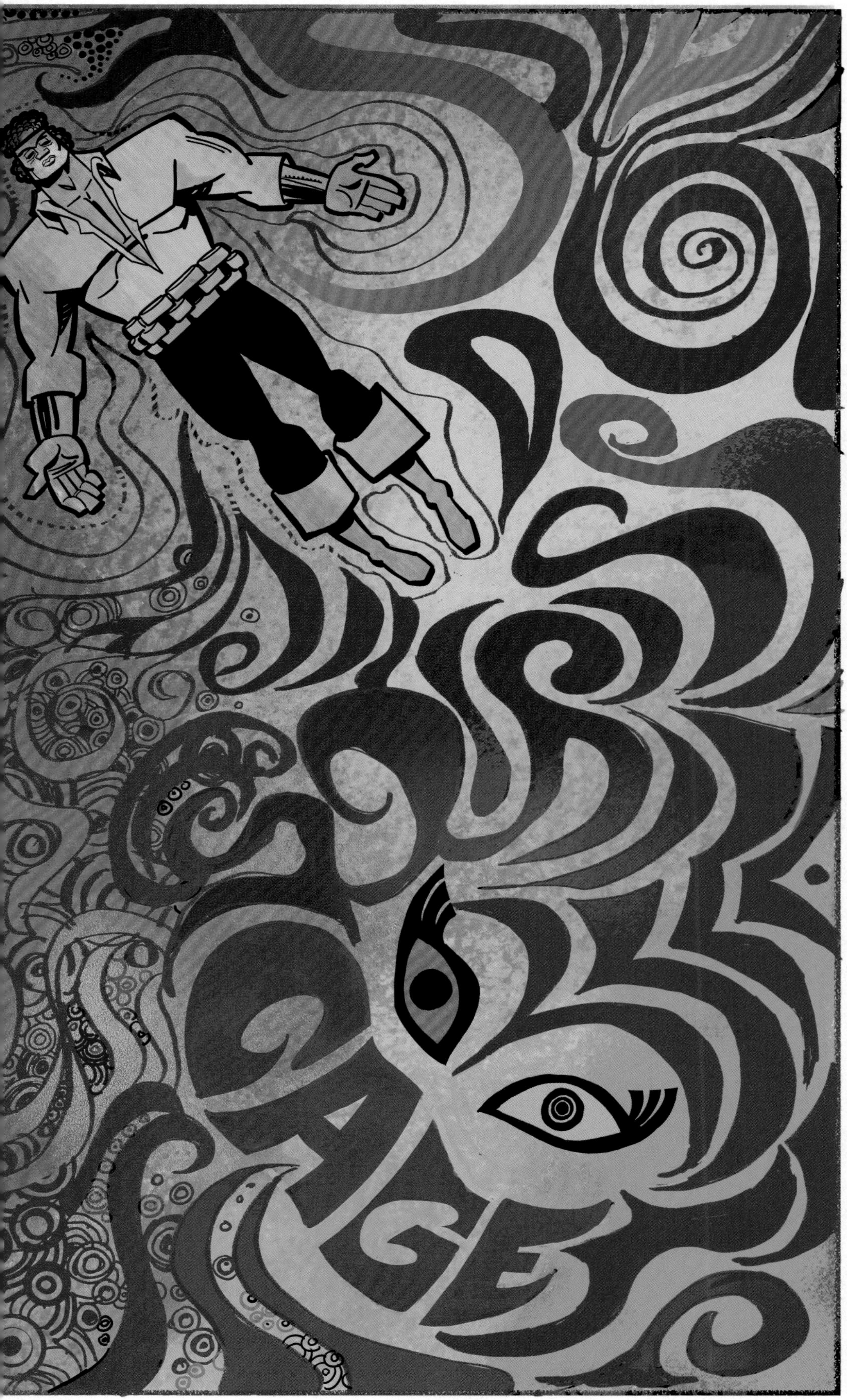

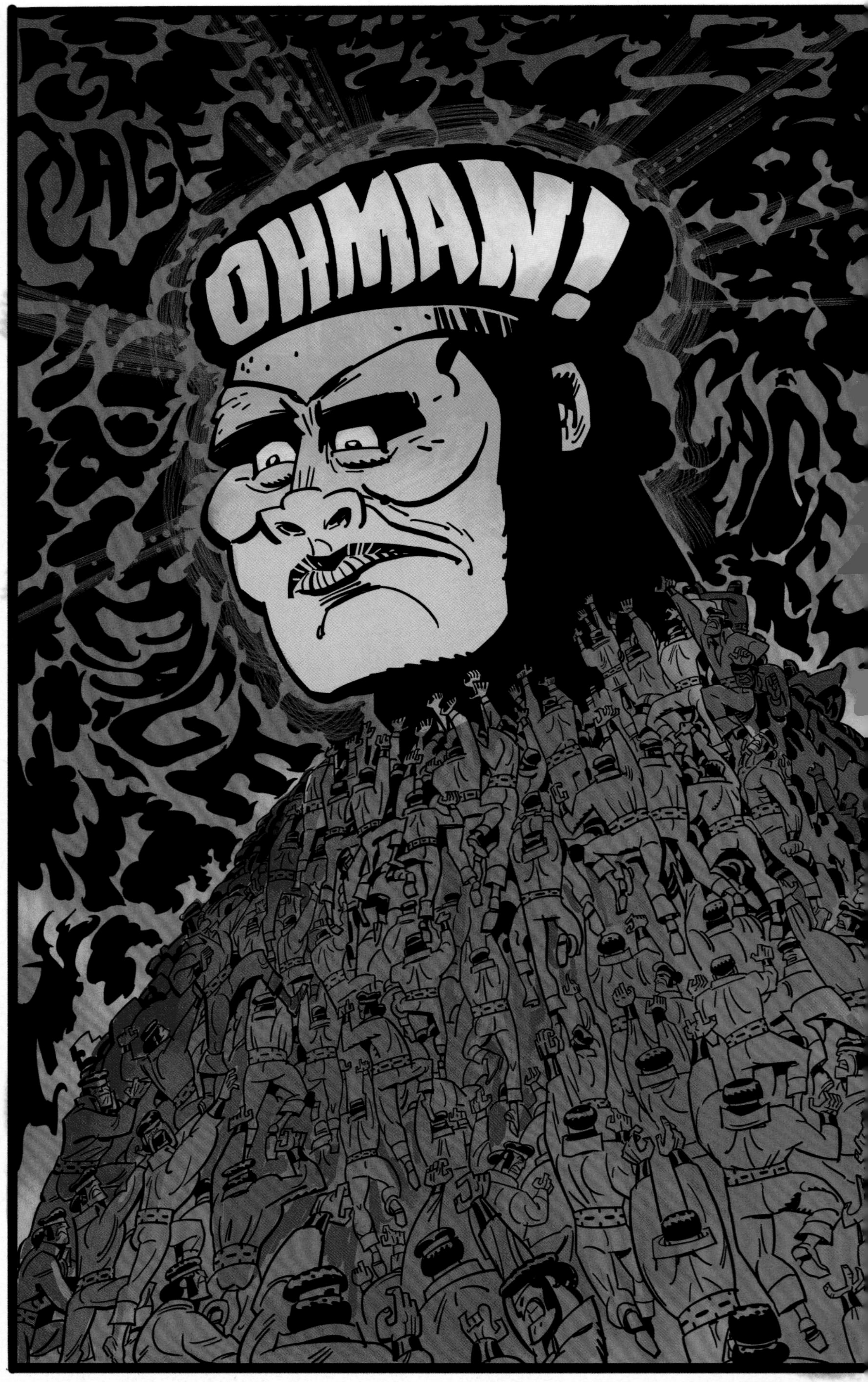
CAGE
OHMAN!

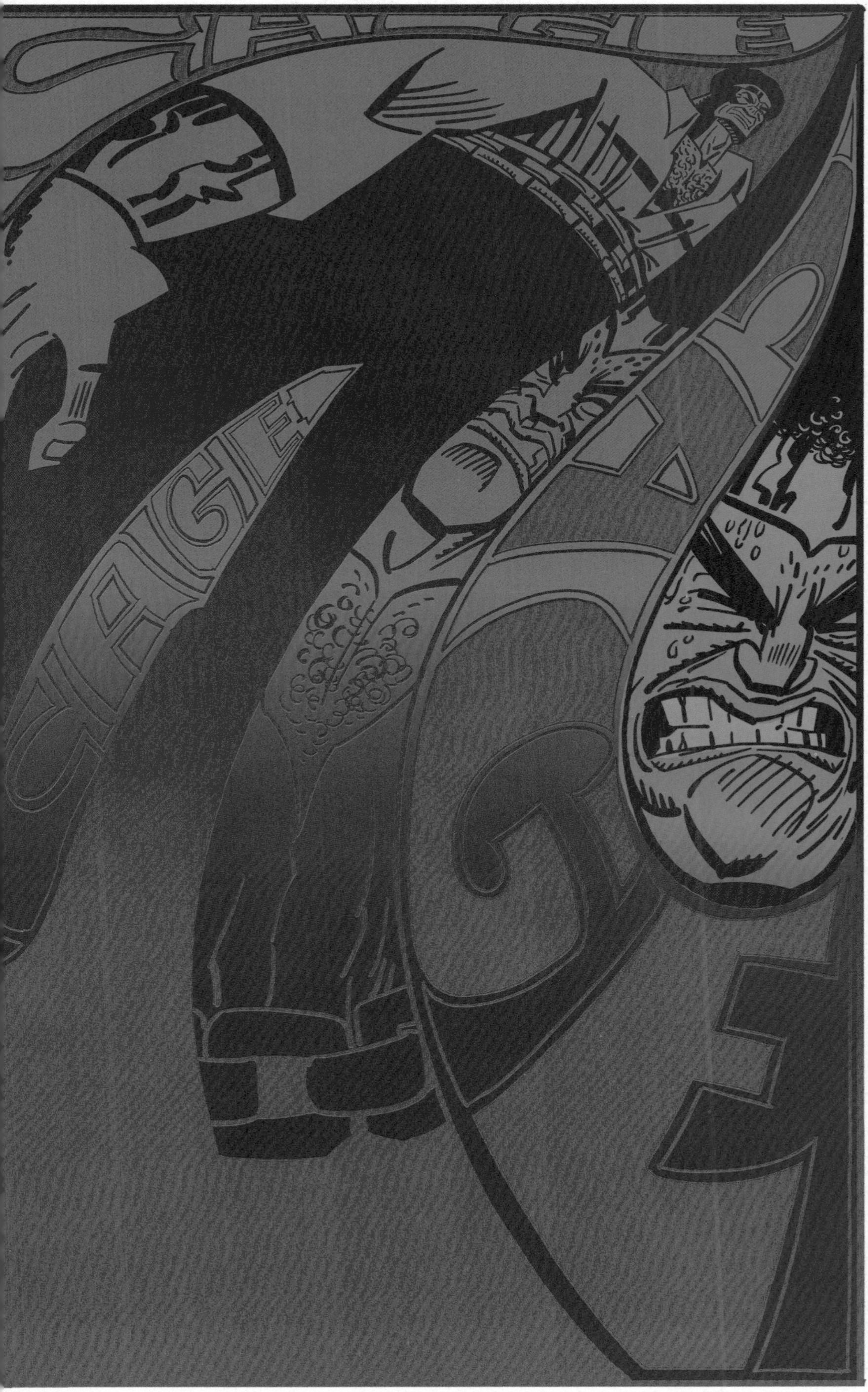

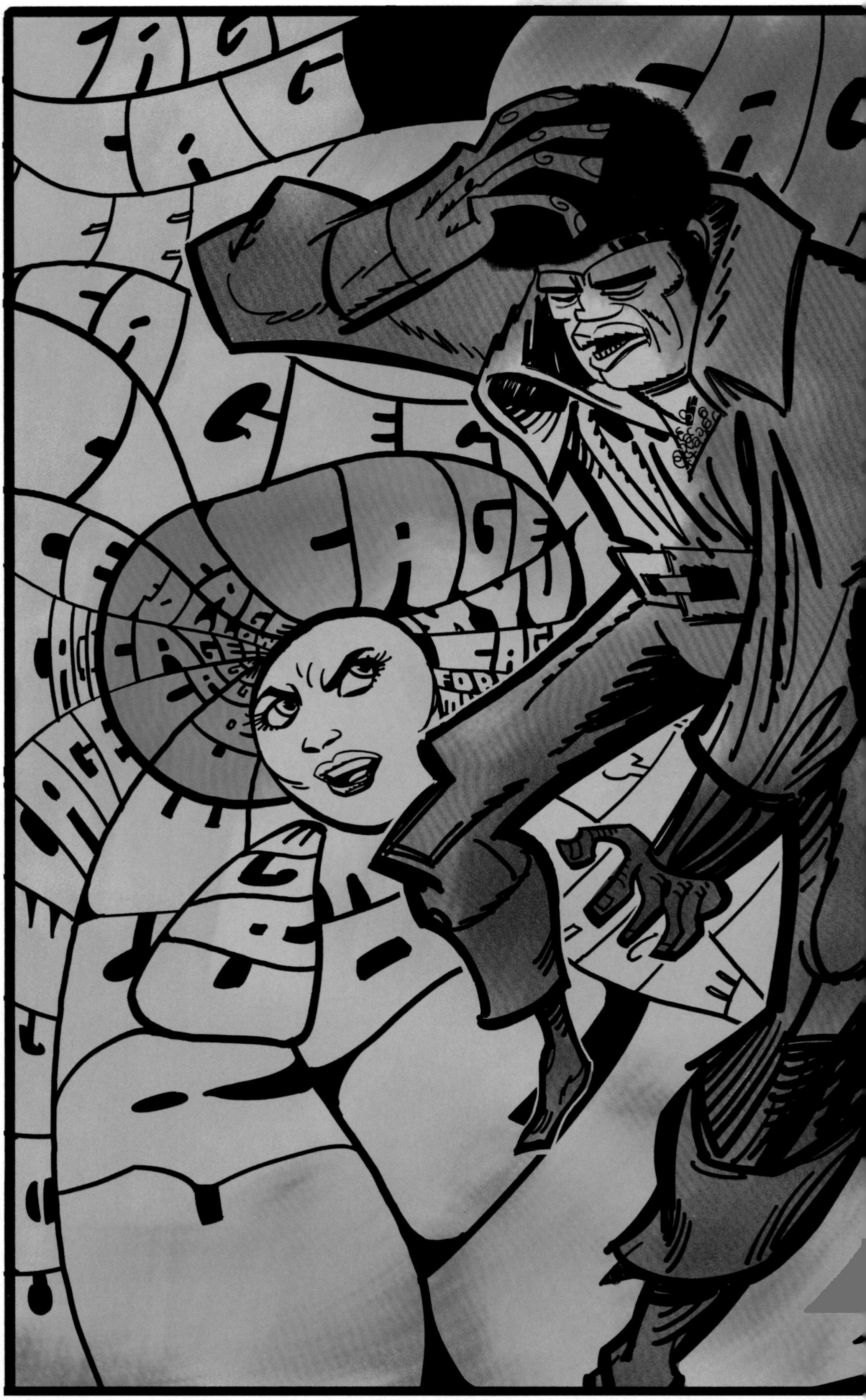
CAGE

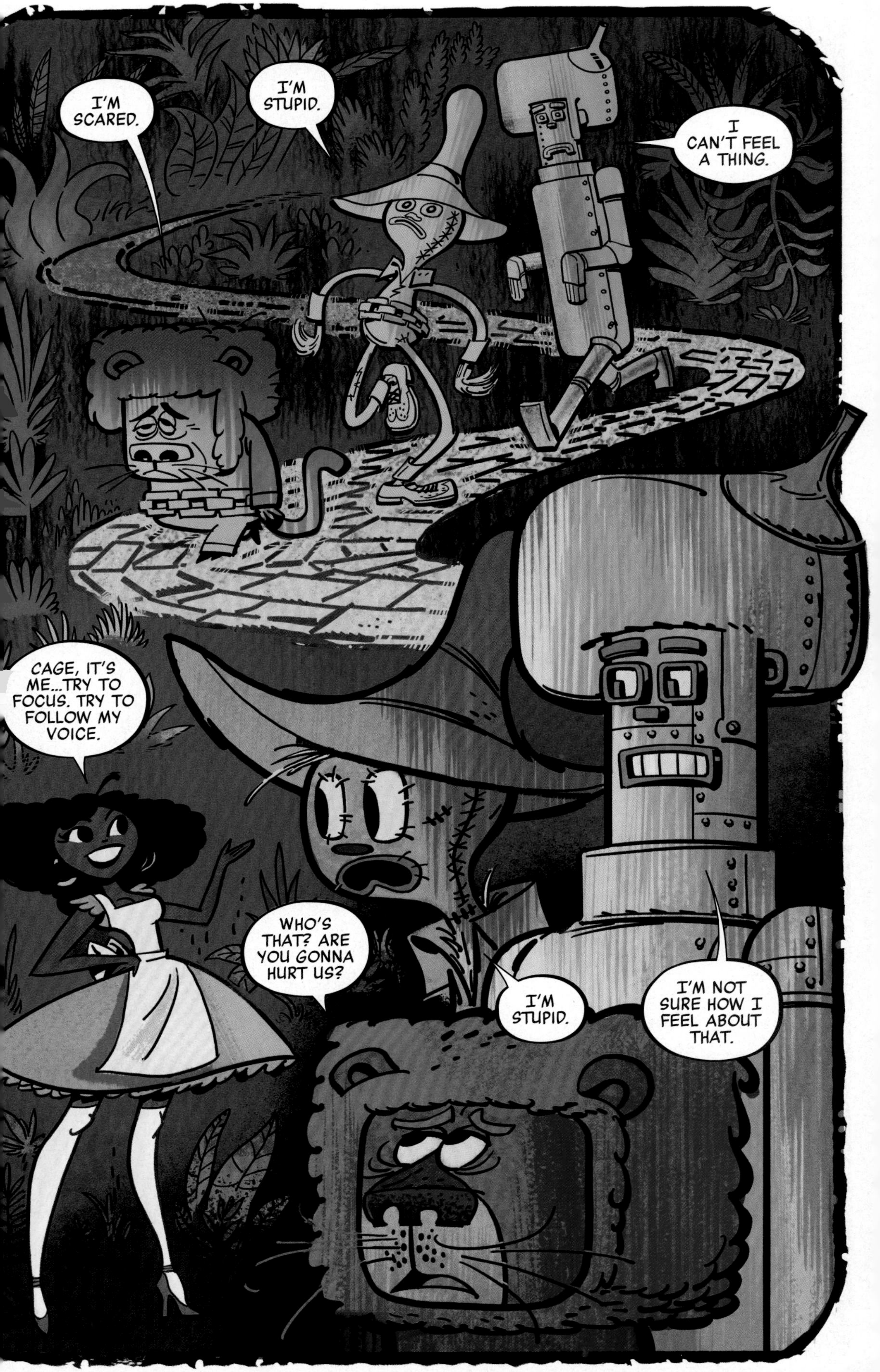
I'M SCARED.
I'M STUPID.
I CAN'T FEEL A THING.
CAGE, IT'S ME...TRY TO FOCUS. TRY TO FOLLOW MY VOICE.
WHO'S THAT? ARE YOU GONNA HURT US?
I'M STUPID.
I'M NOT SURE HOW I FEEL ABOUT THAT.

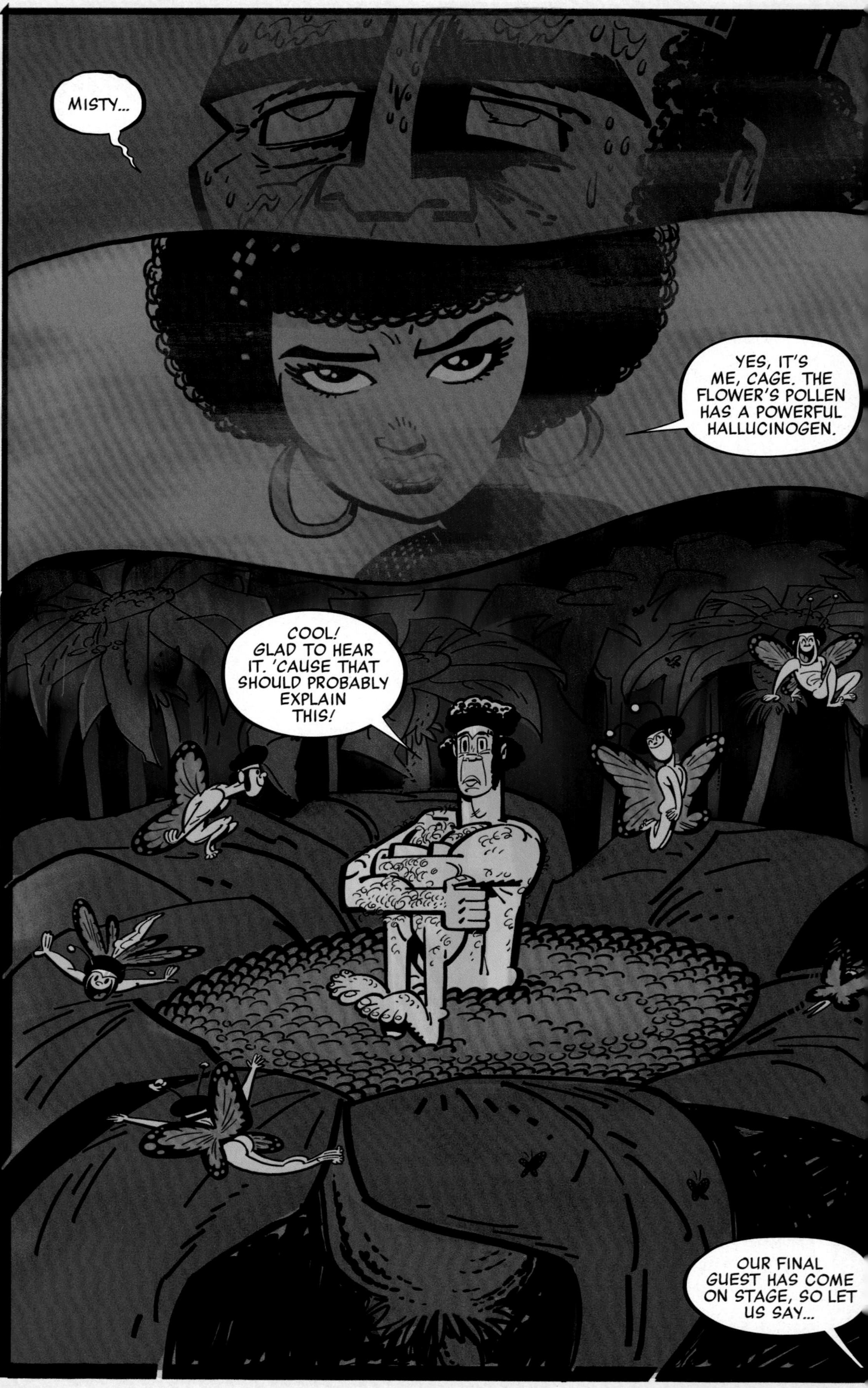
MISTY...
YES, IT'S ME, CAGE. THE FLOWER'S POLLEN HAS A POWERFUL HALLUCINOGEN.
COOL! GLAD TO HEAR IT. 'CAUSE THAT SHOULD PROBABLY EXPLAIN THIS!
OUR FINAL GUEST HAS COME ON STAGE, SO LET US SAY...

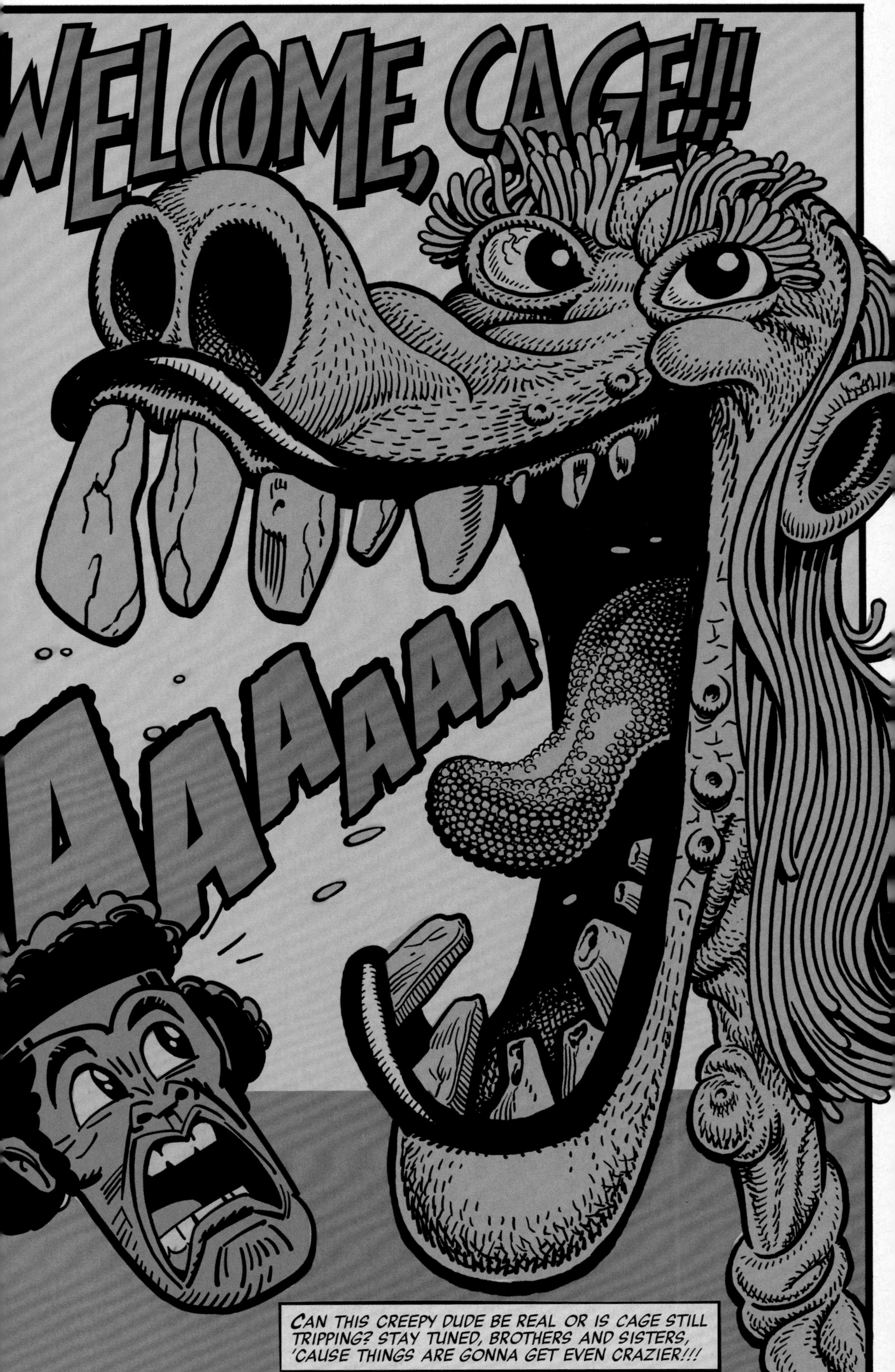
WELCOME, CAGE!!
AAAAAAA
CAN THIS CREEPY DUDE BE REAL OR IS CAGE STILL TRIPPING? STAY TUNED, BROTHERS AND SISTERS, 'CAUSE THINGS ARE GONNA GET EVEN CRAZIER!!!

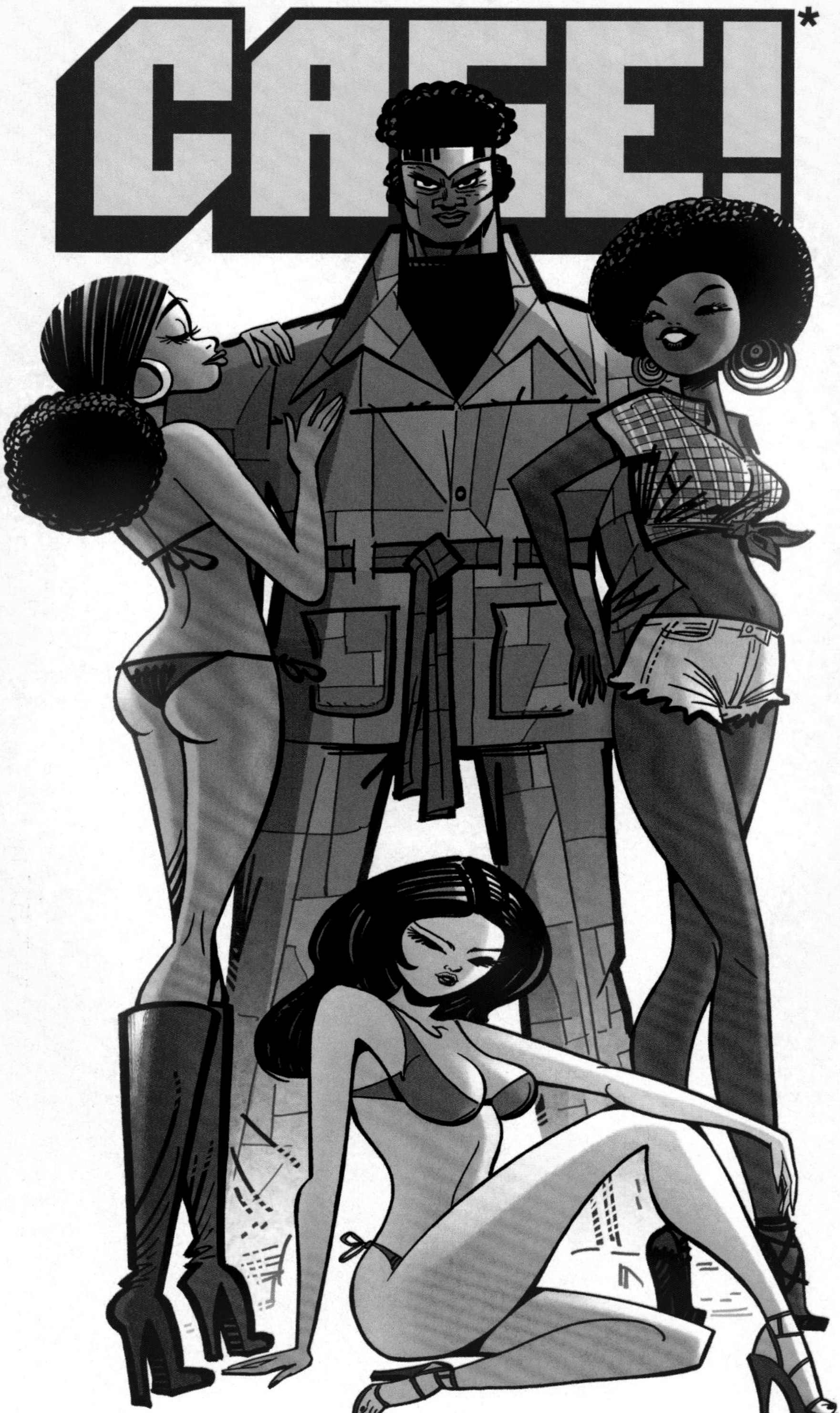
CAGE!*

*This cover has nothing to do with what's inside

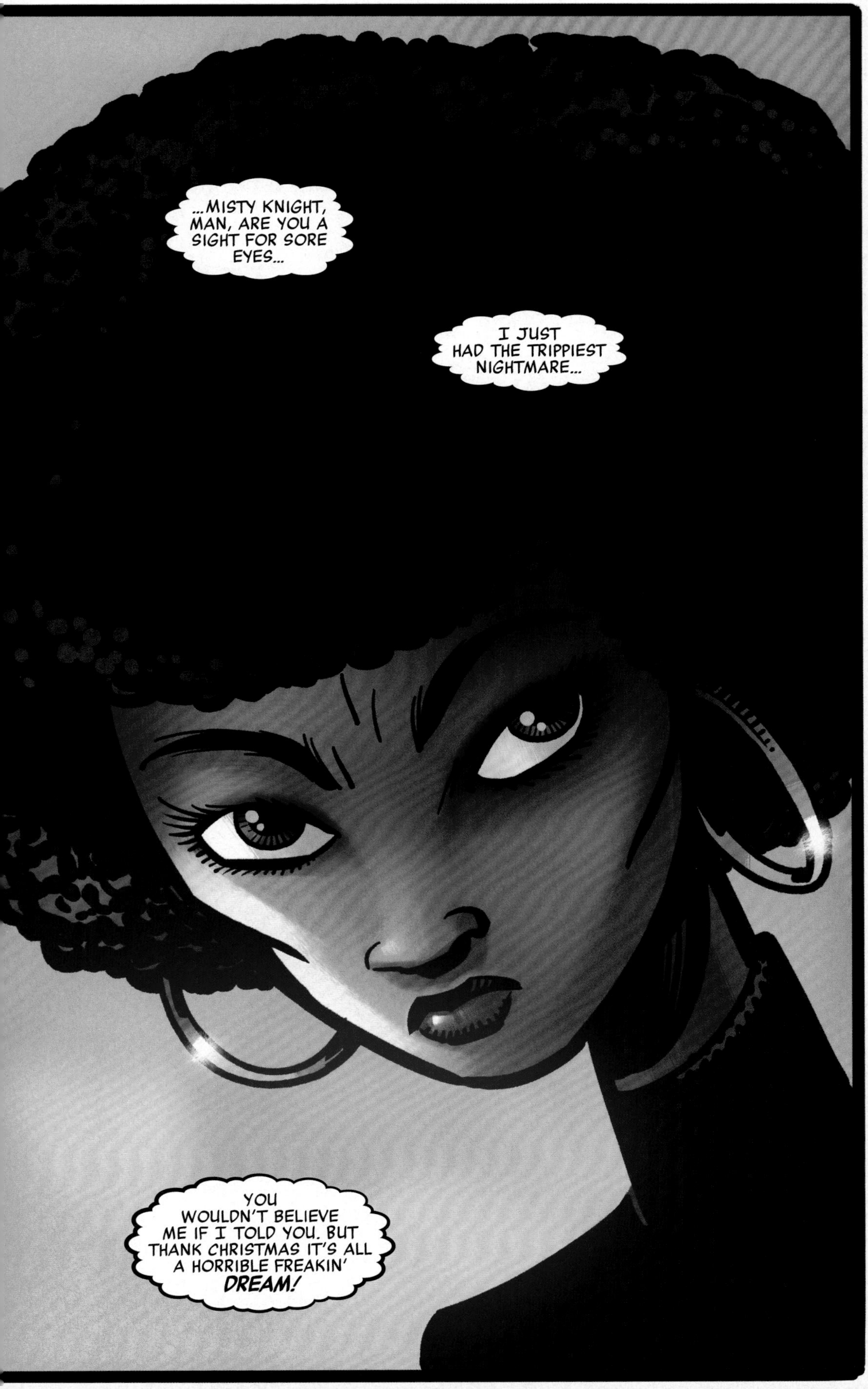
...MISTY KNIGHT, MAN, ARE YOU A SIGHT FOR SORE EYES...
I JUST HAD THE TRIPPIEST NIGHTMARE...
YOU WOULDN'T BELIEVE ME IF I TOLD YOU. BUT THANK CHRISTMAS IT'S ALL A HORRIBLE FREAKIN' DREAM!

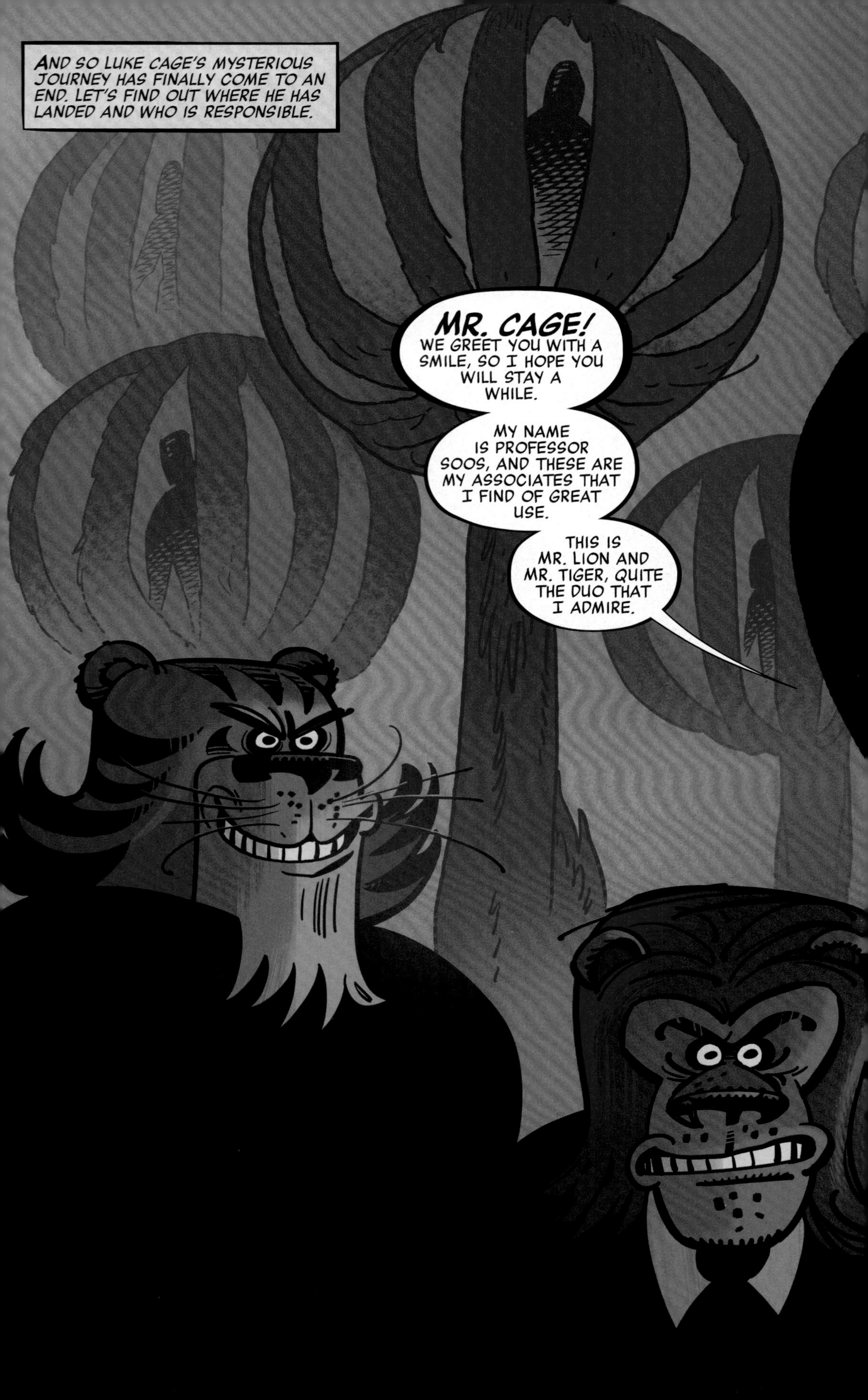
AND SO LUKE CAGE'S MYSTERIOUS JOURNEY HAS FINALLY COME TO AN END. LET'S FIND OUT WHERE HE HAS LANDED AND WHO IS RESPONSIBLE.
MR. CAGE! WE GREET YOU WITH A SMILE, SO I HOPE YOU WILL STAY A WHILE.
MY NAME IS PROFESSOR SOOS, AND THESE ARE MY ASSOCIATES THAT I FIND OF GREAT USE.
THIS IS MR. LION AND MR. TIGER, QUITE THE DUO THAT I ADMIRE.

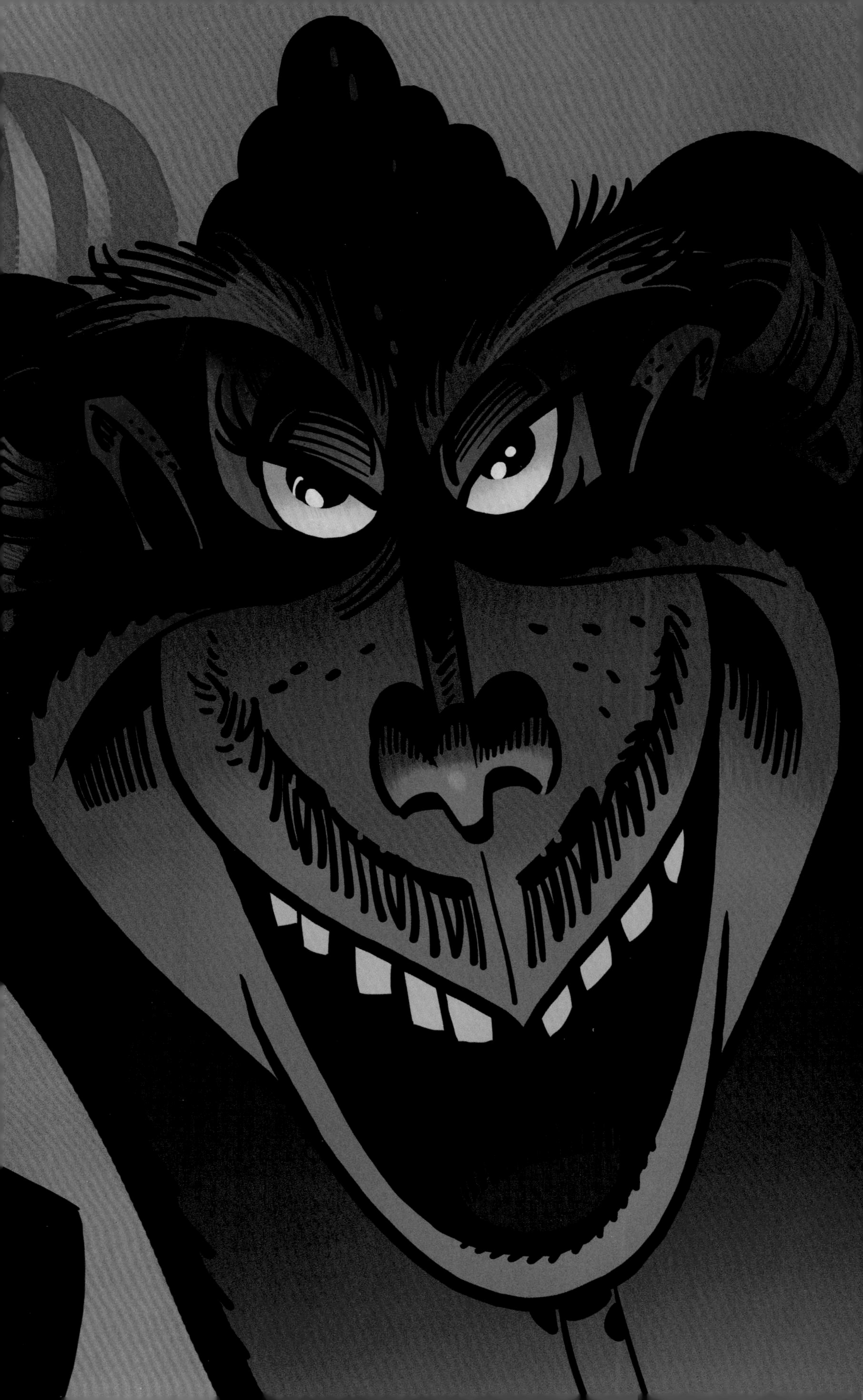

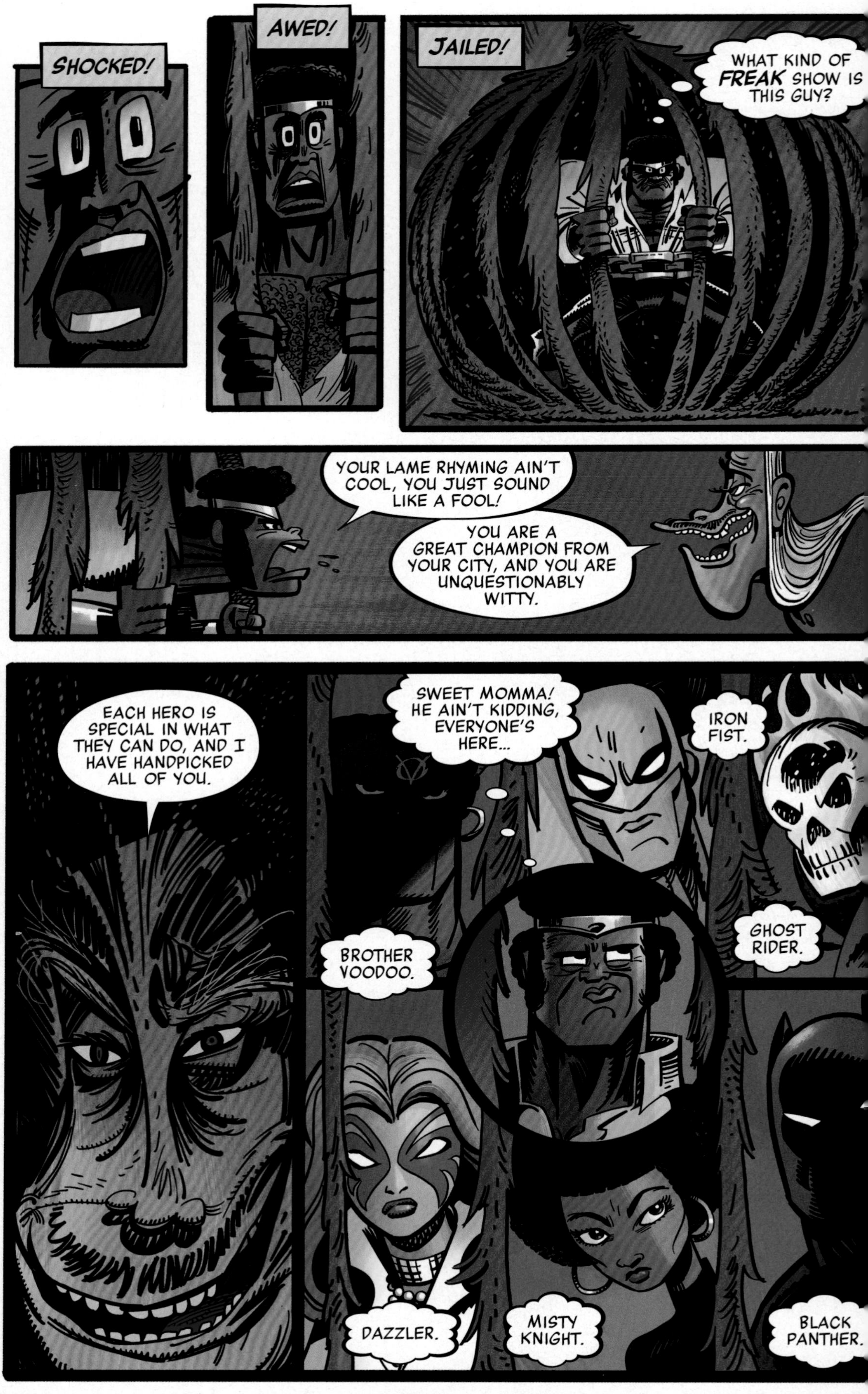
SHOCKED!
AWED!
JAILED!
WHAT KIND OF FREAK SHOW IS THIS GUY?
YOUR LAME RHYMING AIN'T COOL, YOU JUST SOUND LIKE A FOOL!
YOU ARE A GREAT CHAMPION FROM YOUR CITY, AND YOU ARE UNQUESTIONABLY WITTY.
EACH HERO IS SPECIAL IN WHAT THEY CAN DO, AND I HAVE HANDPICKED ALL OF YOU.
SWEET MOMMA! HE AIN'T KIDDING, EVERYONE'S HERE...
IRON FIST.
GHOST RIDER.
BROTHER VOODOO.
DAZZLER.
MISTY KNIGHT.
BLACK PANTHER.

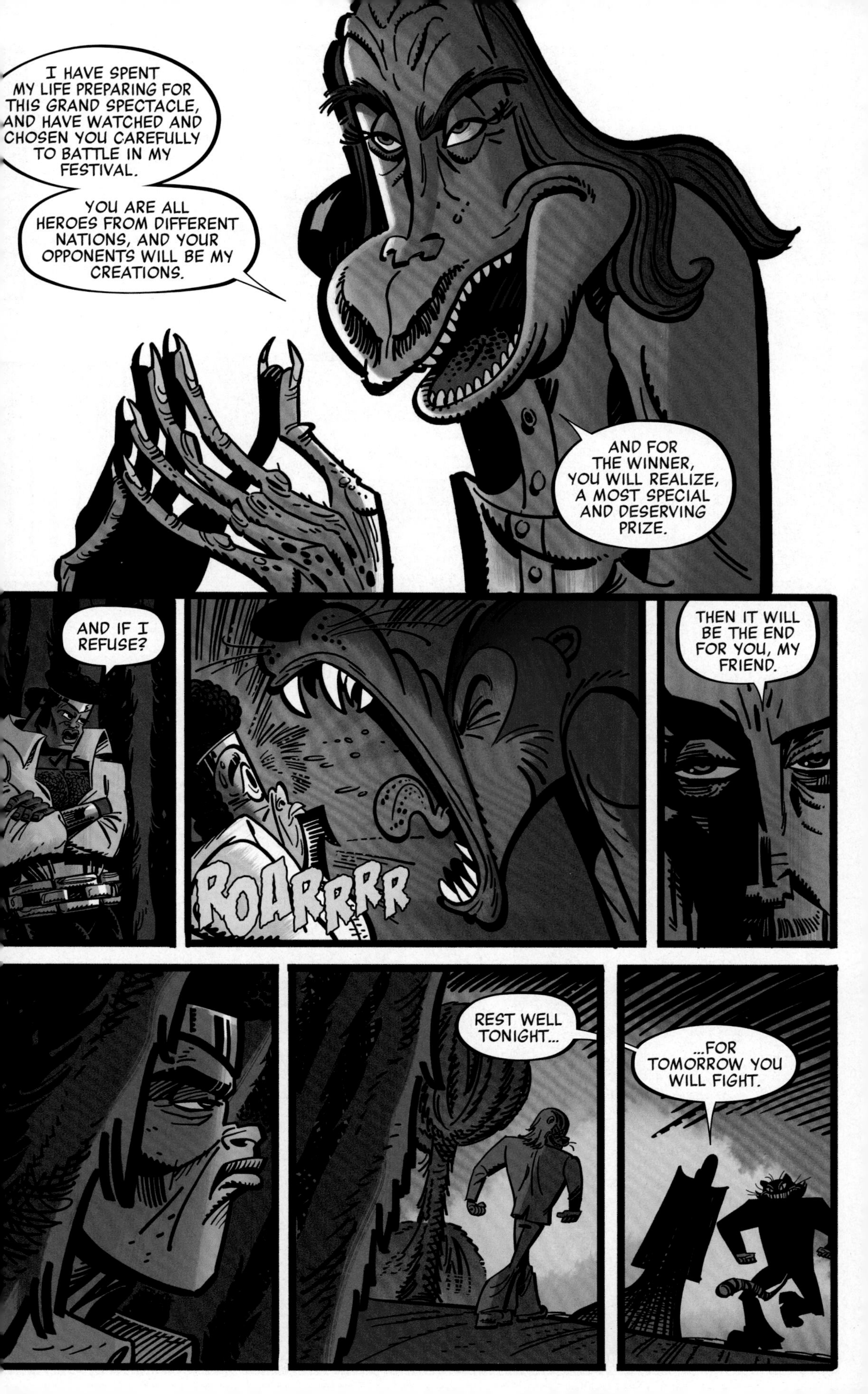
I HAVE SPENT MY LIFE PREPARING FOR THIS GRAND SPECTACLE, AND HAVE WATCHED AND CHOSEN YOU CAREFULLY TO BATTLE IN MY FESTIVAL.
YOU ARE ALL HEROES FROM DIFFERENT NATIONS, AND YOUR OPPONENTS WILL BE MY CREATIONS.
AND FOR THE WINNER, YOU WILL REALIZE, A MOST SPECIAL AND DESERVING PRIZE.
AND IF I REFUSE?
ROARRRR
THEN IT WILL BE THE END FOR YOU, MY FRIEND.
REST WELL TONIGHT...
...FOR TOMORROW YOU WILL FIGHT.

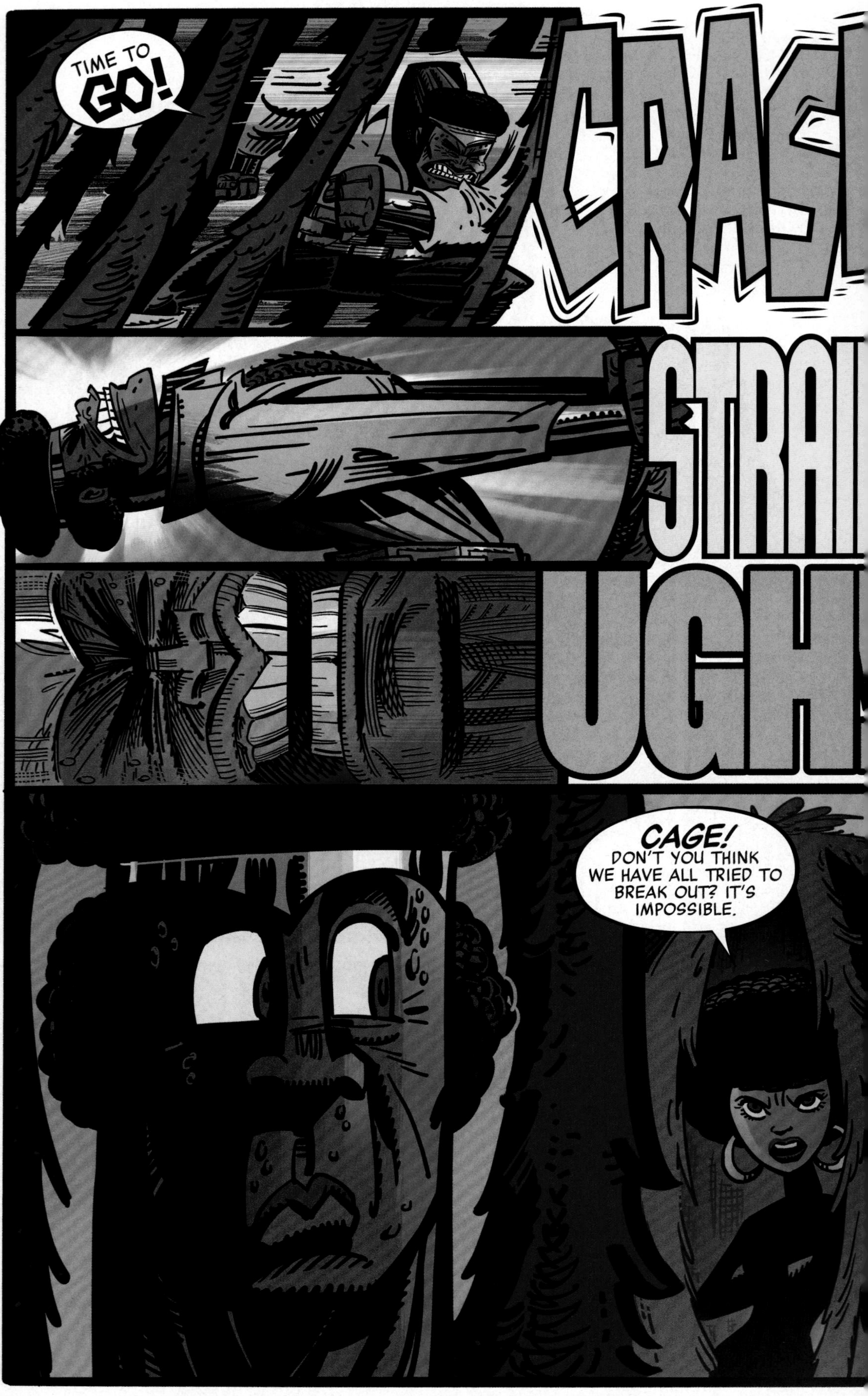
TIME TO GO!
CRAS
STRAI
UGH
CAGE! DON'T YOU THINK WE HAVE ALL TRIED TO BREAK OUT? IT'S IMPOSSIBLE.

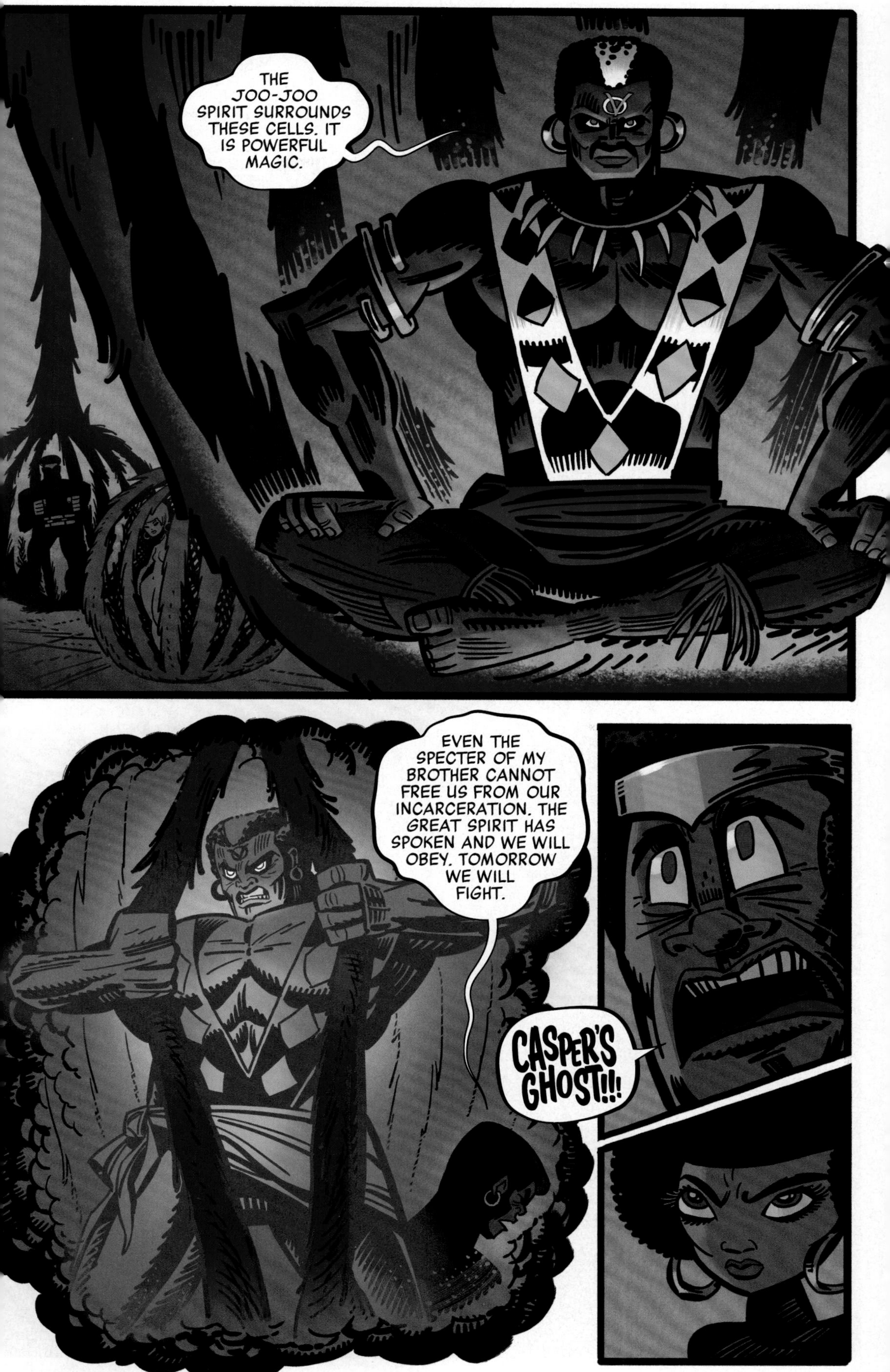
THE JOO-JOO SPIRIT SURROUNDS THESE CELLS. IT IS POWERFUL MAGIC.
EVEN THE SPECTER OF MY BROTHER CANNOT FREE US FROM OUR INCARCERATION. THE GREAT SPIRIT HAS SPOKEN AND WE WILL OBEY. TOMORROW WE WILL FIGHT.
CASPER'S GHOST!!!

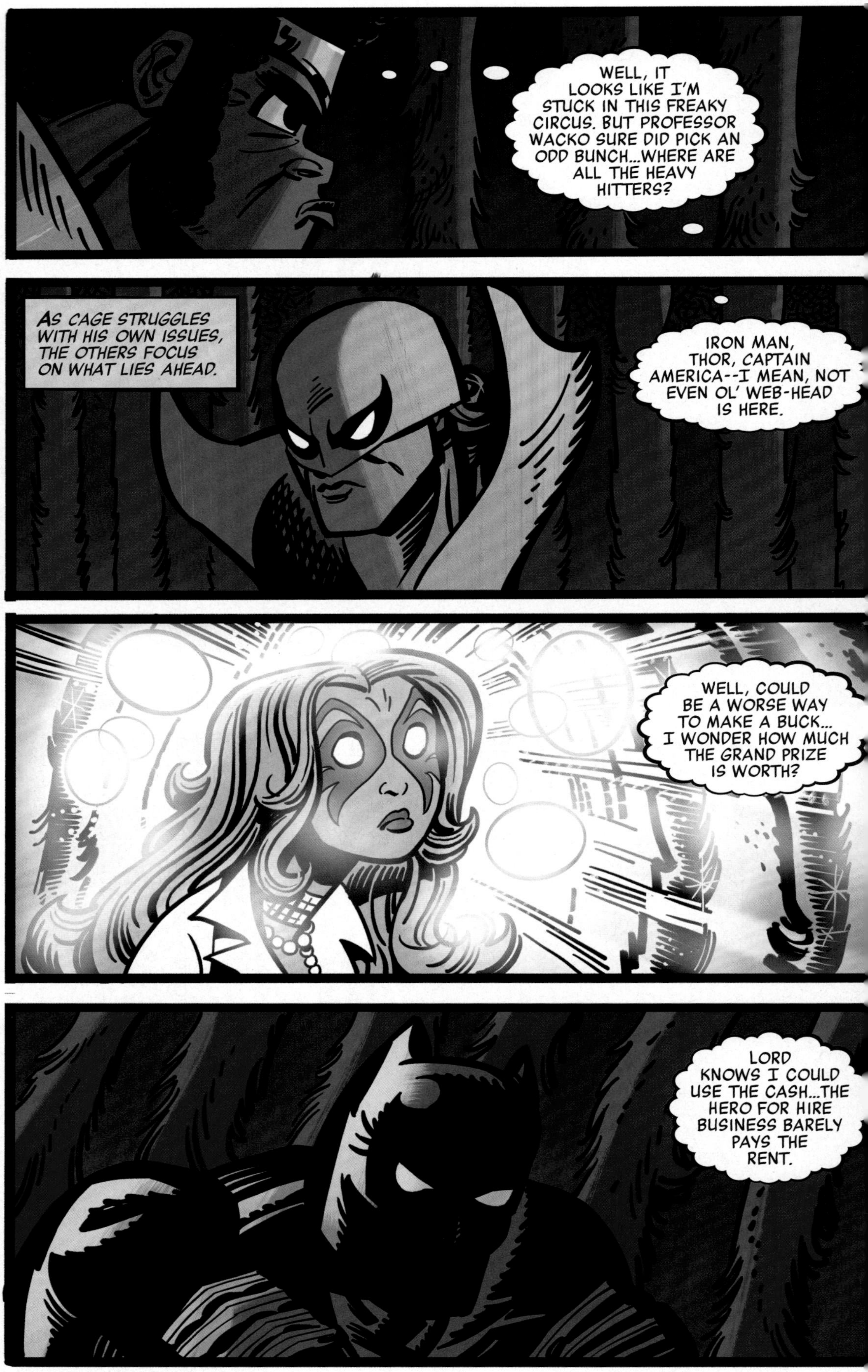
WELL, IT LOOKS LIKE I'M STUCK IN THIS FREAKY CIRCUS. BUT PROFESSOR WACKO SURE DID PICK AN ODD BUNCH...WHERE ARE ALL THE HEAVY HITTERS?
AS CAGE STRUGGLES WITH HIS OWN ISSUES, THE OTHERS FOCUS ON WHAT LIES AHEAD.
IRON MAN, THOR, CAPTAIN AMERICA--I MEAN, NOT EVEN OL' WEB-HEAD IS HERE.
WELL, COULD BE A WORSE WAY TO MAKE A BUCK... I WONDER HOW MUCH THE GRAND PRIZE IS WORTH?
LORD KNOWS I COULD USE THE CASH...THE HERO FOR HIRE BUSINESS BARELY PAYS THE RENT.

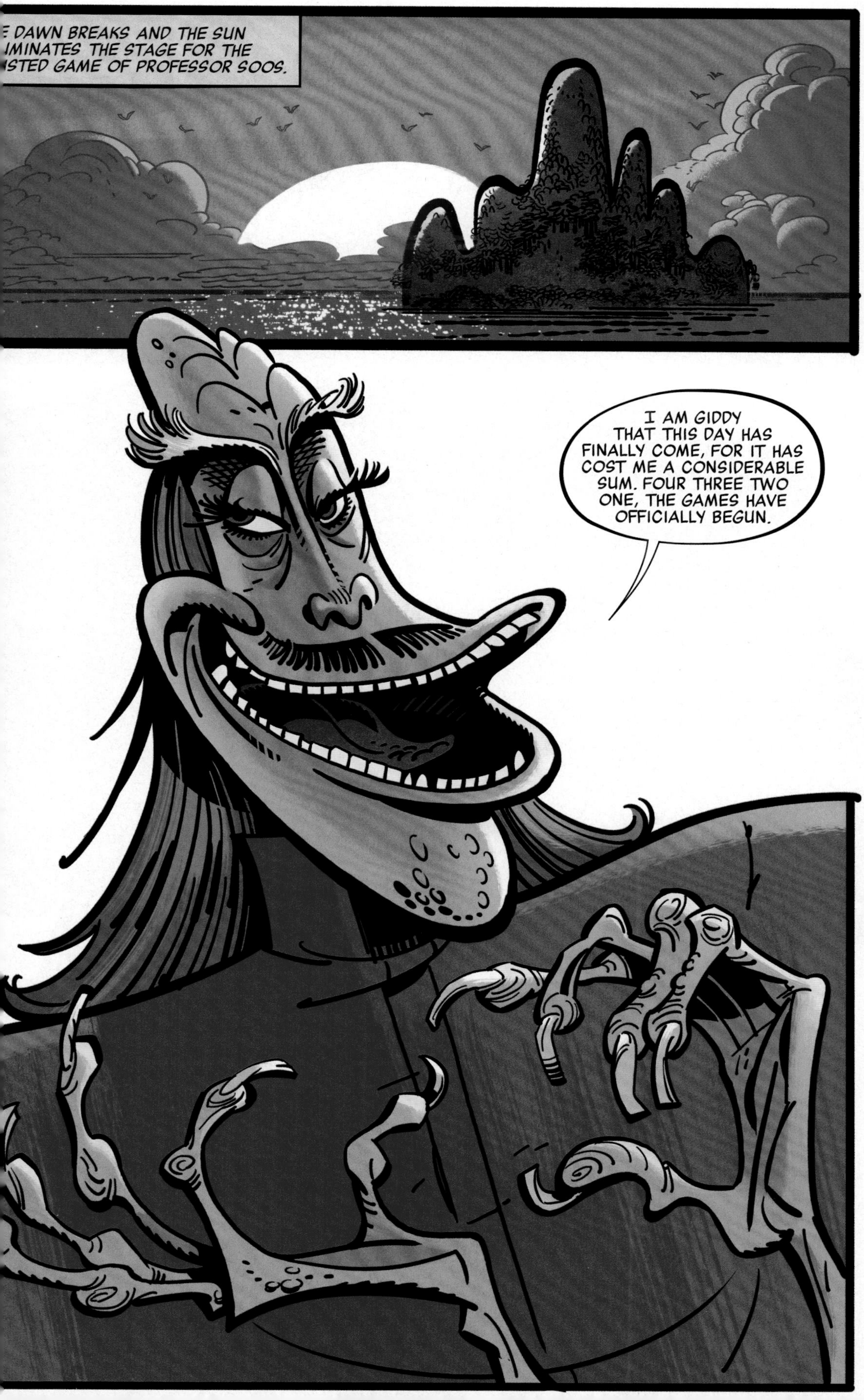
E DAWN BREAKS AND THE SUN IMINATES THE STAGE FOR THE ISTED GAME OF PROFESSOR SOOS.
I AM GIDDY THAT THIS DAY HAS FINALLY COME, FOR IT HAS COST ME A CONSIDERABLE SUM. FOUR THREE TWO ONE, THE GAMES HAVE OFFICIALLY BEGUN.

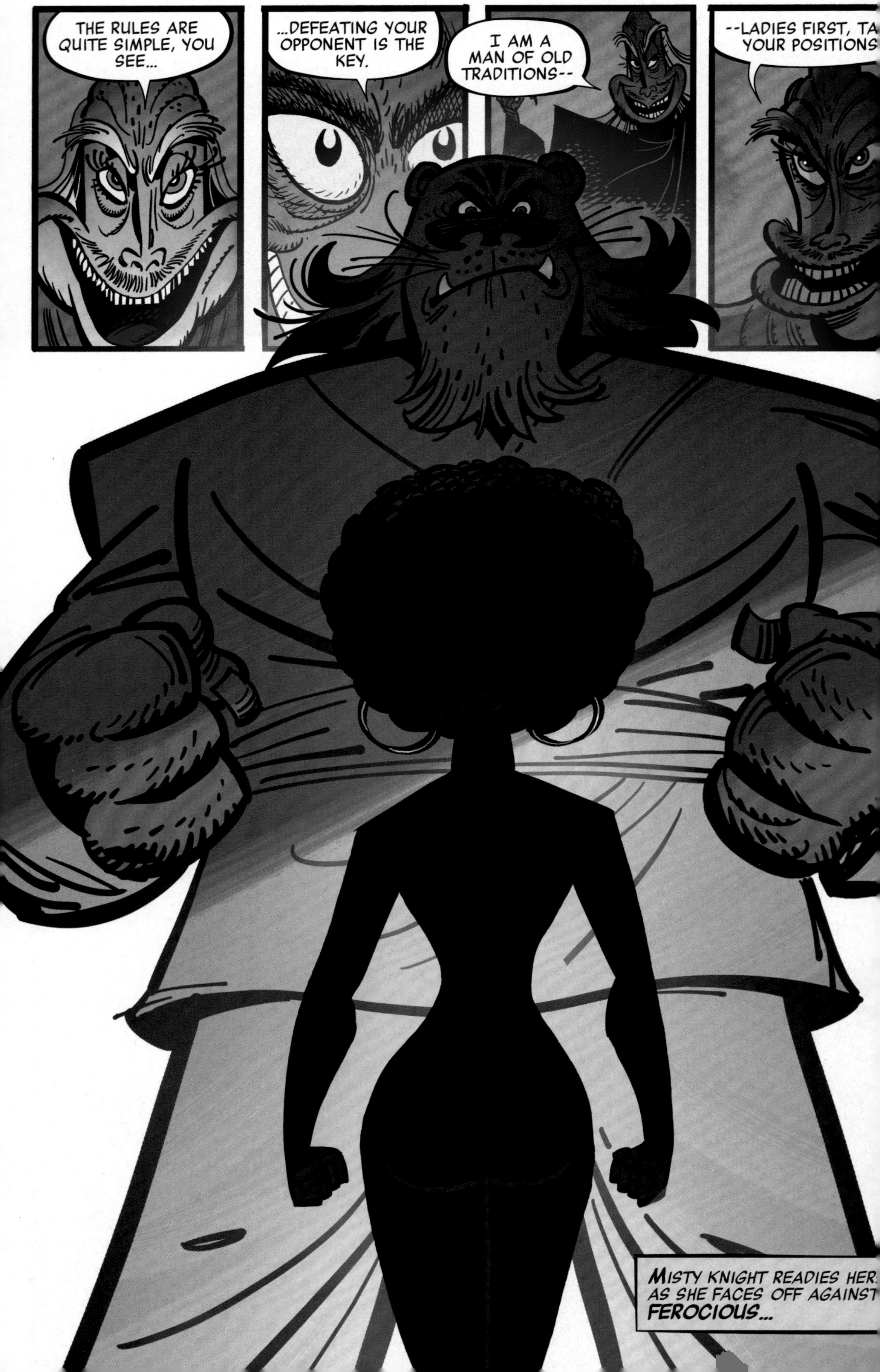
THE RULES ARE QUITE SIMPLE, YOU SEE...
...DEFEATING YOUR OPPONENT IS THE KEY.
I AM A MAN OF OLD TRADITIONS--
--LADIES FIRST, TA YOUR POSITIONS
MISTY KNIGHT READIES HER AS SHE FACES OFF AGAINST FEROCIOUS...

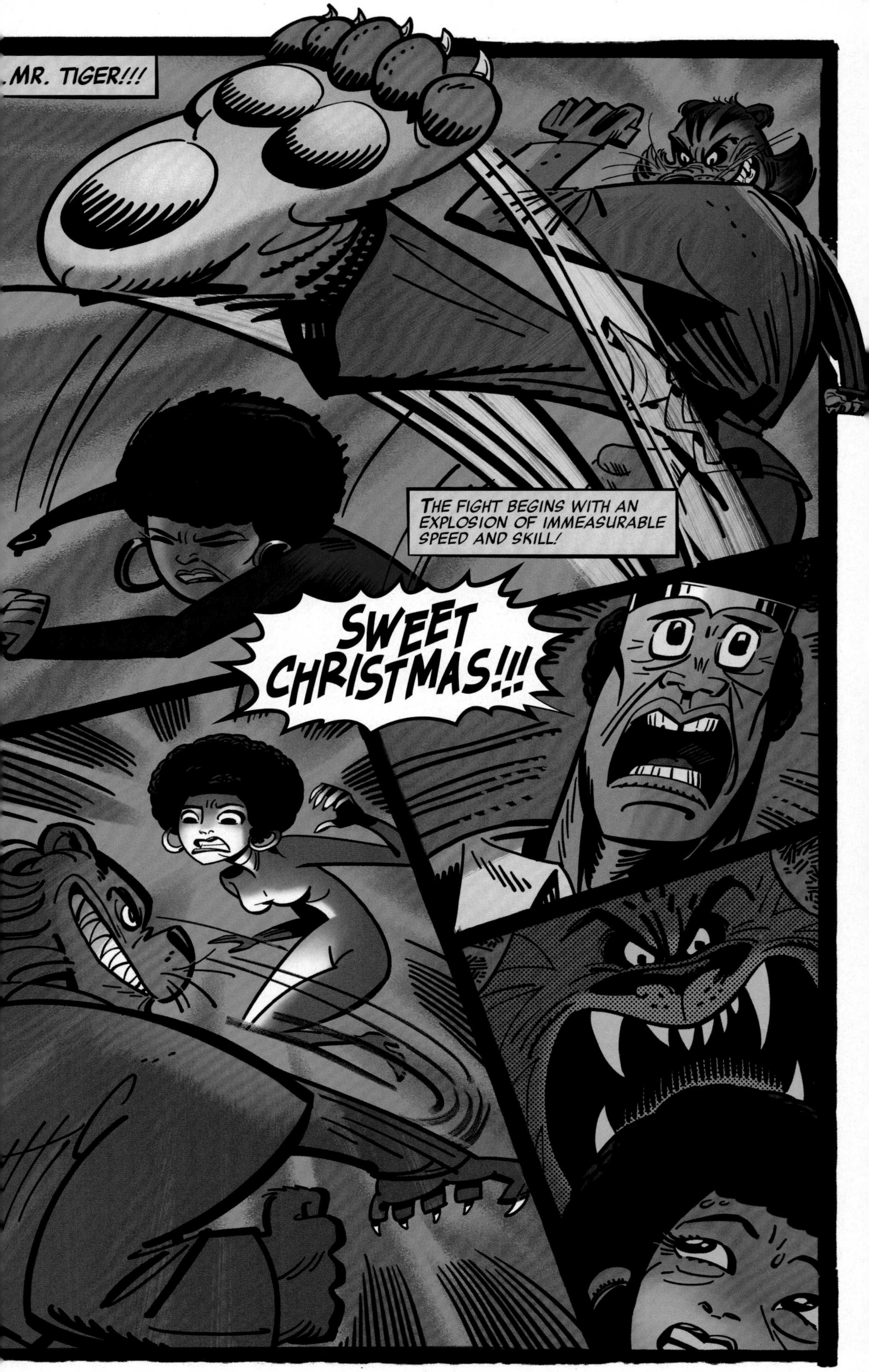
...MR. TIGER!!!
THE FIGHT BEGINS WITH AN EXPLOSION OF IMMEASURABLE SPEED AND SKILL!
SWEET CHRISTMAS!!!

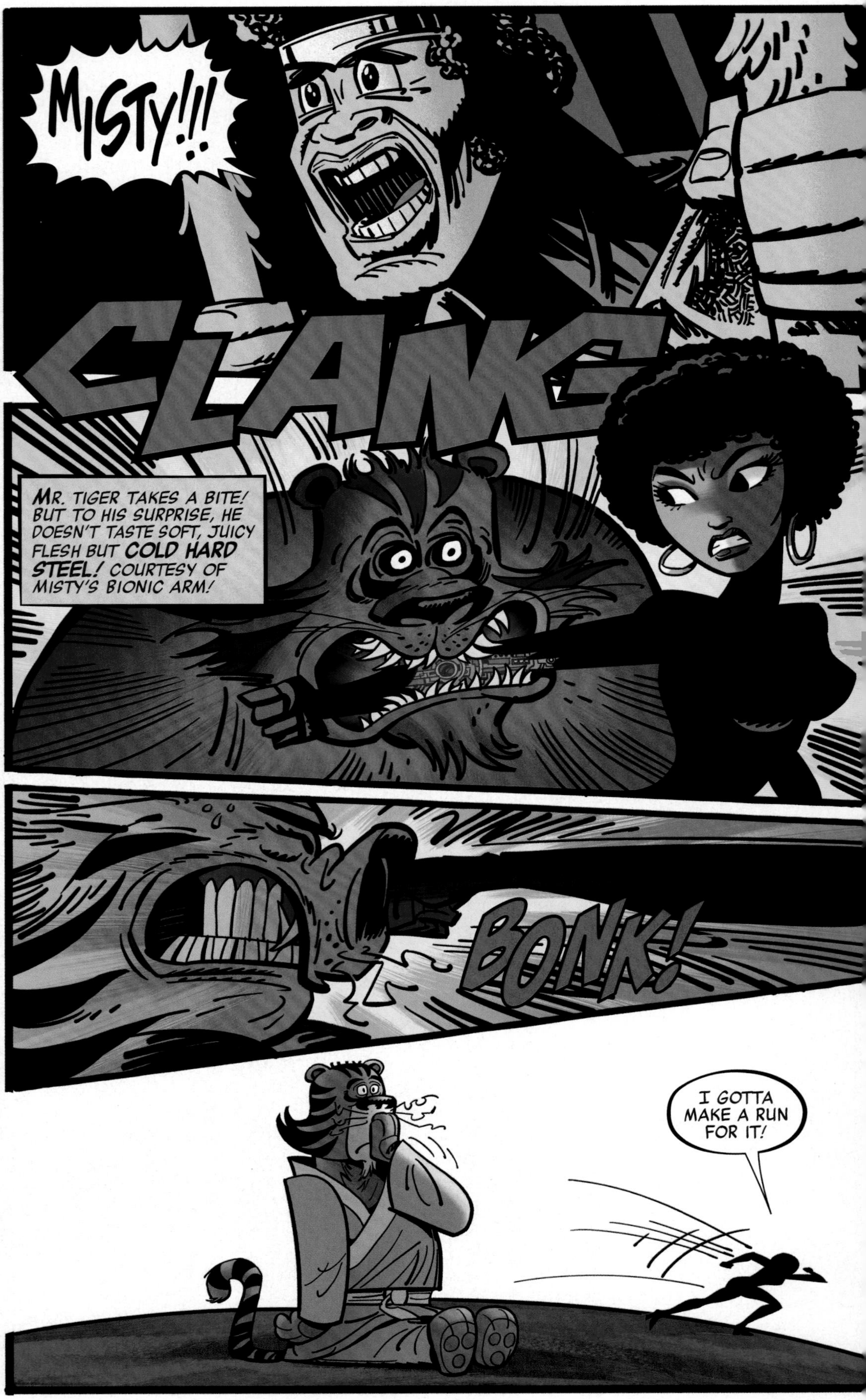
MISTY!!!
CLANG
MR. TIGER TAKES A BITE! BUT TO HIS SURPRISE, HE DOESN'T TASTE SOFT, JUICY FLESH BUT COLD HARD STEEL! COURTESY OF MISTY'S BIONIC ARM!
BONK!
I GOTTA MAKE A RUN FOR IT!

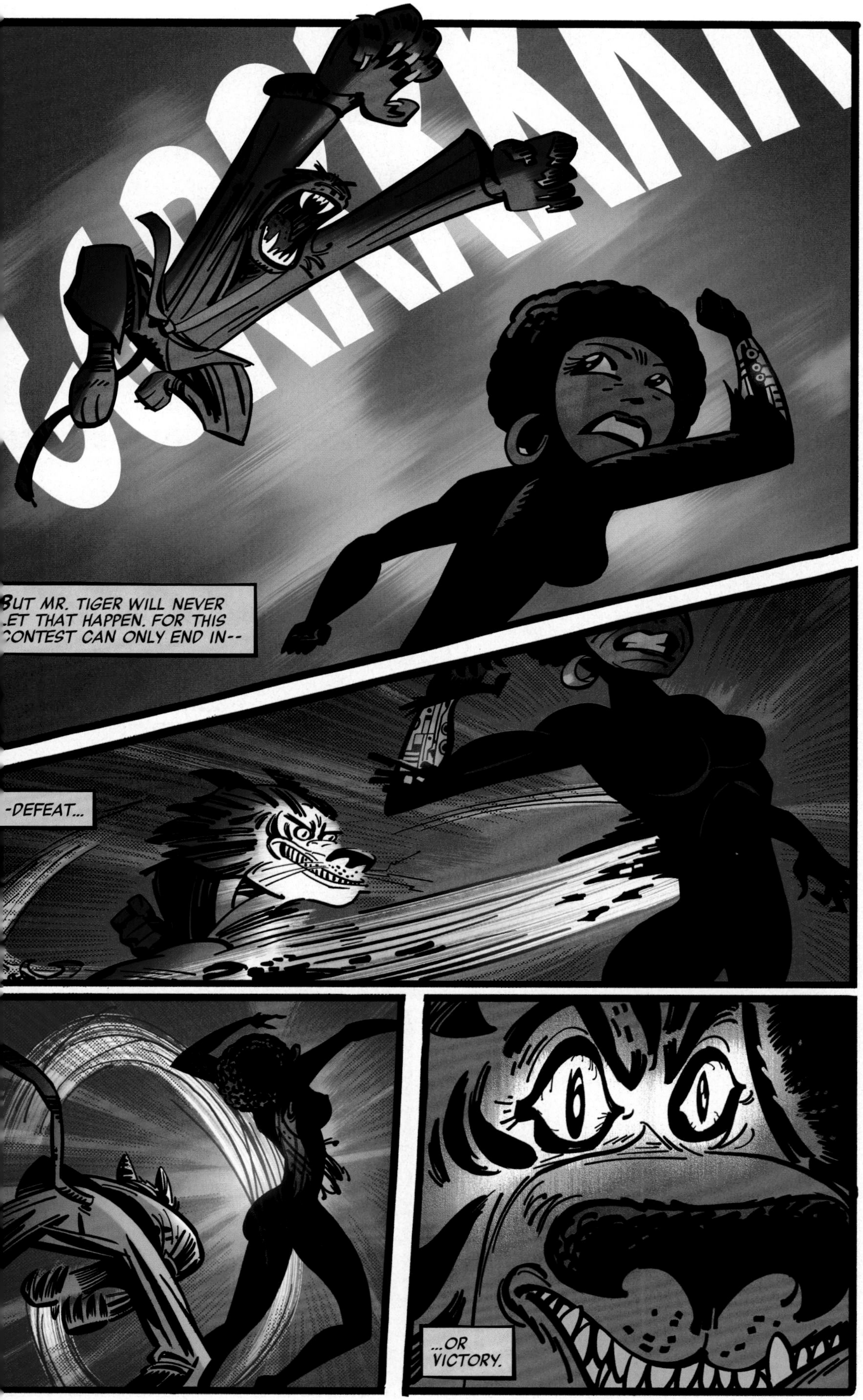
BUT MR. TIGER WILL NEVER LET THAT HAPPEN. FOR THIS CONTEST CAN ONLY END IN--
-DEFEAT...
...OR VICTORY.

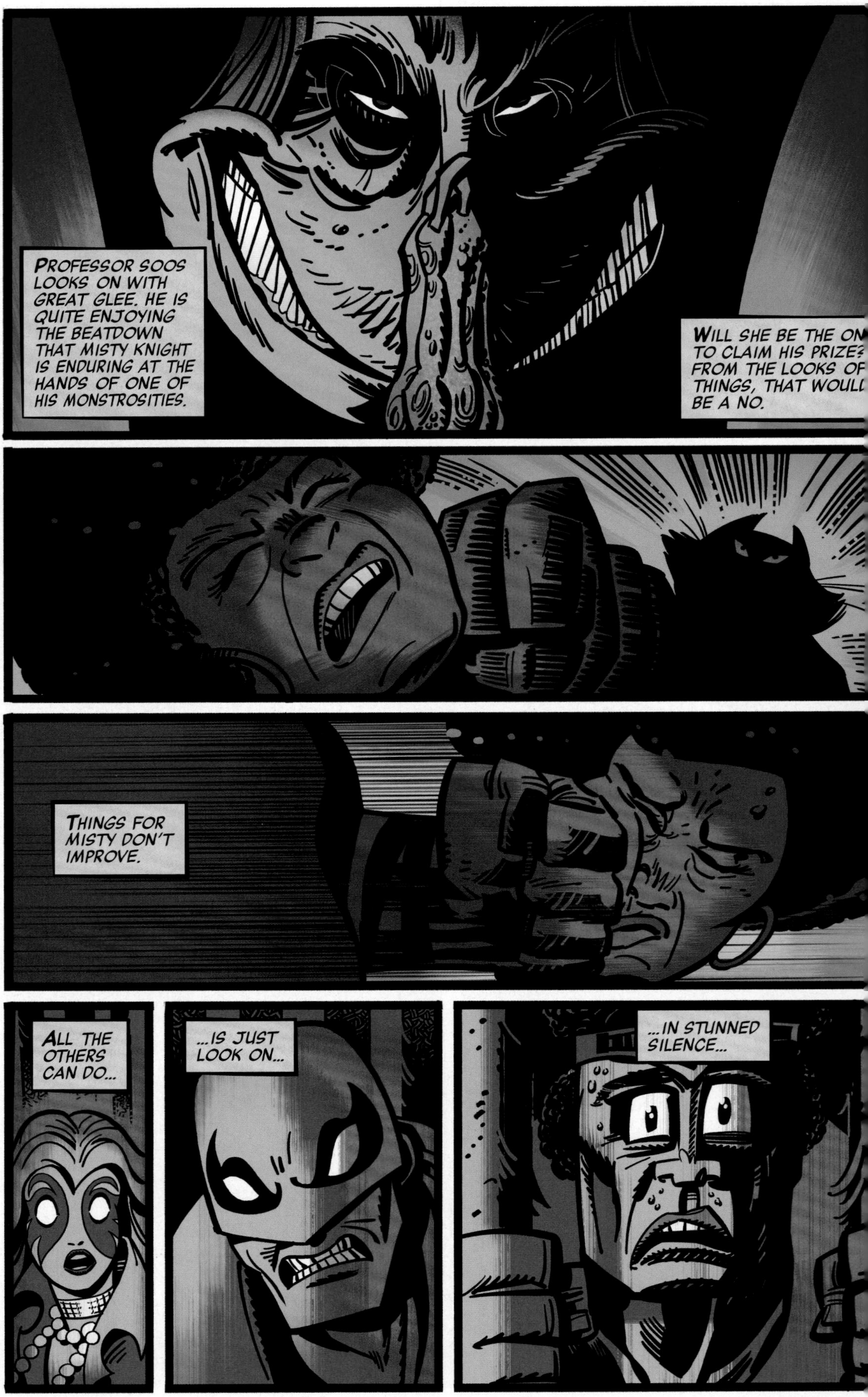
PROFESSOR SOOS LOOKS ON WITH GREAT GLEE. HE IS QUITE ENJOYING THE BEATDOWN THAT MISTY KNIGHT IS ENDURING AT THE HANDS OF ONE OF HIS MONSTROSITIES.
WILL SHE BE THE ON TO CLAIM HIS PRIZE? FROM THE LOOKS OF THINGS, THAT WOUL BE A NO.
THINGS FOR MISTY DON'T IMPROVE.
ALL THE OTHERS CAN DO...
...IS JUST LOOK ON...
...IN STUNNED SILENCE...

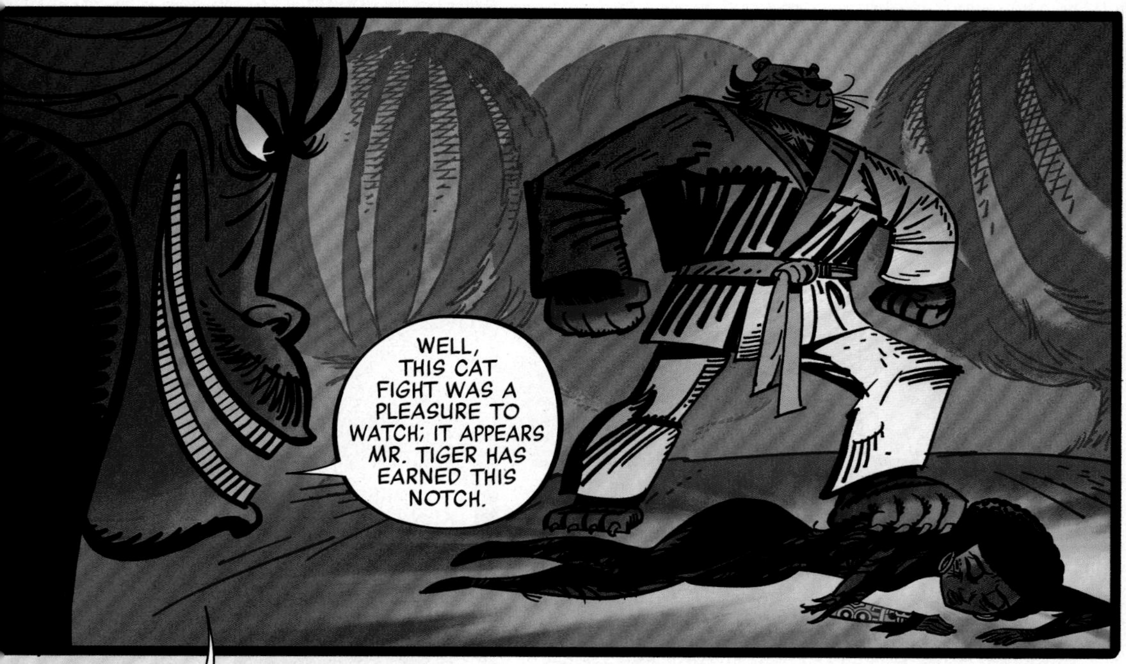
WELL, THIS CAT FIGHT WAS A PLEASURE TO WATCH; IT APPEARS MR. TIGER HAS EARNED THIS NOTCH.

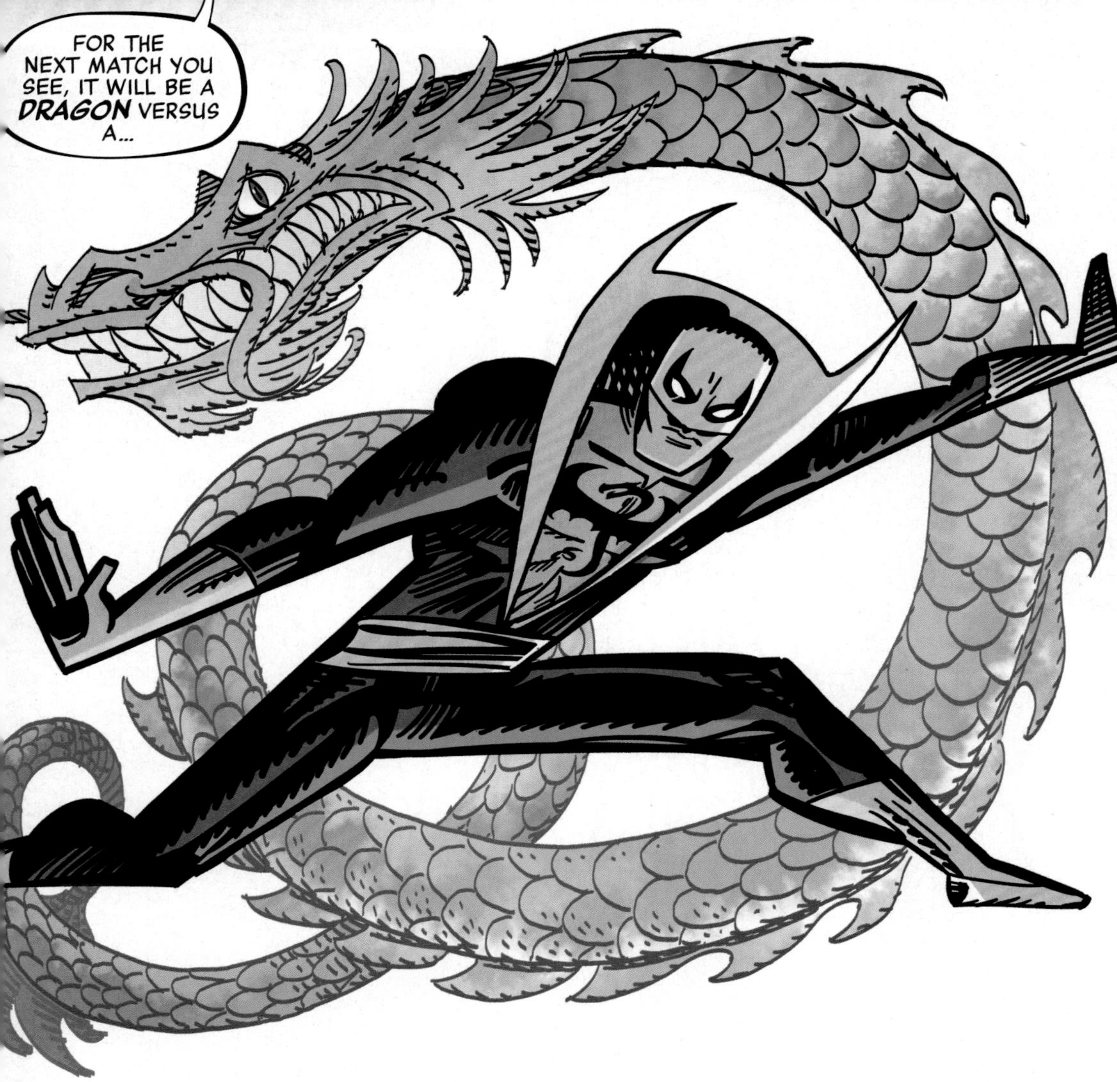
FOR THE NEXT MATCH YOU SEE, IT WILL BE A DRAGON VERSUS A...

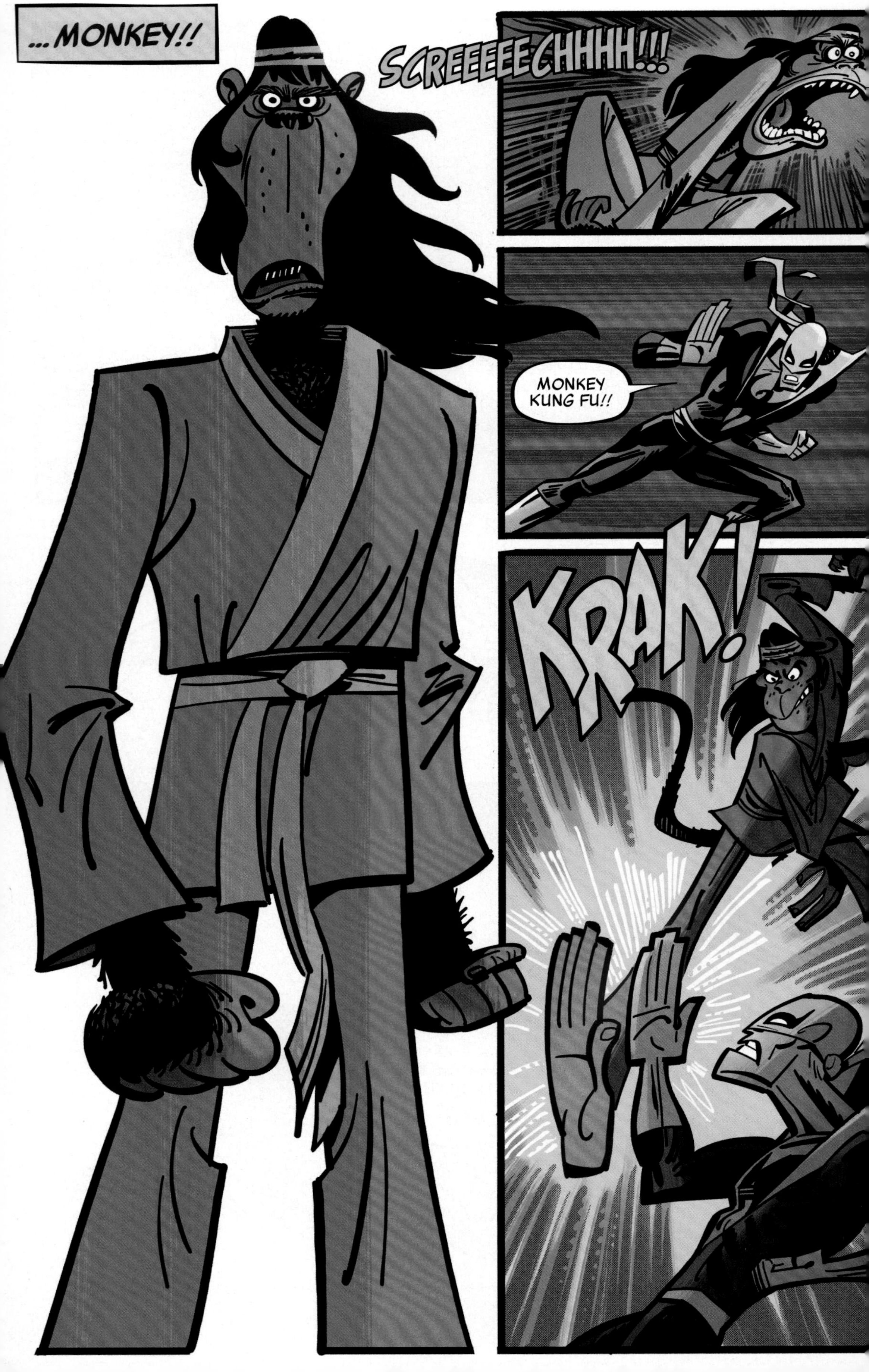

...MONKEY!!
SCREEEEEECHHHH!!!
MONKEY KUNG FU!!
KRAK!

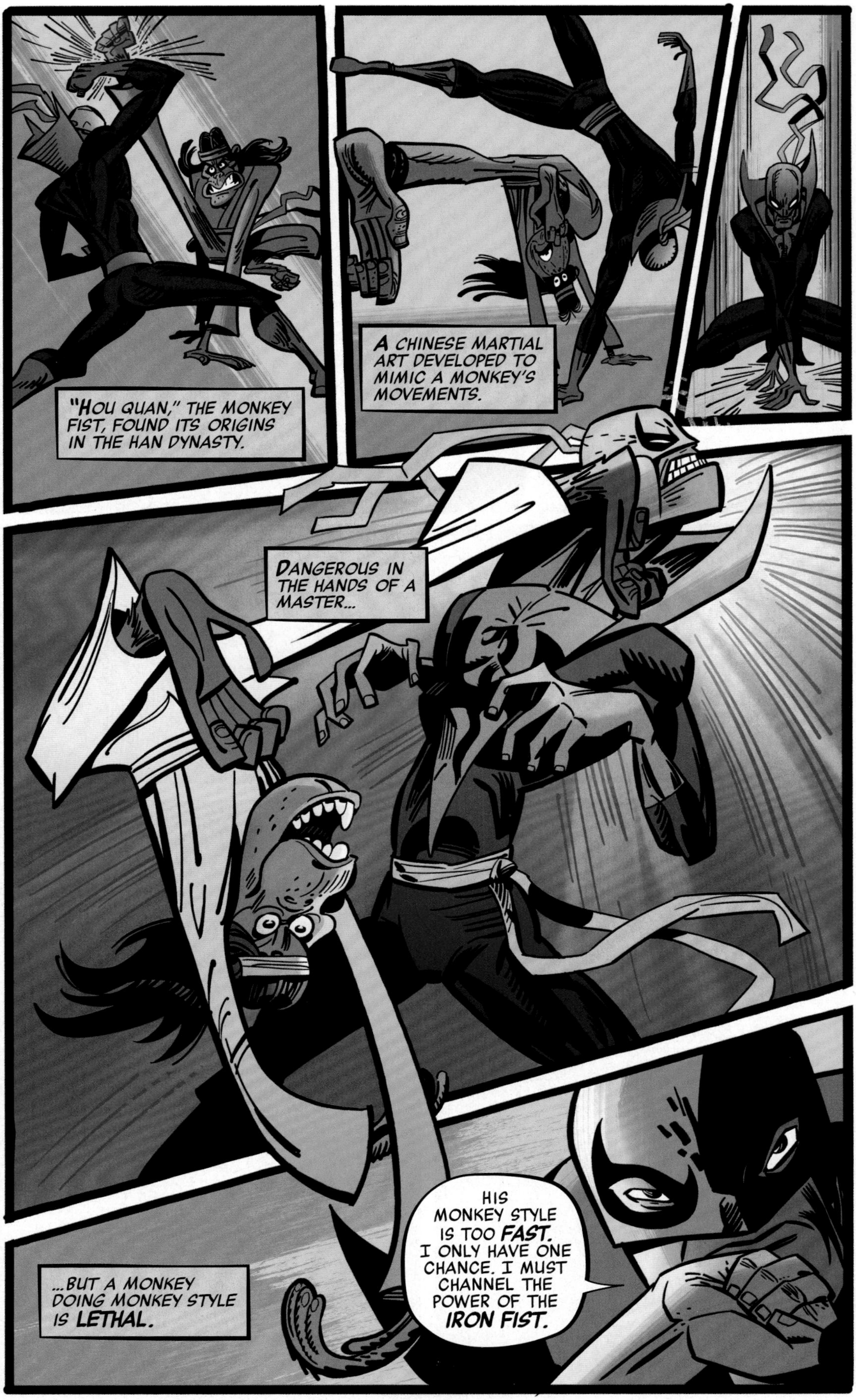
"HOU QUAN," THE MONKEY FIST, FOUND ITS ORIGINS IN THE HAN DYNASTY.
A CHINESE MARTIAL ART DEVELOPED TO MIMIC A MONKEY'S MOVEMENTS.
DANGEROUS IN THE HANDS OF A MASTER...
...BUT A MONKEY DOING MONKEY STYLE IS LETHAL.
HIS MONKEY STYLE IS TOO FAST. I ONLY HAVE ONE CHANCE. I MUST CHANNEL THE POWER OF THE IRON FIST.

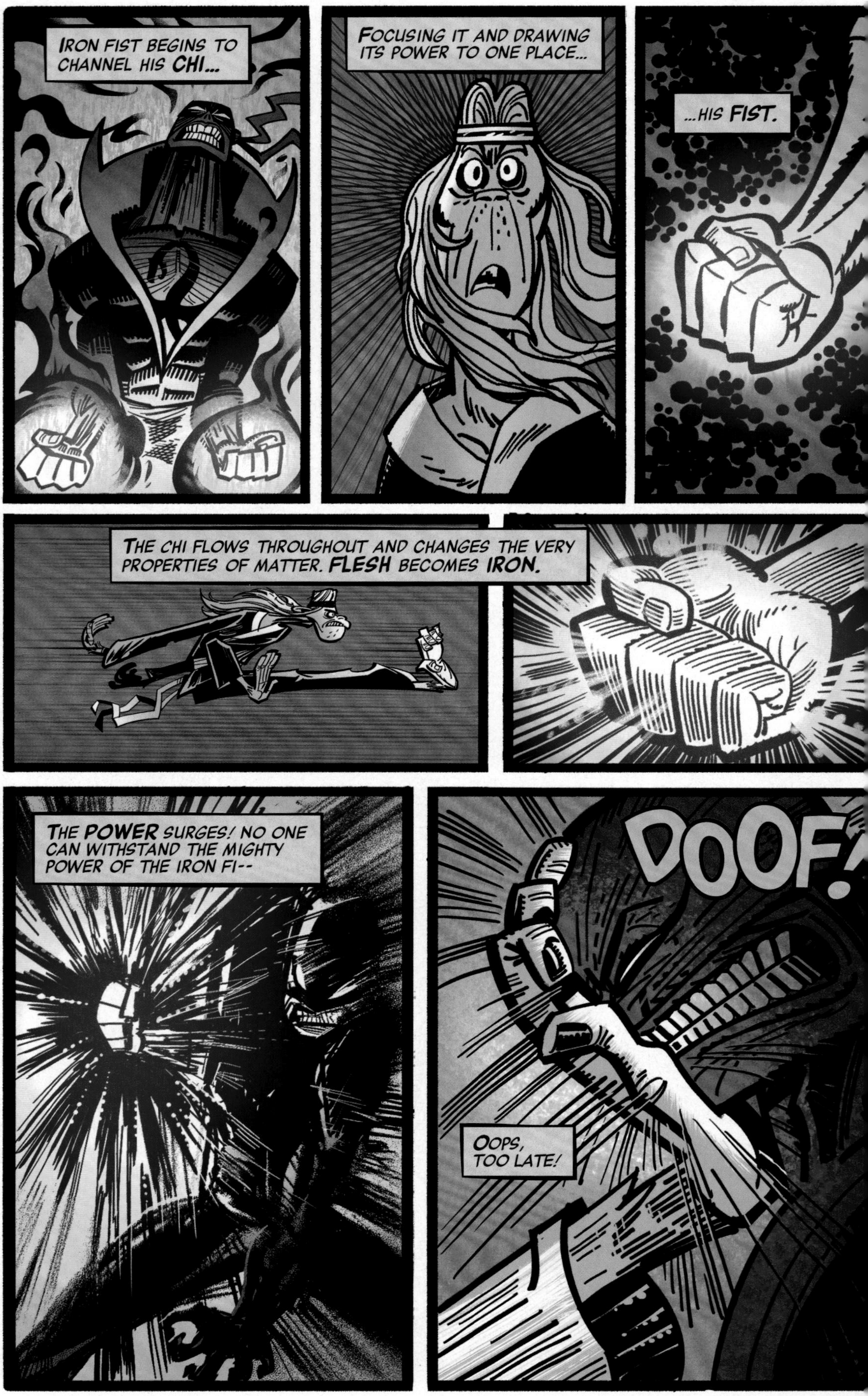
IRON FIST BEGINS TO CHANNEL HIS CHI...
FOCUSING IT AND DRAWING ITS POWER TO ONE PLACE...
...HIS FIST.
THE CHI FLOWS THROUGHOUT AND CHANGES THE VERY PROPERTIES OF MATTER. FLESH BECOMES IRON.
THE POWER SURGES! NO ONE CAN WITHSTAND THE MIGHTY POWER OF THE IRON FI--
DOOF!
OOPS, TOO LATE!

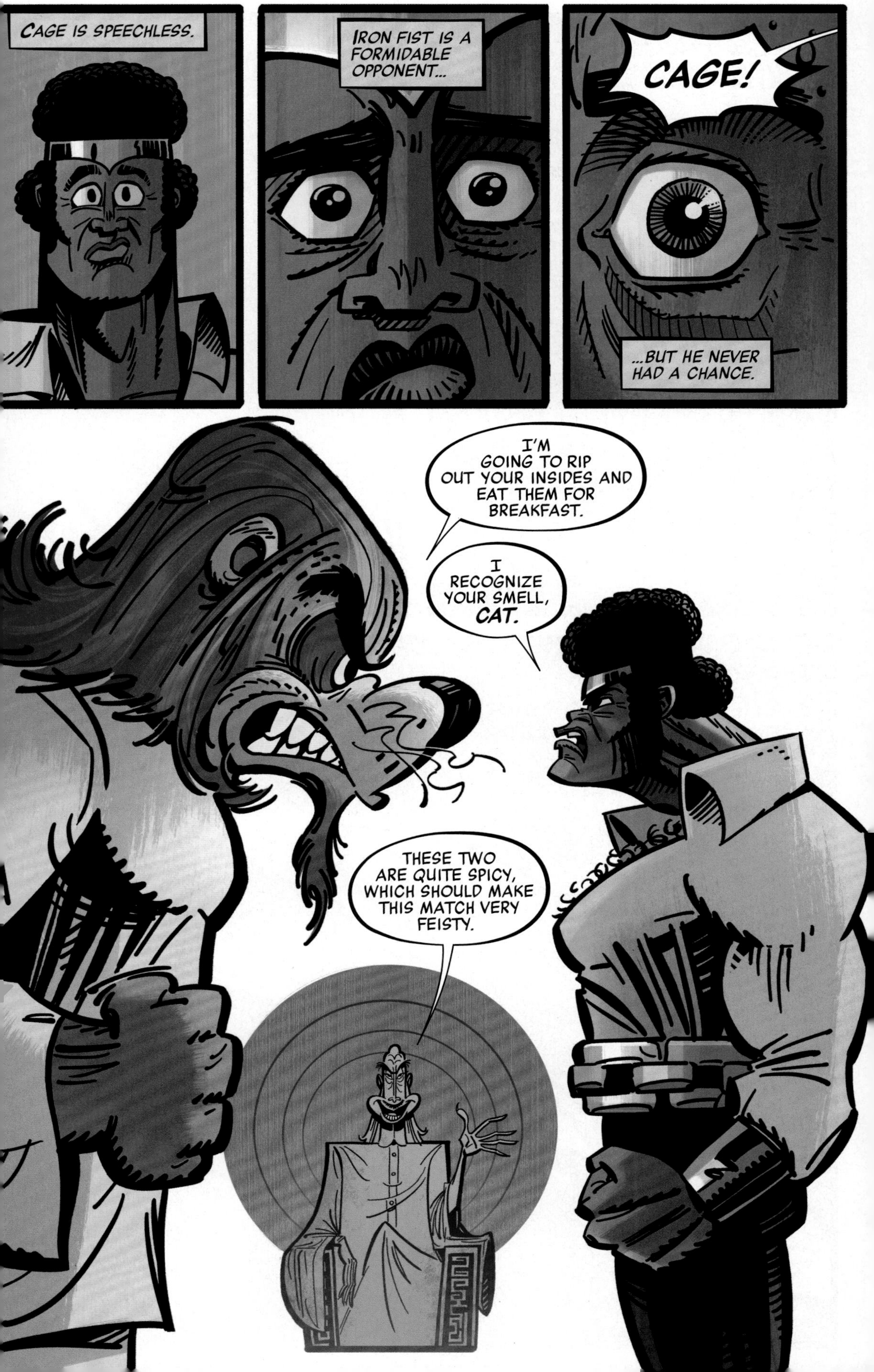
CAGE IS SPEECHLESS.
IRON FIST IS A FORMIDABLE OPPONENT...
CAGE!
...BUT HE NEVER HAD A CHANCE.
I'M GOING TO RIP OUT YOUR INSIDES AND EAT THEM FOR BREAKFAST.
I RECOGNIZE YOUR SMELL, CAT.
THESE TWO ARE QUITE SPICY, WHICH SHOULD MAKE THIS MATCH VERY FEISTY.

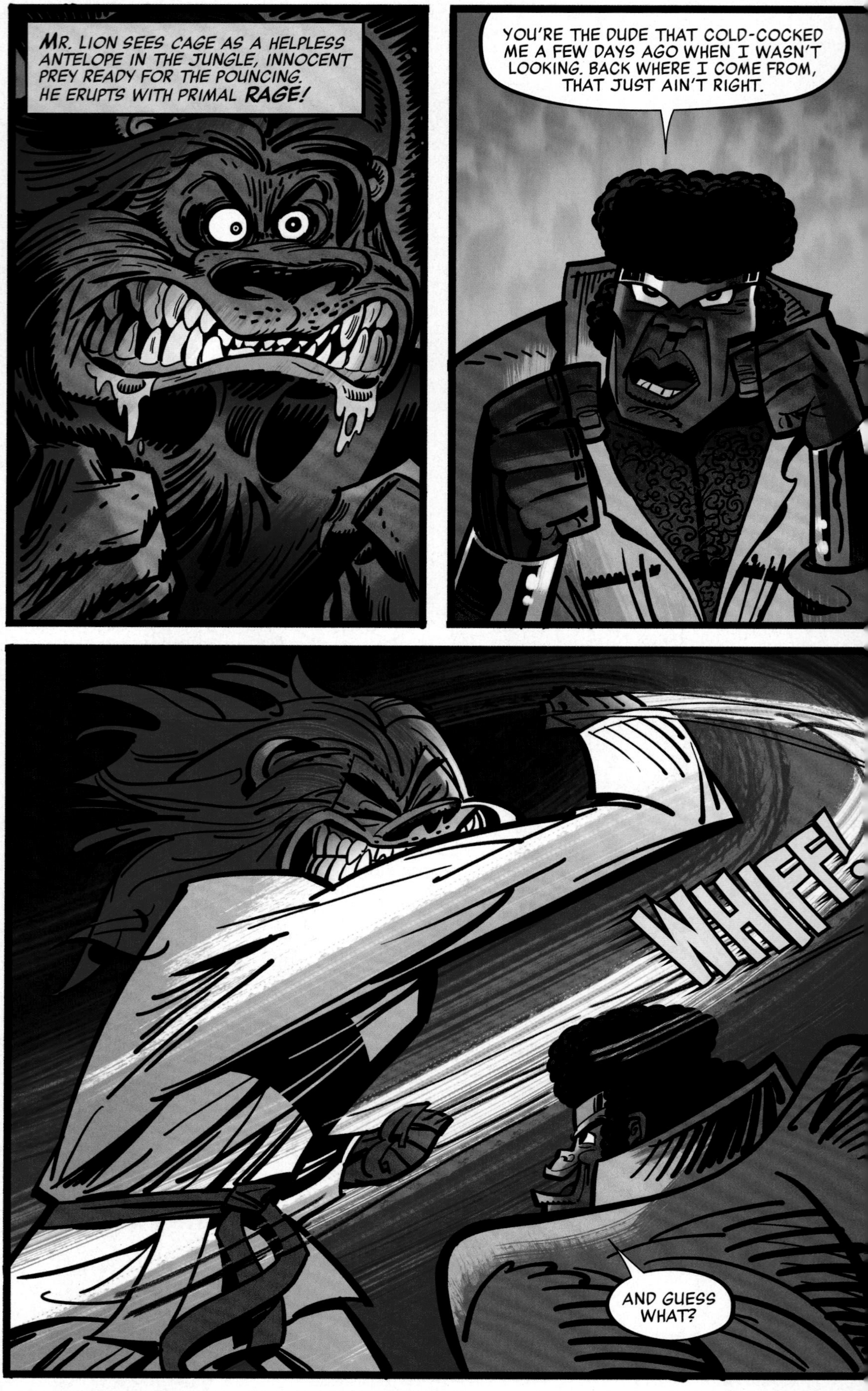
MR. LION SEES CAGE AS A HELPLESS ANTELOPE IN THE JUNGLE, INNOCENT PREY READY FOR THE POUNCING. HE ERUPTS WITH PRIMAL RAGE!
YOU'RE THE DUDE THAT COLD-COCKED ME A FEW DAYS AGO WHEN I WASN'T LOOKING. BACK WHERE I COME FROM, THAT JUST AIN'T RIGHT.
WHIFF!
AND GUESS WHAT?

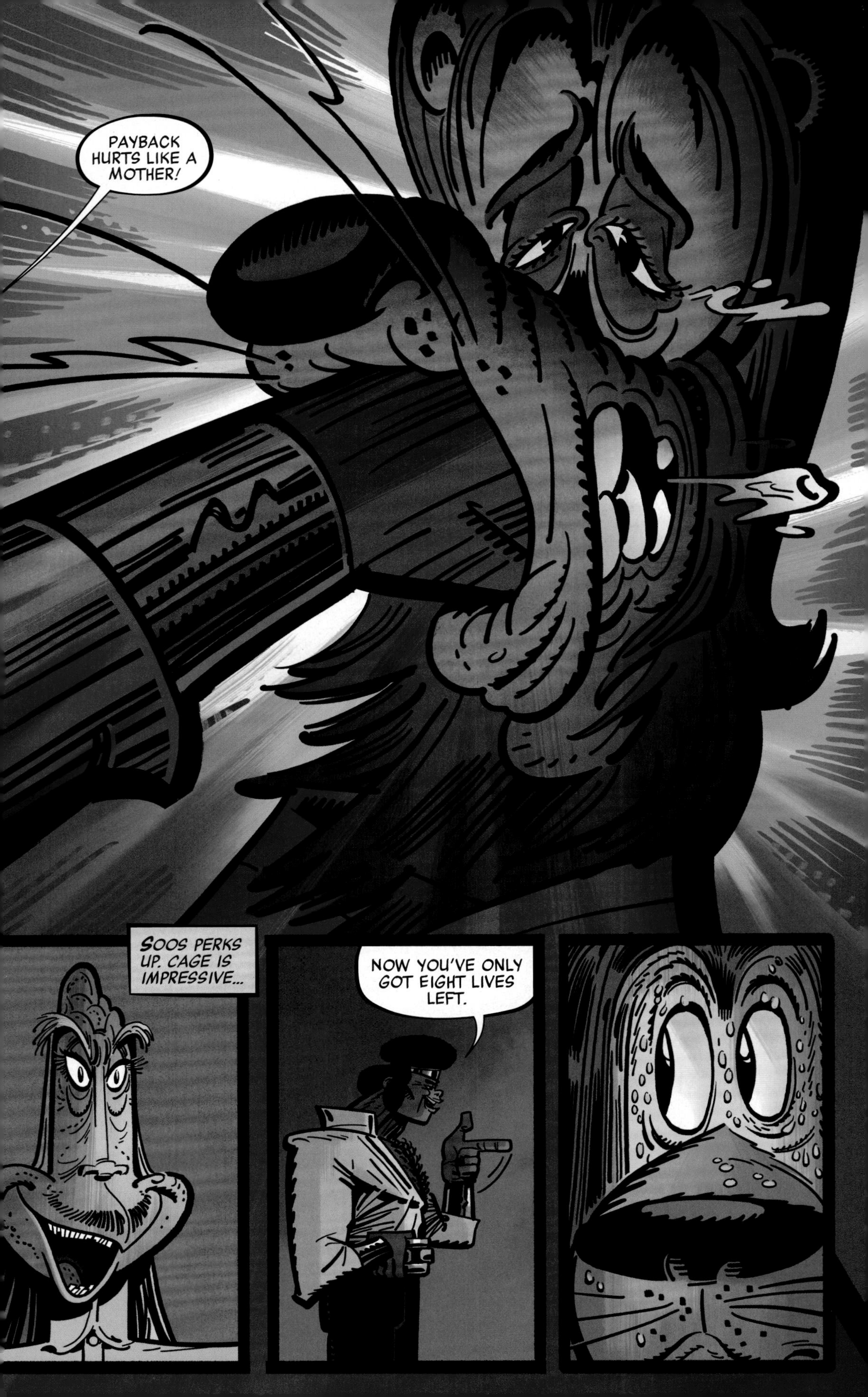
PAYBACK HURTS LIKE A MOTHER!
SOOS PERKS UP. CAGE IS IMPRESSIVE...
NOW YOU'VE ONLY GOT EIGHT LIVES LEFT.

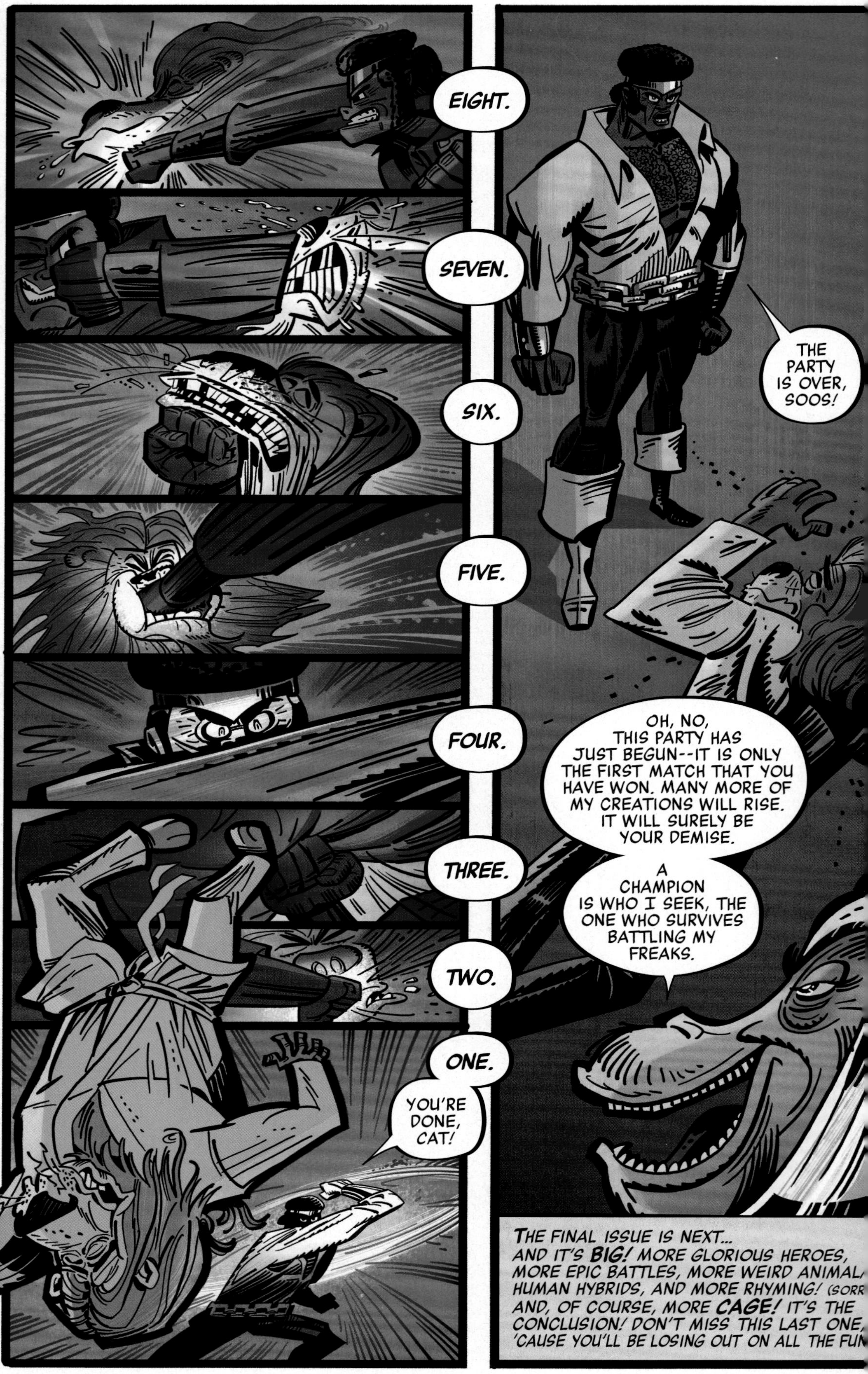
EIGHT.
SEVEN.
SIX.
FIVE.
FOUR.
THREE.
TWO.
ONE.
YOU'RE DONE, CAT!
THE PARTY IS OVER, SOOS!
OH, NO, THIS PARTY HAS JUST BEGUN--IT IS ONLY THE FIRST MATCH THAT YOU HAVE WON. MANY MORE OF MY CREATIONS WILL RISE. IT WILL SURELY BE YOUR DEMISE.
A CHAMPION IS WHO I SEEK, THE ONE WHO SURVIVES BATTLING MY FREAKS.
THE FINAL ISSUE IS NEXT...
AND IT'S BIG! MORE GLORIOUS HEROES,
MORE EPIC BATTLES, MORE WEIRD ANIMAL
HUMAN HYBRIDS, AND MORE RHYMING! (SORR
AND, OF COURSE, MORE CAGE! IT'S THE
CONCLUSION! DON'T MISS THIS LAST ONE,
'CAUSE YOU'LL BE LOSING OUT ON ALL THE FU

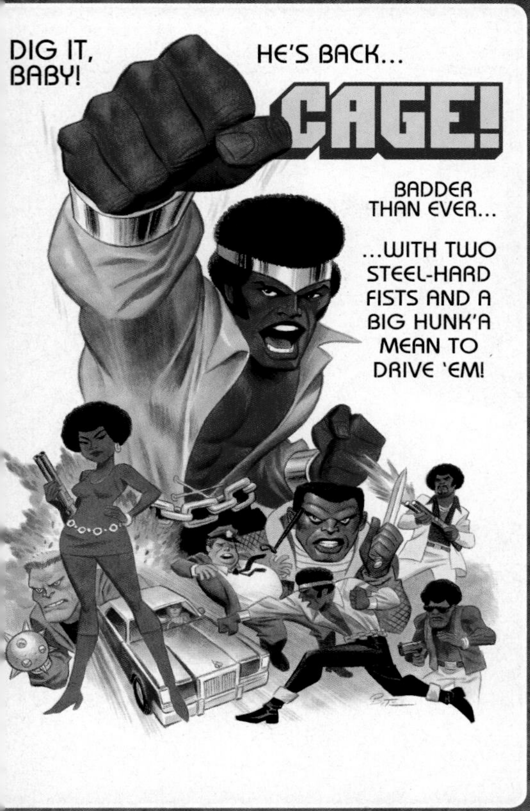
DIG IT, BABY!
HE'S BACK...
CAGE!
BADDER THAN EVER...
...WITH TWO STEEL-HARD FISTS AND A BIG HUNK'A MEAN TO DRIVE 'EM!

**BRUCE TIMM**
2 variant

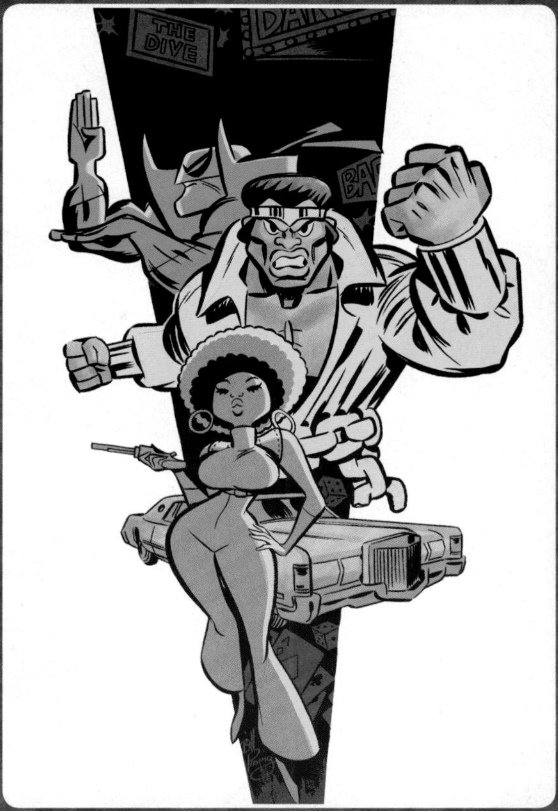
THE DIVE

**BILL PRESSING**
3 variant

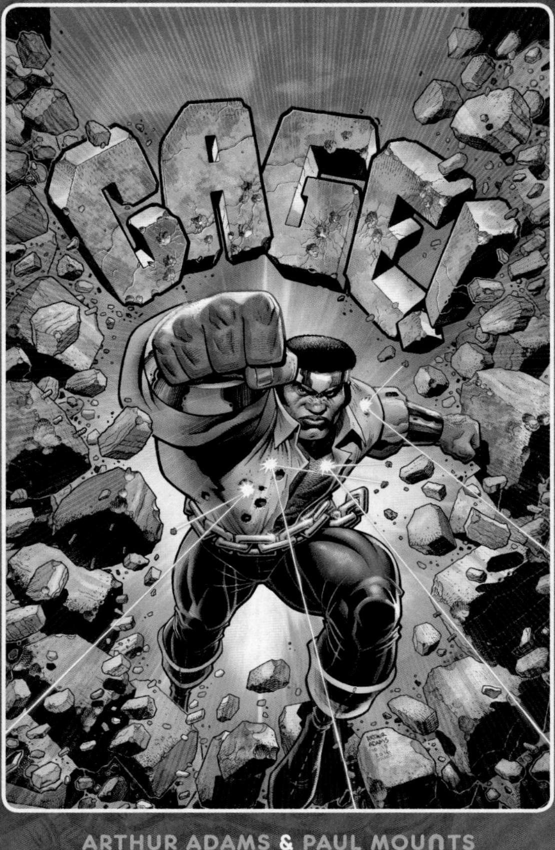
CAGE!

**ARTHUR ADAMS & PAUL MOUNTS**
4 variant

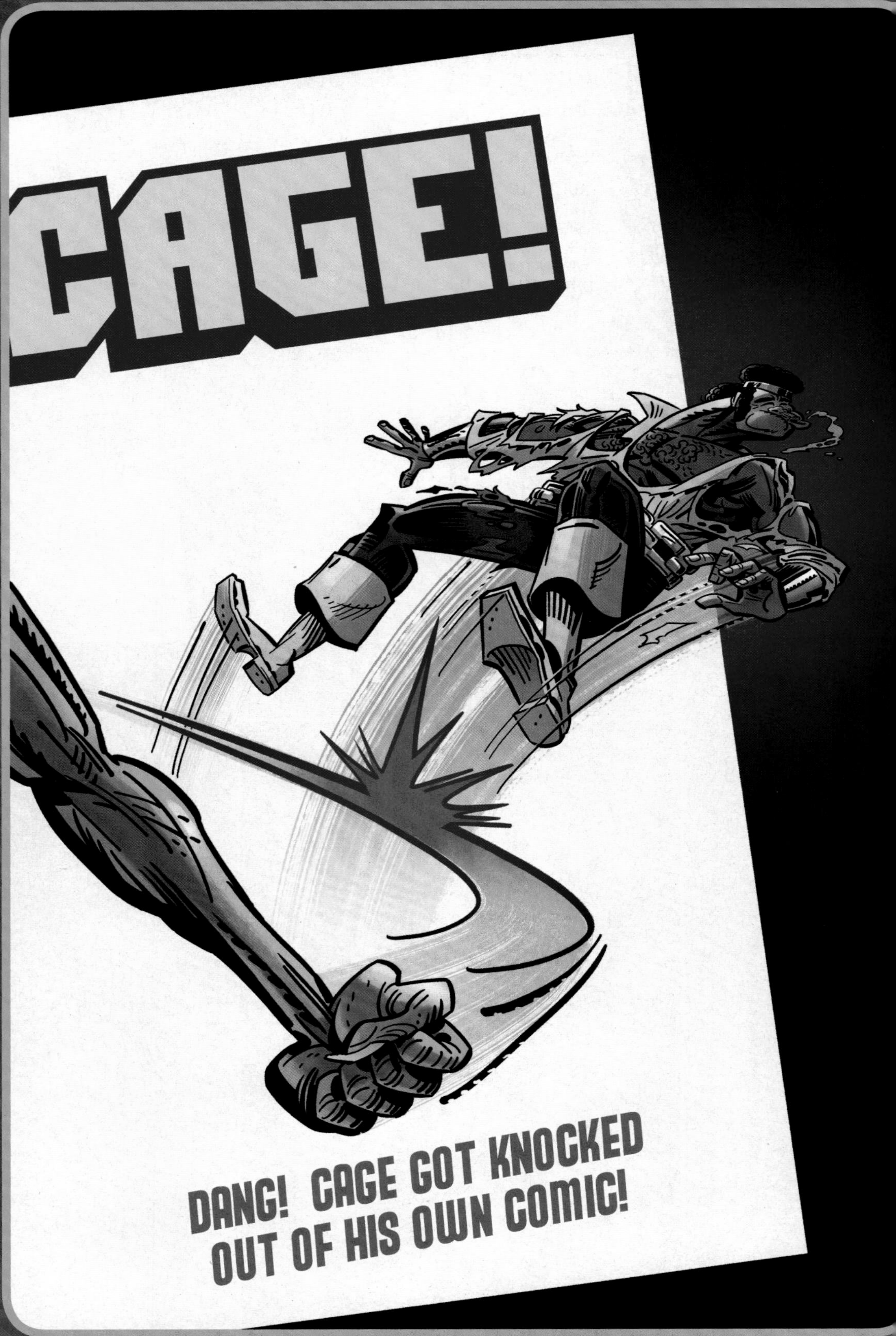
CAGE!
DANG! CAGE GOT KNOCKED OUT OF HIS OWN COMIC!

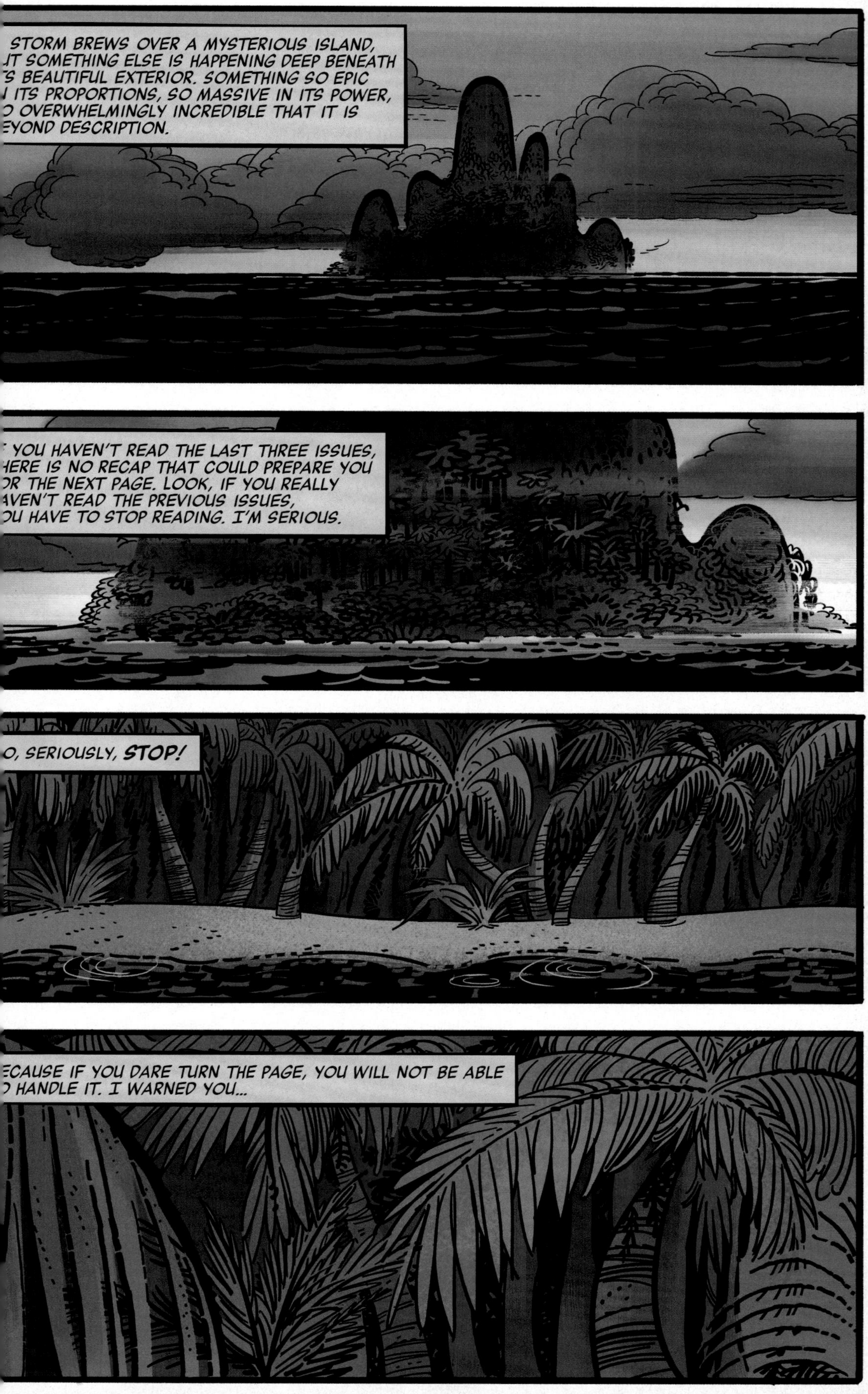
STORM BREWS OVER A MYSTERIOUS ISLAND,
IT SOMETHING ELSE IS HAPPENING DEEP BENEATH
S BEAUTIFUL EXTERIOR. SOMETHING SO EPIC
ITS PROPORTIONS, SO MASSIVE IN ITS POWER,
O OVERWHELMINGLY INCREDIBLE THAT IT IS
EYOND DESCRIPTION.
YOU HAVEN'T READ THE LAST THREE ISSUES,
HERE IS NO RECAP THAT COULD PREPARE YOU
OR THE NEXT PAGE. LOOK, IF YOU REALLY
AVEN'T READ THE PREVIOUS ISSUES,
OU HAVE TO STOP READING. I'M SERIOUS.
O, SERIOUSLY, STOP!
ECAUSE IF YOU DARE TURN THE PAGE, YOU WILL NOT BE ABLE
O HANDLE IT. I WARNED YOU...

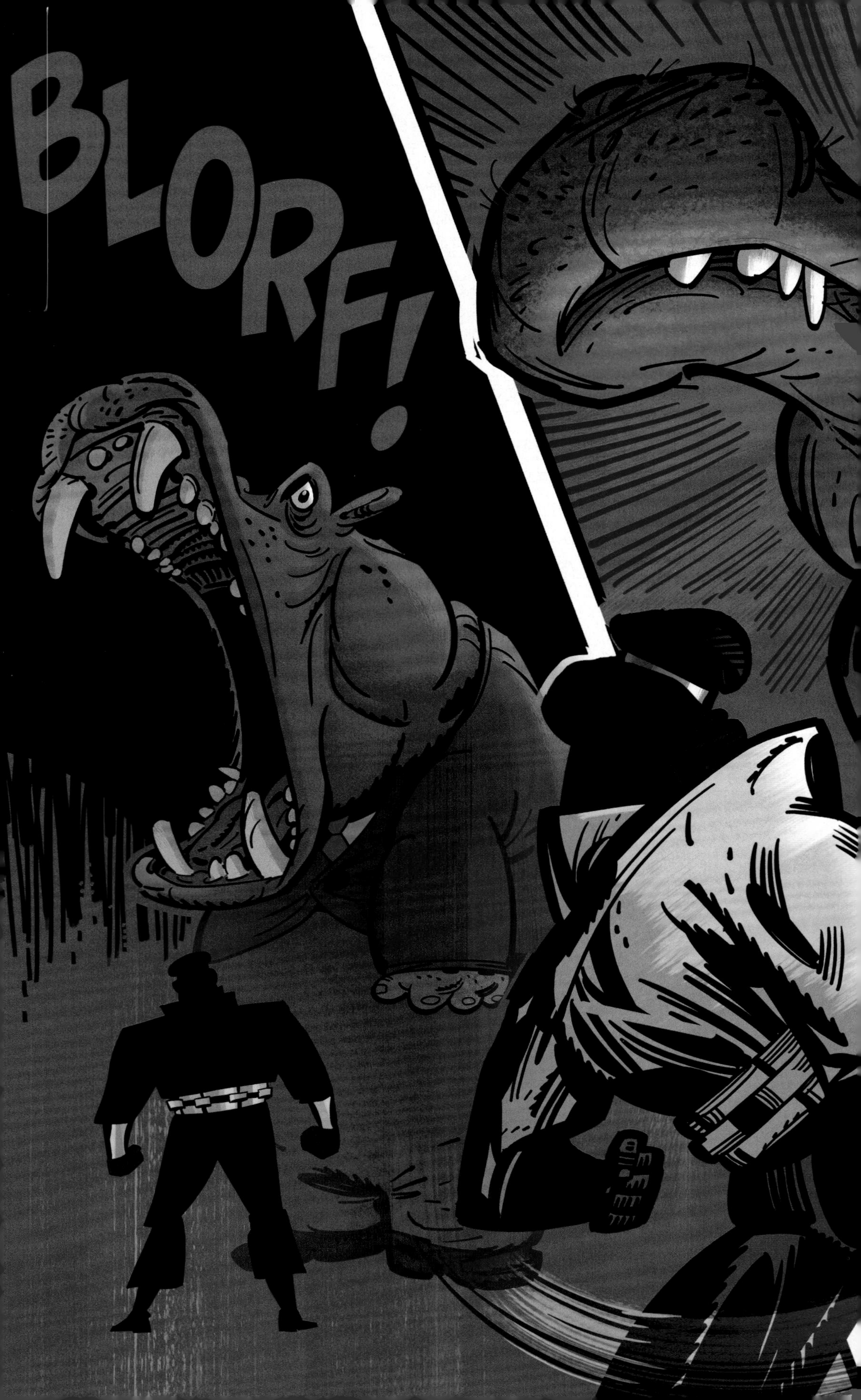
BLORF!

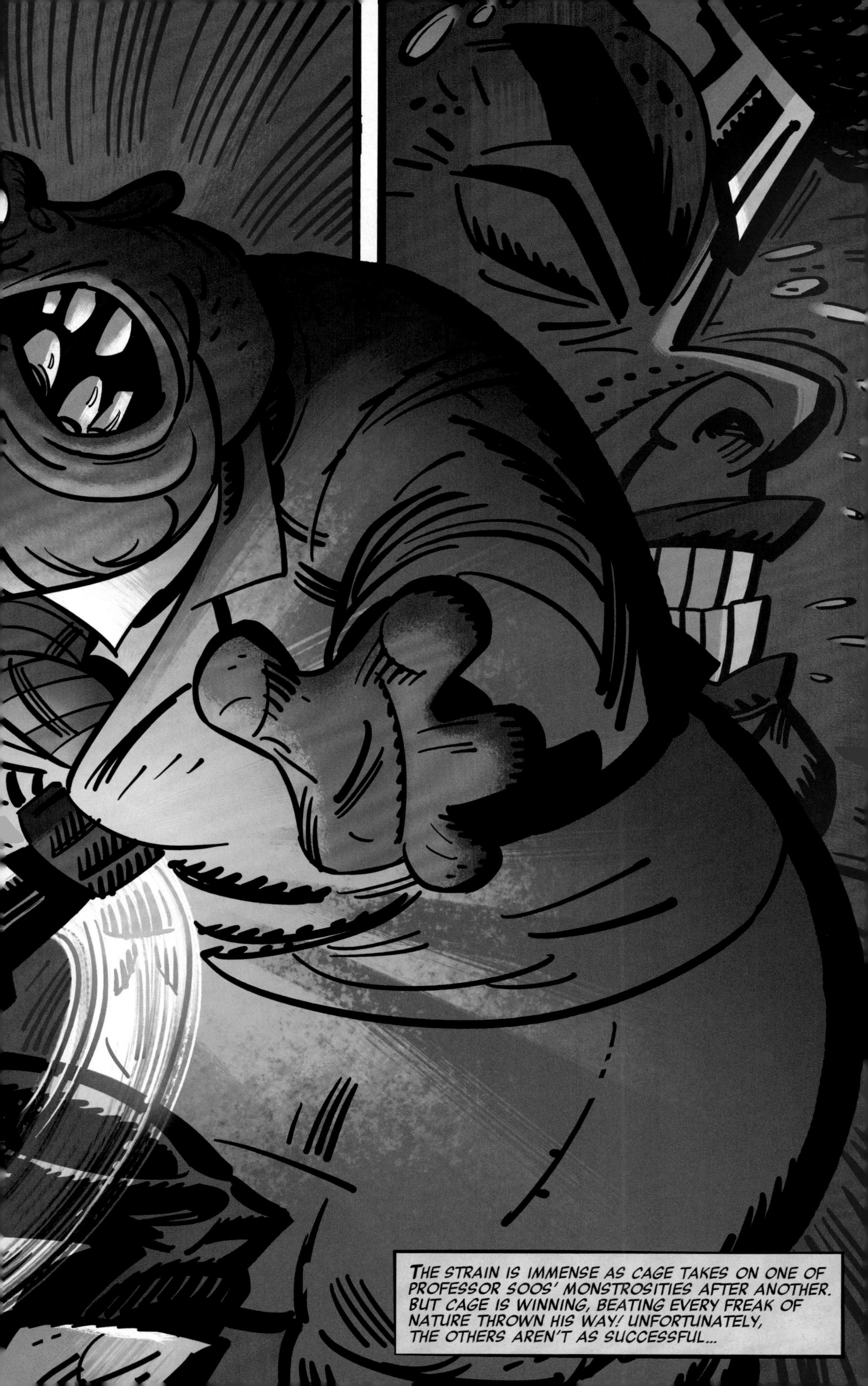
THE STRAIN IS IMMENSE AS CAGE TAKES ON ONE OF PROFESSOR SOOS' MONSTROSITIES AFTER ANOTHER. BUT CAGE IS WINNING, BEATING EVERY FREAK OF NATURE THROWN HIS WAY! UNFORTUNATELY, THE OTHERS AREN'T AS SUCCESSFUL...

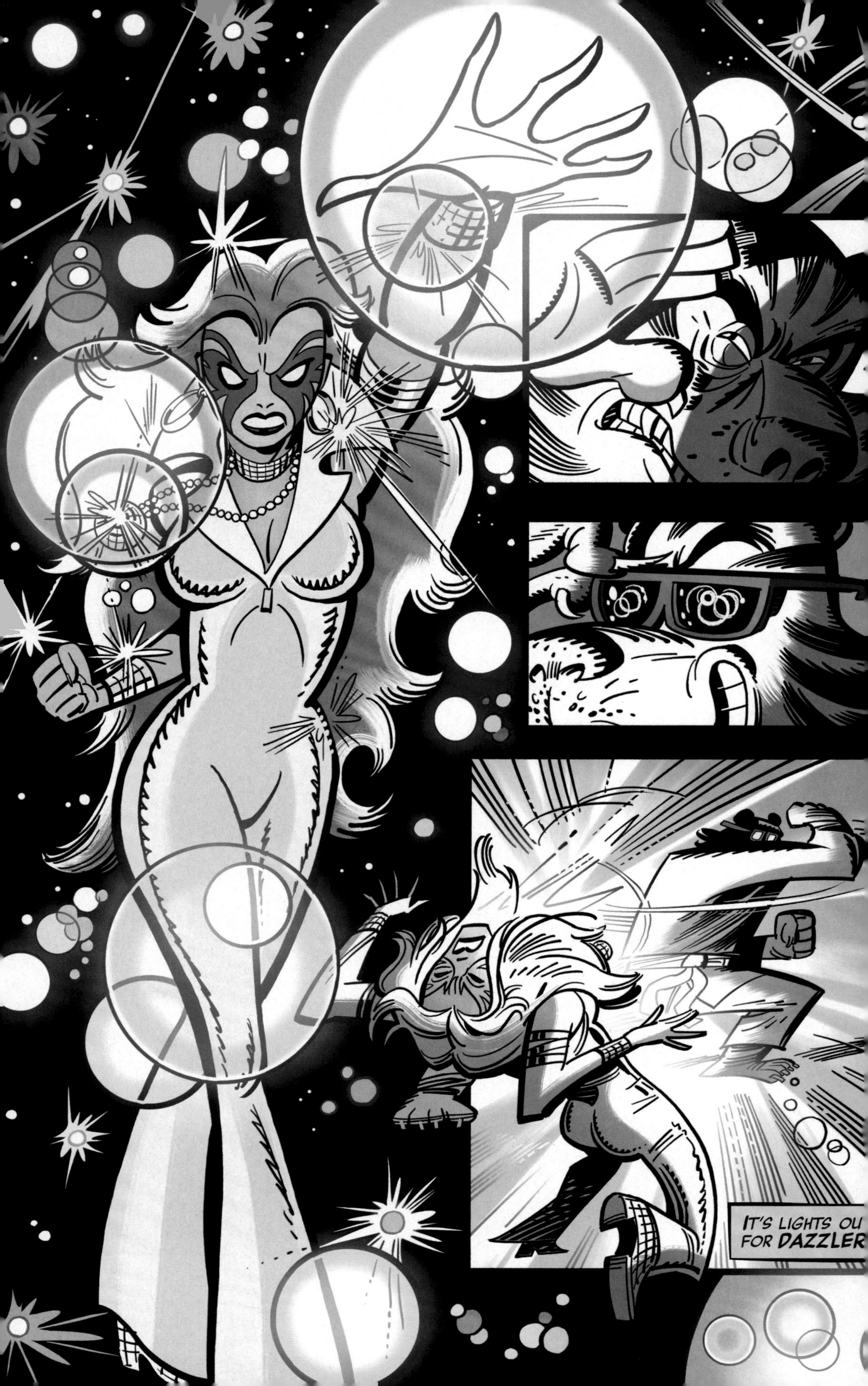
IT'S LIGHTS OU
FOR DAZZLER

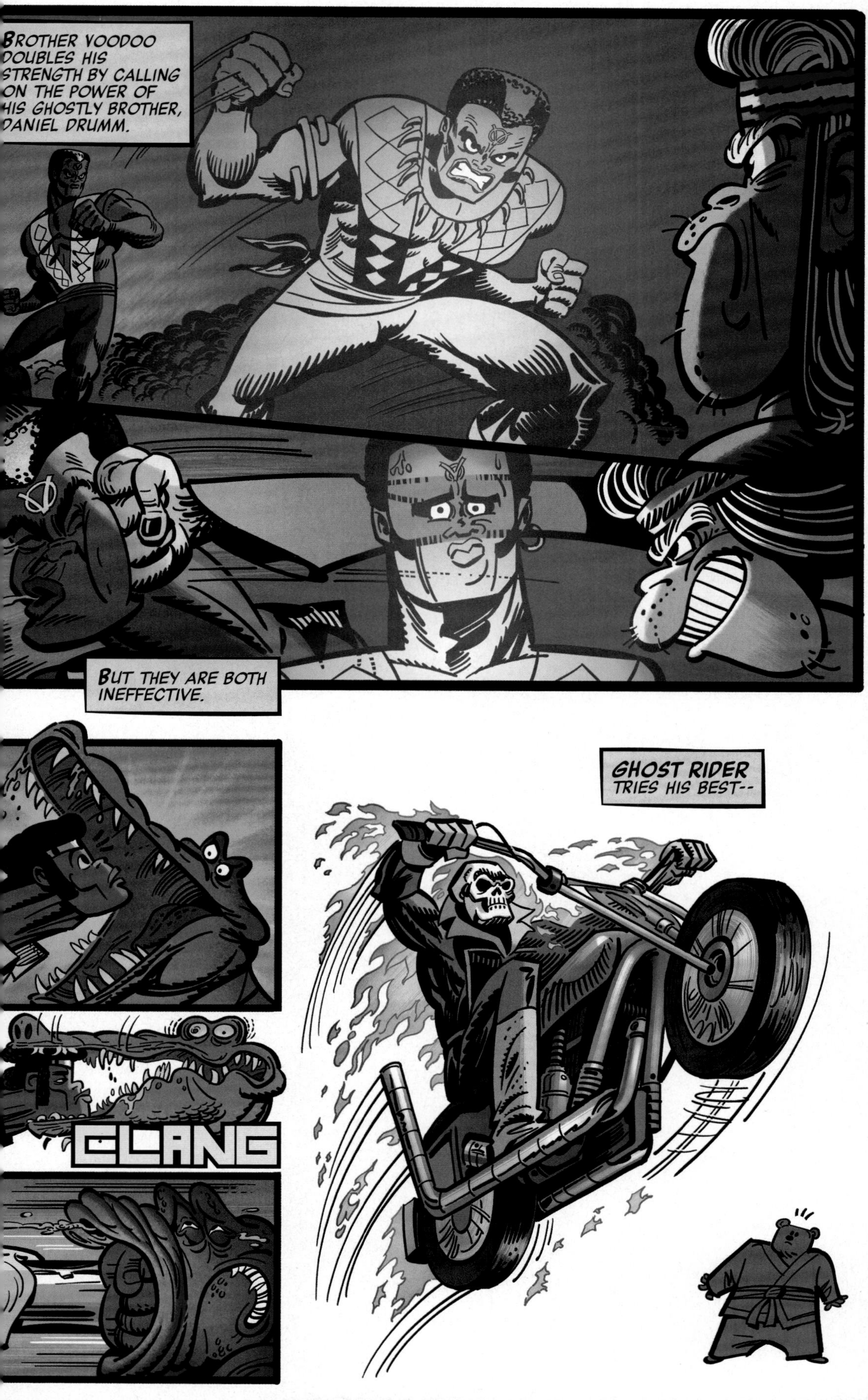
BROTHER VOODOO DOUBLES HIS STRENGTH BY CALLING ON THE POWER OF HIS GHOSTLY BROTHER, DANIEL DRUMM.
BUT THEY ARE BOTH INEFFECTIVE.
CLANG
GHOST RIDER TRIES HIS BEST--

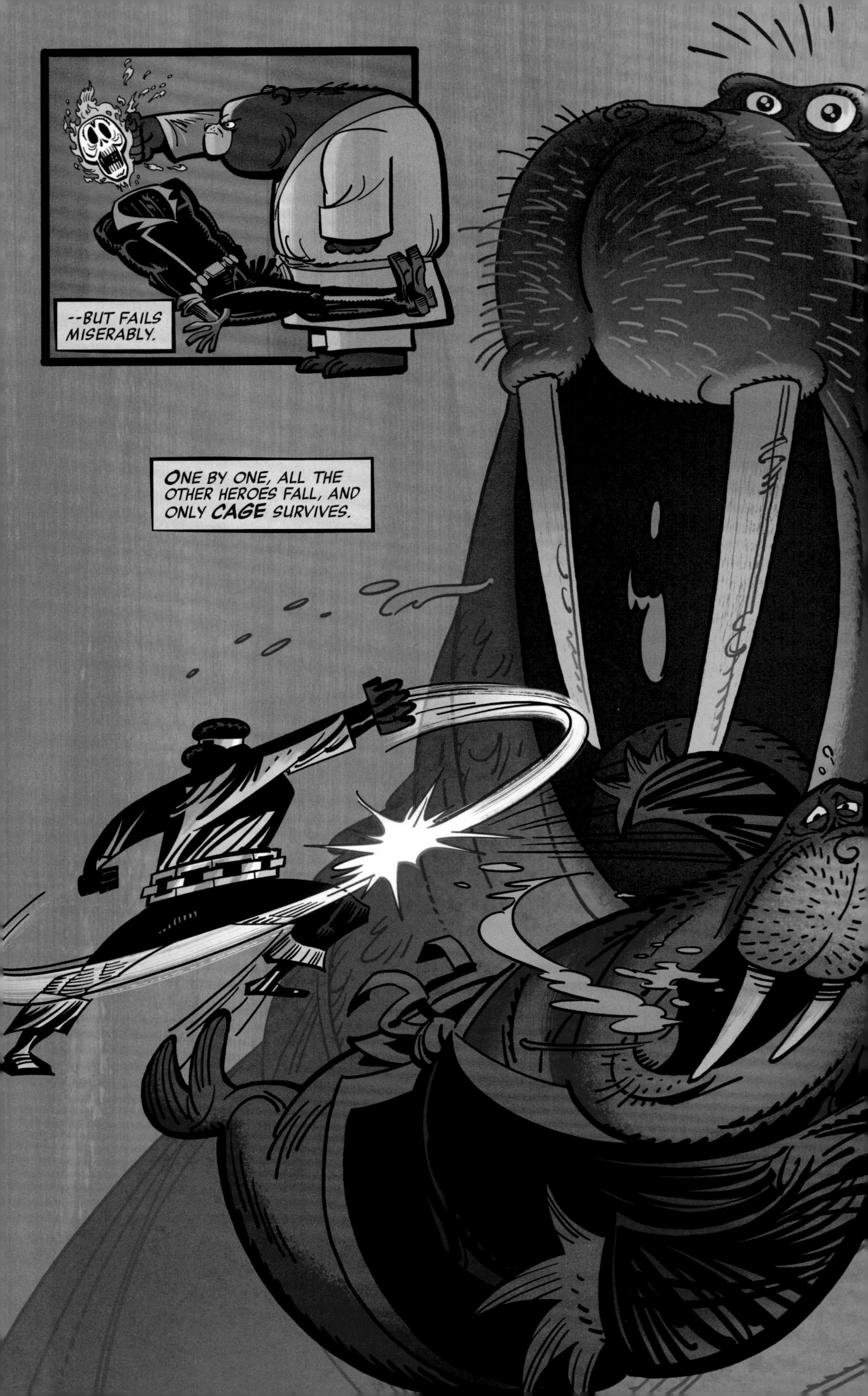
--BUT FAILS MISERABLY.
ONE BY ONE, ALL THE OTHER HEROES FALL, AND ONLY CAGE SURVIVES.

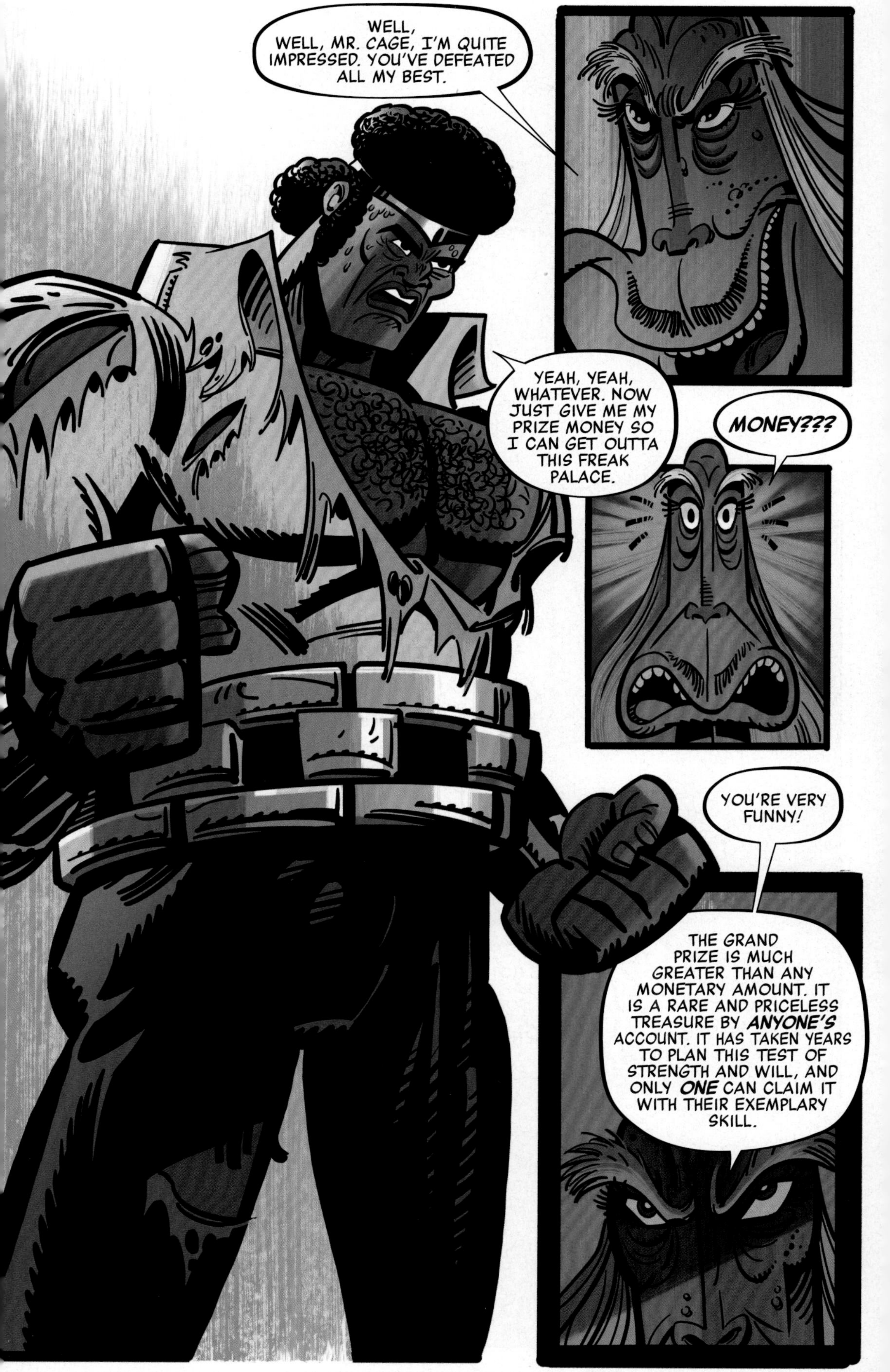
WELL, WELL, MR. CAGE, I'M QUITE IMPRESSED. YOU'VE DEFEATED ALL MY BEST.
YEAH, YEAH, WHATEVER. NOW JUST GIVE ME MY PRIZE MONEY SO I CAN GET OUTTA THIS FREAK PALACE.
MONEY???
YOU'RE VERY FUNNY!
THE GRAND PRIZE IS MUCH GREATER THAN ANY MONETARY AMOUNT. IT IS A RARE AND PRICELESS TREASURE BY ANYONE'S ACCOUNT. IT HAS TAKEN YEARS TO PLAN THIS TEST OF STRENGTH AND WILL, AND ONLY ONE CAN CLAIM IT WITH THEIR EXEMPLARY SKILL.

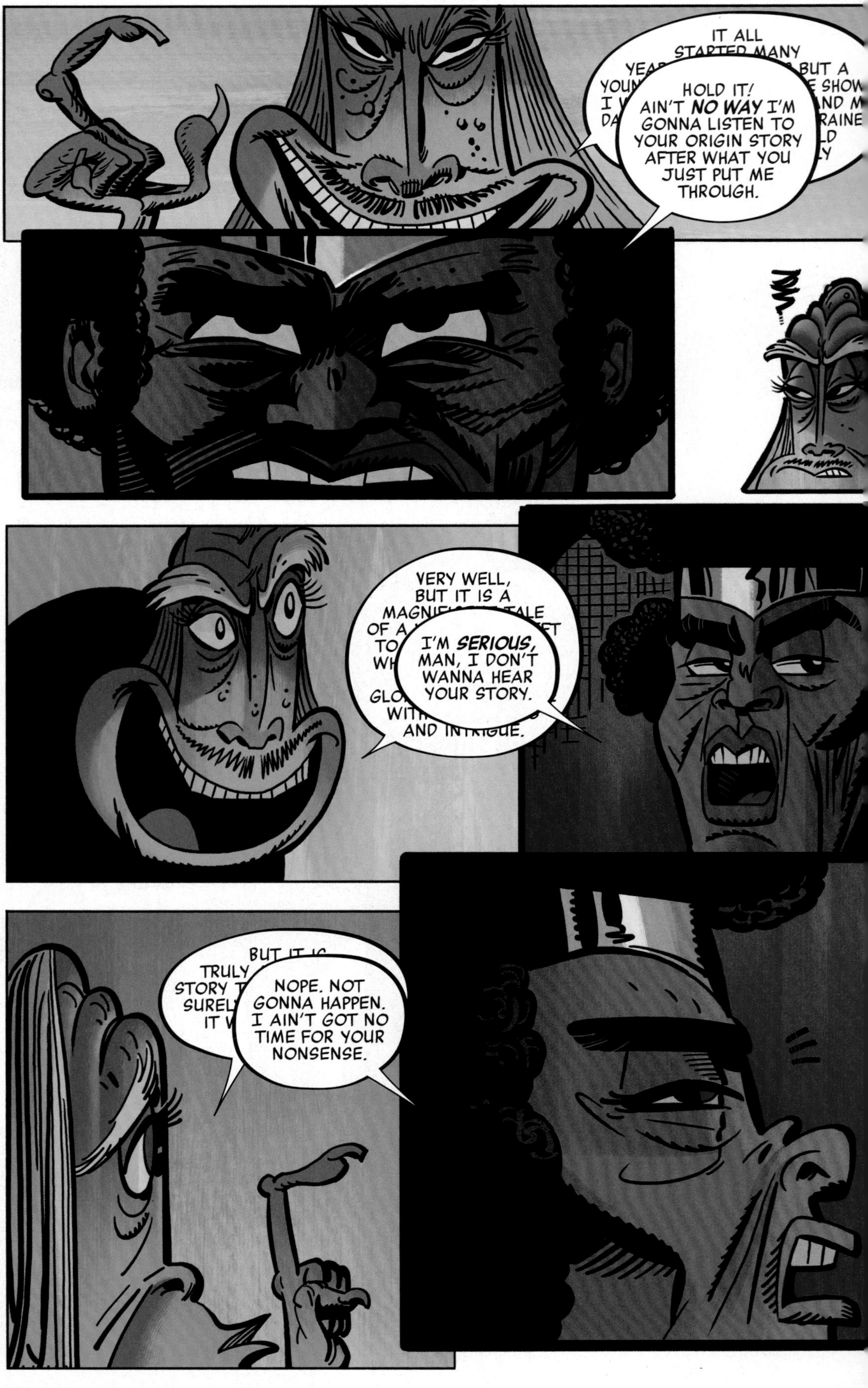
IT ALL STARTED MANY
HOLD IT! AIN'T **NO WAY** I'M GONNA LISTEN TO YOUR ORIGIN STORY AFTER WHAT YOU JUST PUT ME THROUGH.
VERY WELL, BUT IT IS A
I'M ***SERIOUS***, MAN, I DON'T WANNA HEAR YOUR STORY.
AND INTRIGUE.
TRULY
NOPE. NOT GONNA HAPPEN. I AIN'T GOT NO TIME FOR YOUR NONSENSE.

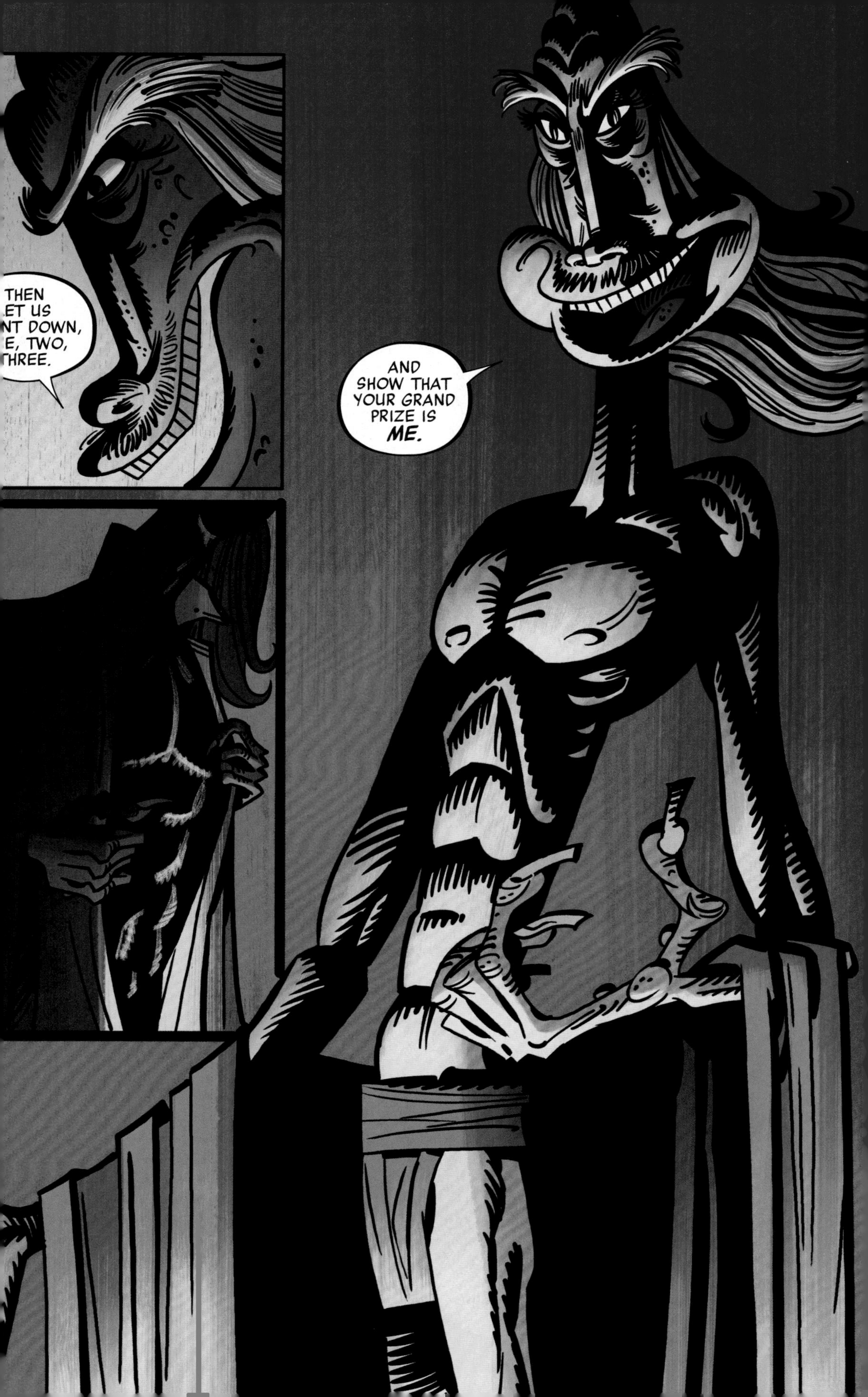
THEN
.ET US
NT DOWN,
E, TWO,
THREE.
AND SHOW THAT YOUR GRAND PRIZE IS *ME.*

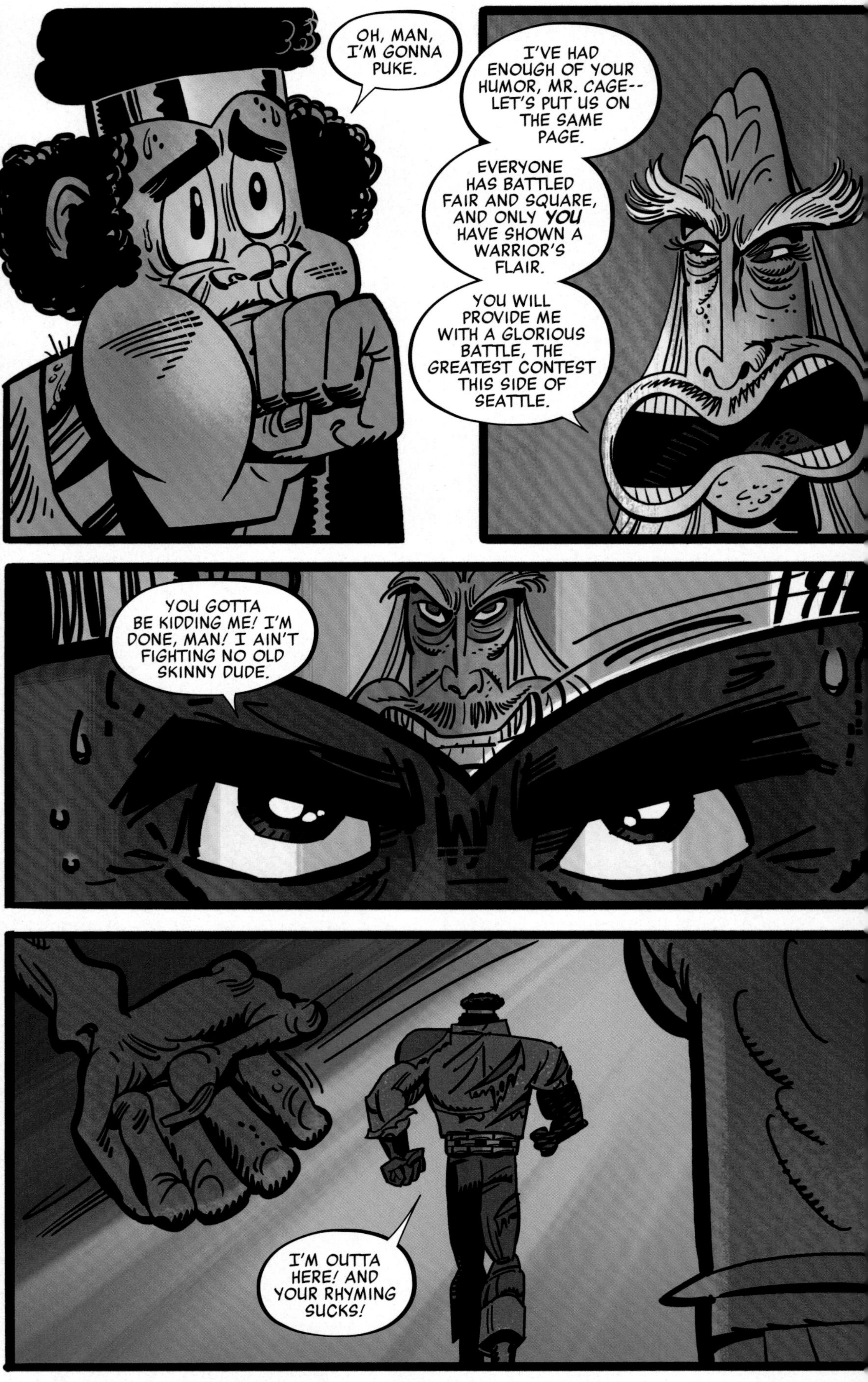
OH, MAN, I'M GONNA PUKE.
I'VE HAD ENOUGH OF YOUR HUMOR, MR. CAGE--LET'S PUT US ON THE SAME PAGE.
EVERYONE HAS BATTLED FAIR AND SQUARE, AND ONLY *YOU* HAVE SHOWN A WARRIOR'S FLAIR.
YOU WILL PROVIDE ME WITH A GLORIOUS BATTLE, THE GREATEST CONTEST THIS SIDE OF SEATTLE.
YOU GOTTA BE KIDDING ME! I'M DONE, MAN! I AIN'T FIGHTING NO OLD SKINNY DUDE.
I'M OUTTA HERE! AND YOUR RHYMING SUCKS!

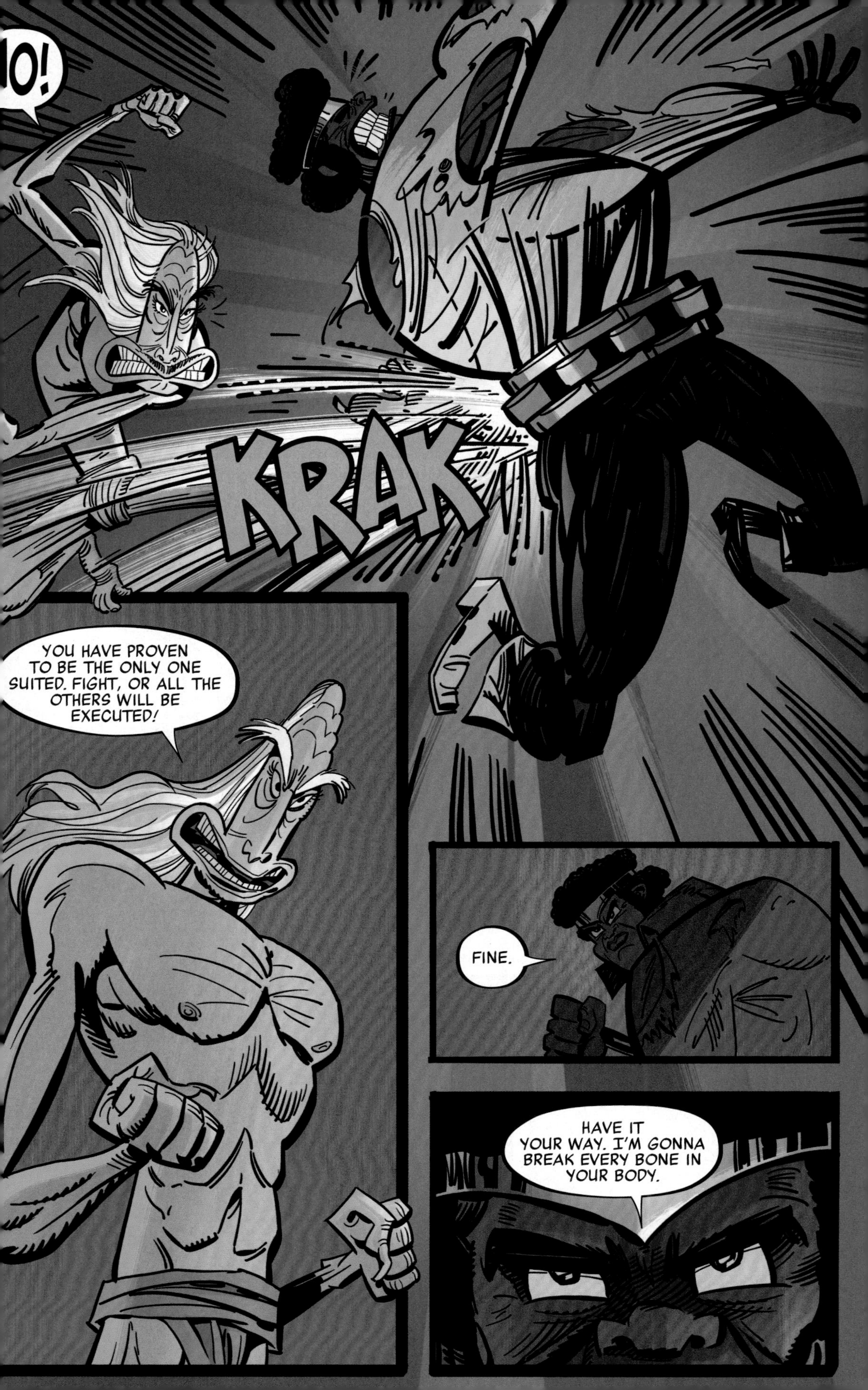

O!
KRAK
YOU HAVE PROVEN TO BE THE ONLY ONE SUITED. FIGHT, OR ALL THE OTHERS WILL BE EXECUTED!
FINE.
HAVE IT YOUR WAY. I'M GONNA BREAK EVERY BONE IN YOUR BODY.

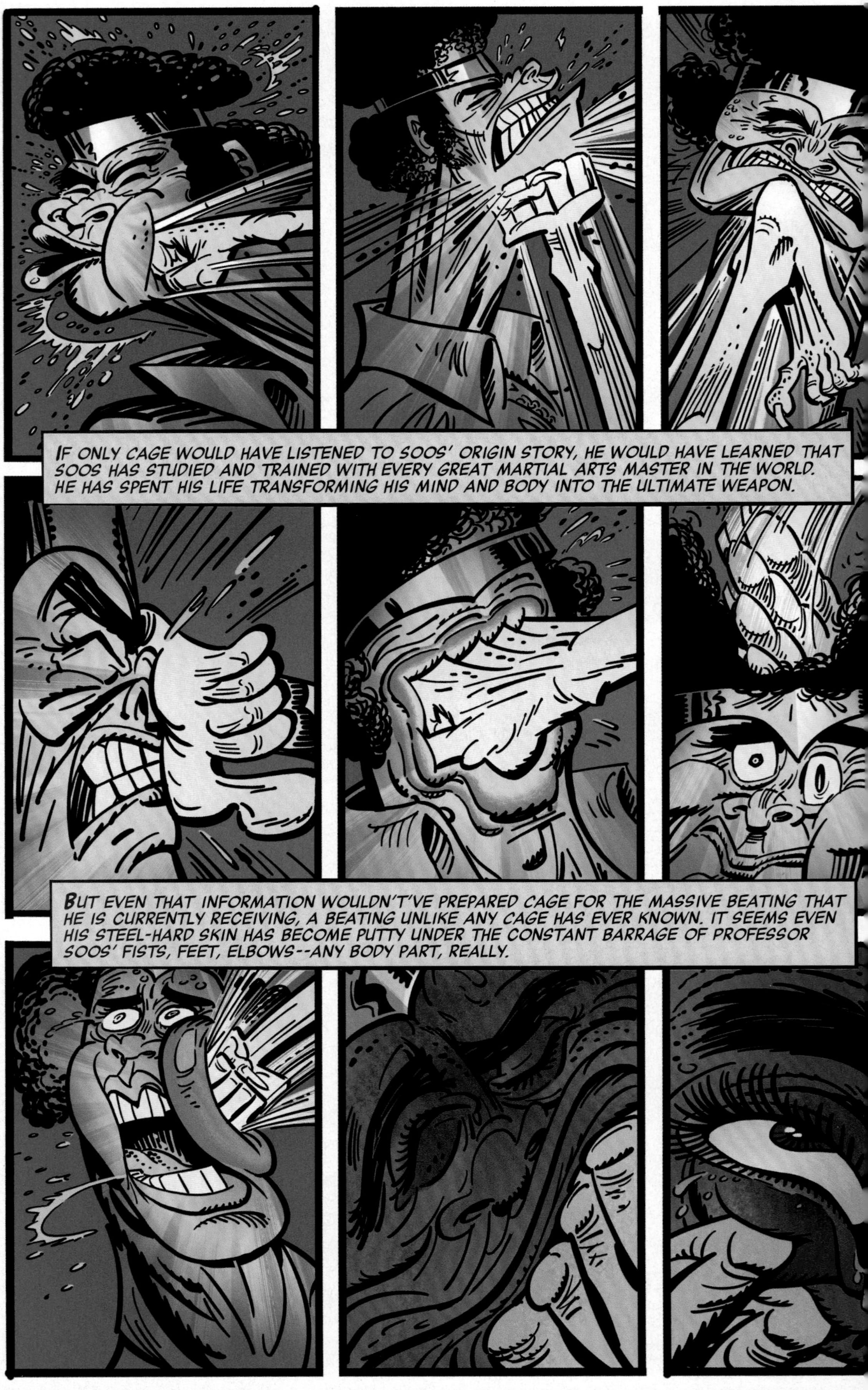
IF ONLY CAGE WOULD HAVE LISTENED TO SOOS' ORIGIN STORY, HE WOULD HAVE LEARNED THAT SOOS HAS STUDIED AND TRAINED WITH EVERY GREAT MARTIAL ARTS MASTER IN THE WORLD. HE HAS SPENT HIS LIFE TRANSFORMING HIS MIND AND BODY INTO THE ULTIMATE WEAPON.
BUT EVEN THAT INFORMATION WOULDN'T'VE PREPARED CAGE FOR THE MASSIVE BEATING THAT HE IS CURRENTLY RECEIVING, A BEATING UNLIKE ANY CAGE HAS EVER KNOWN. IT SEEMS EVEN HIS STEEL-HARD SKIN HAS BECOME PUTTY UNDER THE CONSTANT BARRAGE OF PROFESSOR SOOS' FISTS, FEET, ELBOWS--ANY BODY PART, REALLY.

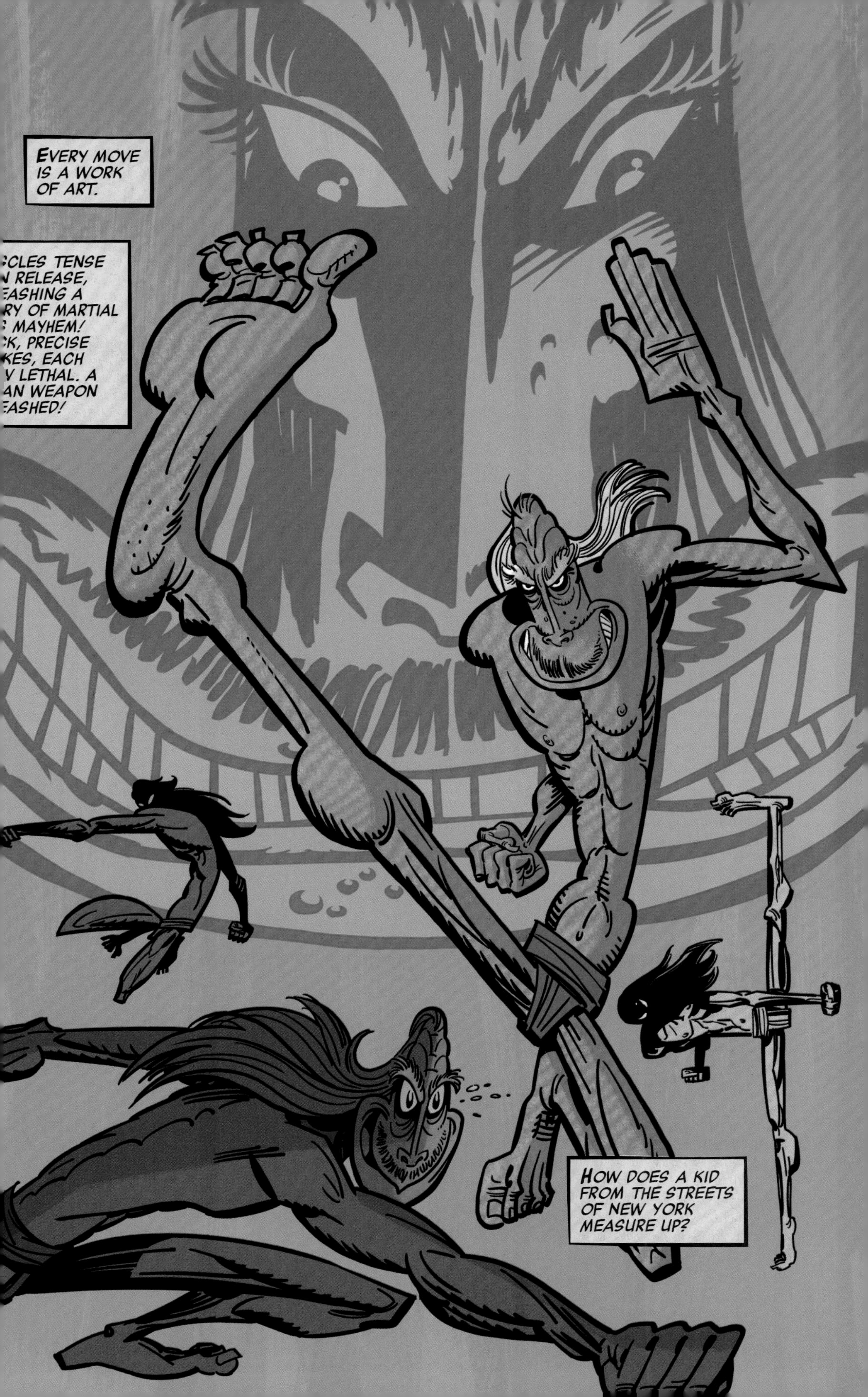
EVERY MOVE IS A WORK OF ART.
CLES TENSE N RELEASE, EASHING A RY OF MARTIAL MAYHEM! CK, PRECISE KES, EACH Y LETHAL. A AN WEAPON EASHED!
HOW DOES A KID FROM THE STREETS OF NEW YORK MEASURE UP?

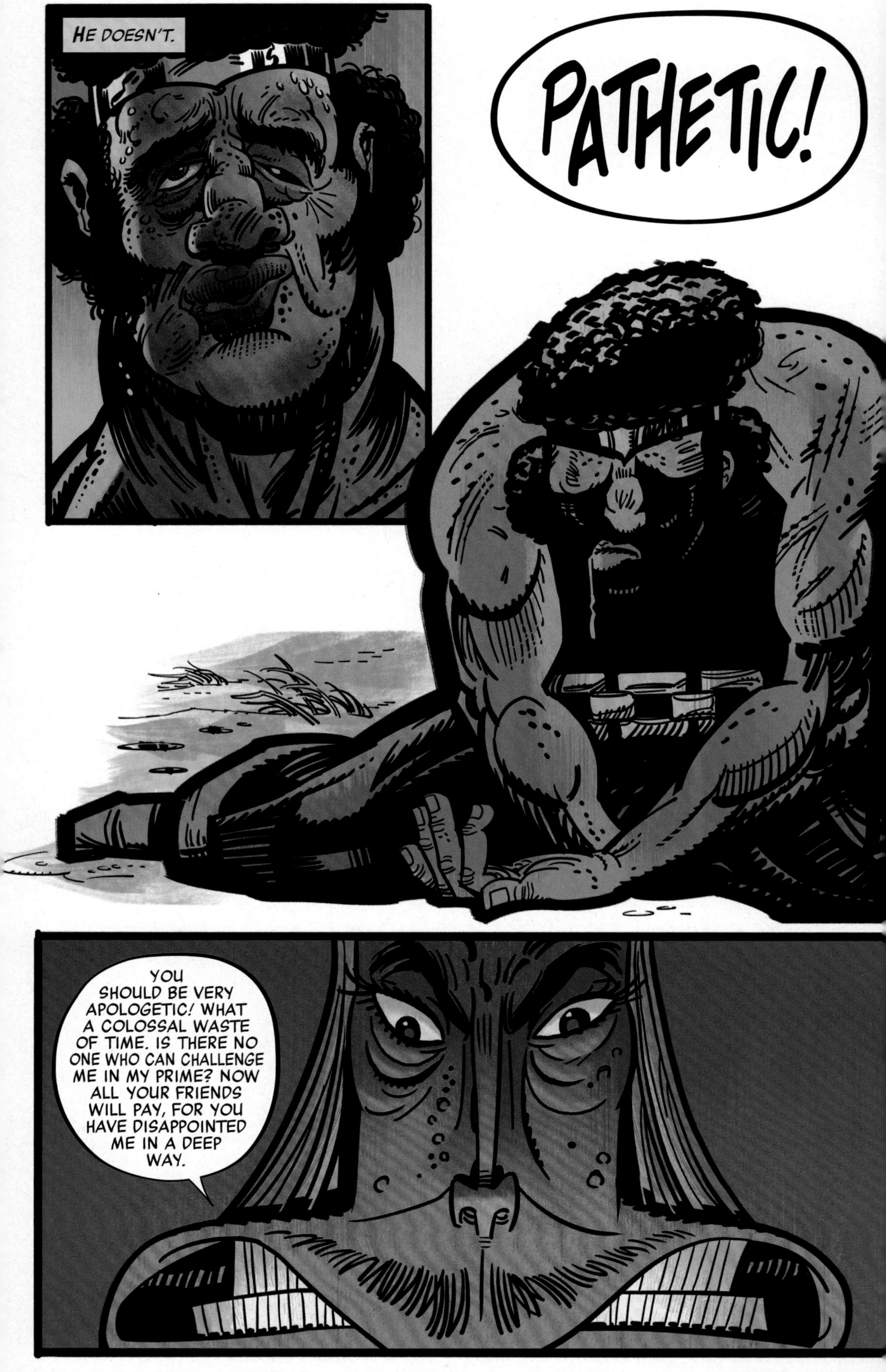
HE DOESN'T.
PATHETIC!
YOU SHOULD BE VERY APOLOGETIC! WHAT A COLOSSAL WASTE OF TIME. IS THERE NO ONE WHO CAN CHALLENGE ME IN MY PRIME? NOW ALL YOUR FRIENDS WILL PAY, FOR YOU HAVE DISAPPOINTED ME IN A DEEP WAY.

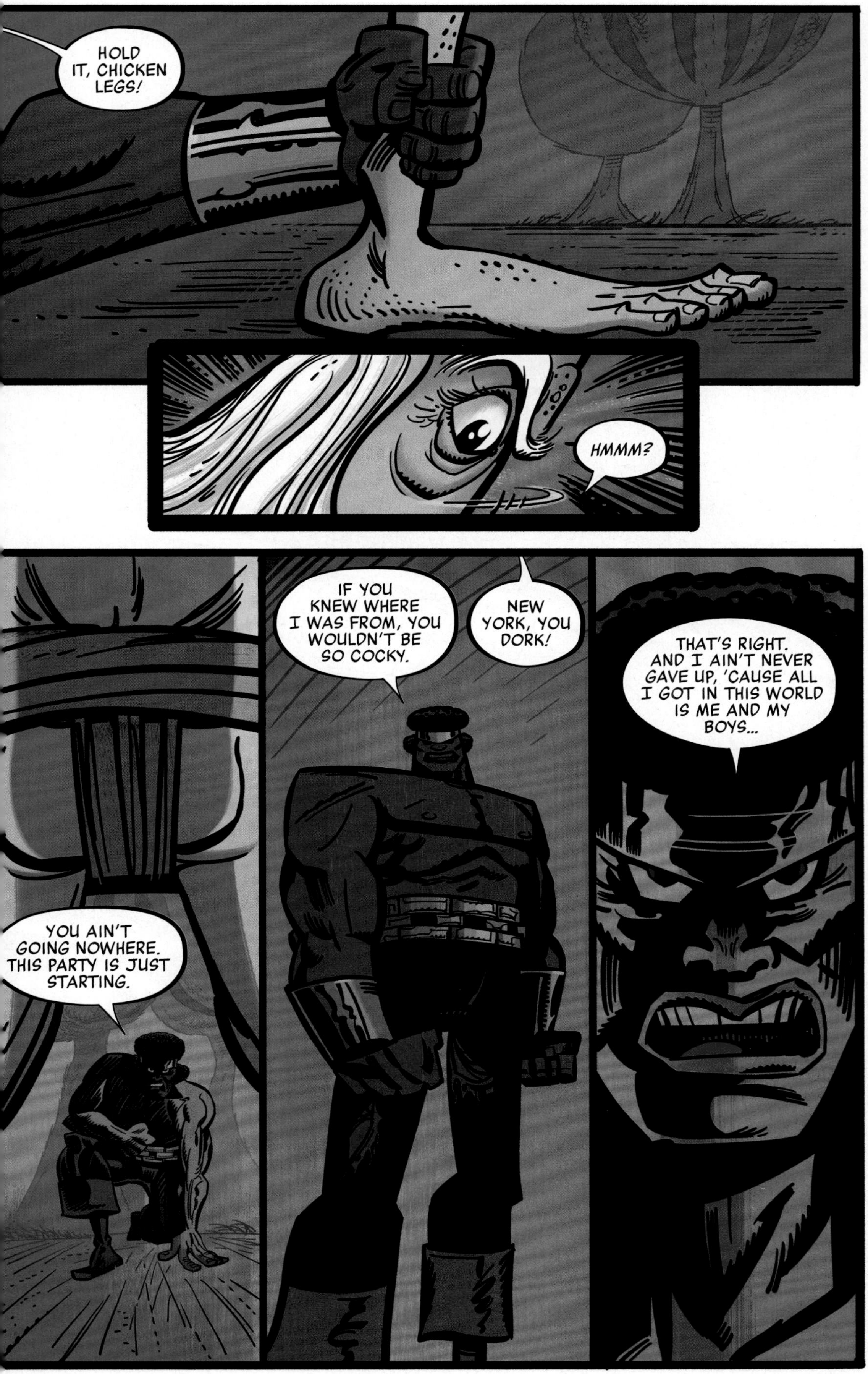
HOLD IT, CHICKEN LEGS!
HMMM?
YOU AIN'T GOING NOWHERE. THIS PARTY IS JUST STARTING.
IF YOU KNEW WHERE I WAS FROM, YOU WOULDN'T BE SO COCKY.
NEW YORK, YOU DORK!
THAT'S RIGHT. AND I AIN'T NEVER GAVE UP, 'CAUSE ALL I GOT IN THIS WORLD IS ME AND MY BOYS...

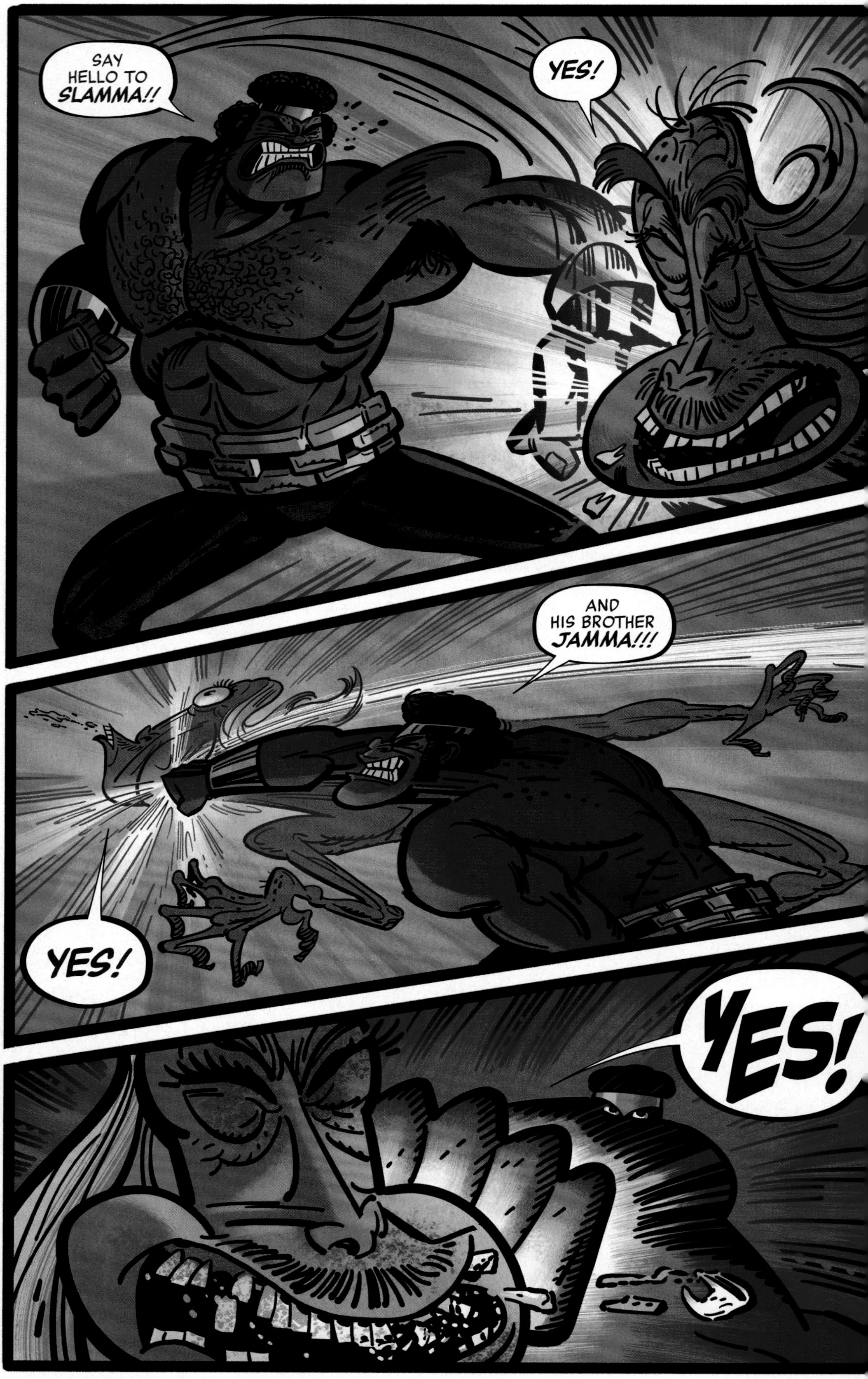
SAY HELLO TO SLAMMA!!
YES!
AND HIS BROTHER JAMMA!!!
YES!
YES!

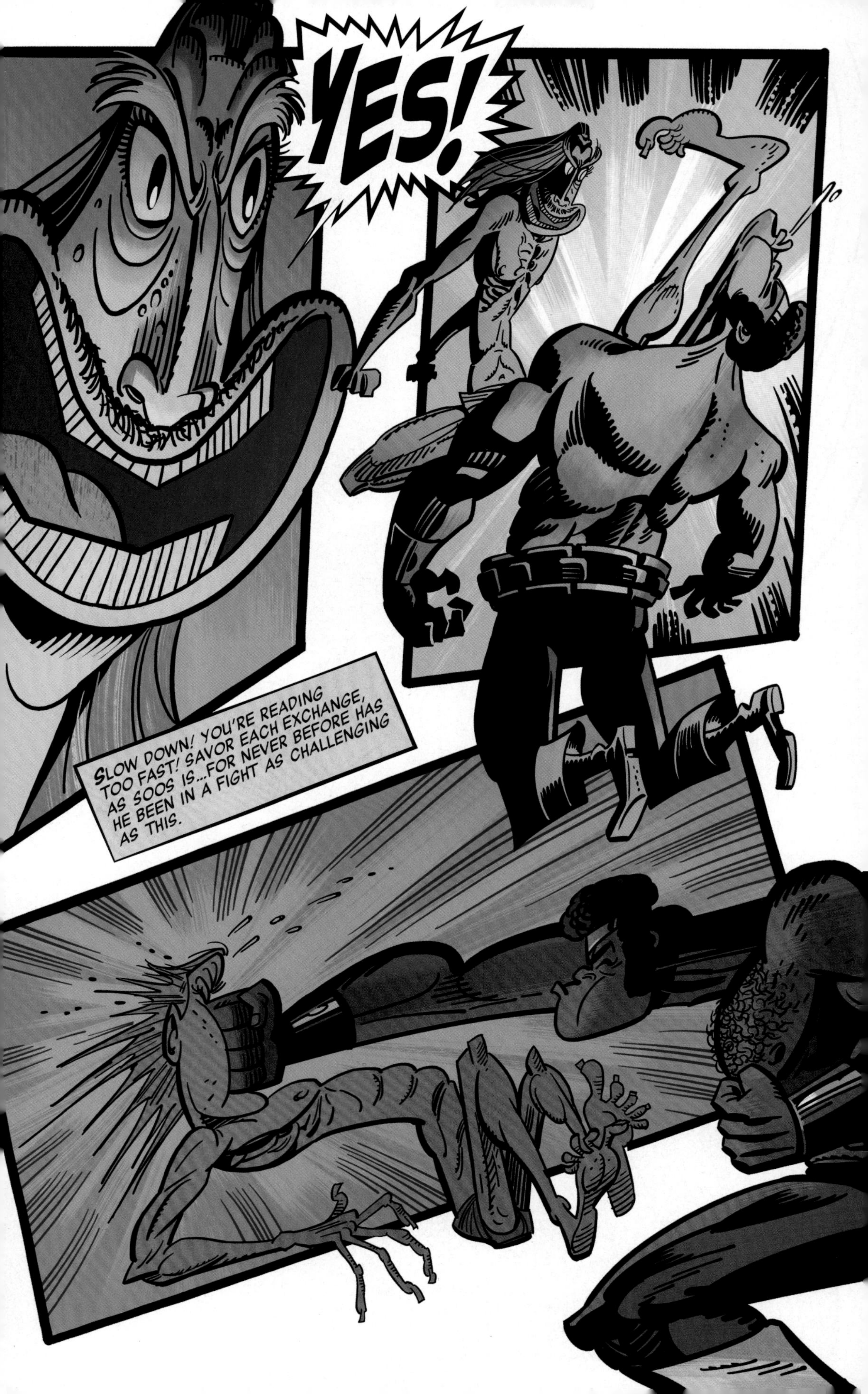
YES!
SLOW DOWN! YOU'RE READING TOO FAST! SAVOR EACH EXCHANGE, AS SOOS IS...FOR NEVER BEFORE HAS HE BEEN IN A FIGHT AS CHALLENGING AS THIS.

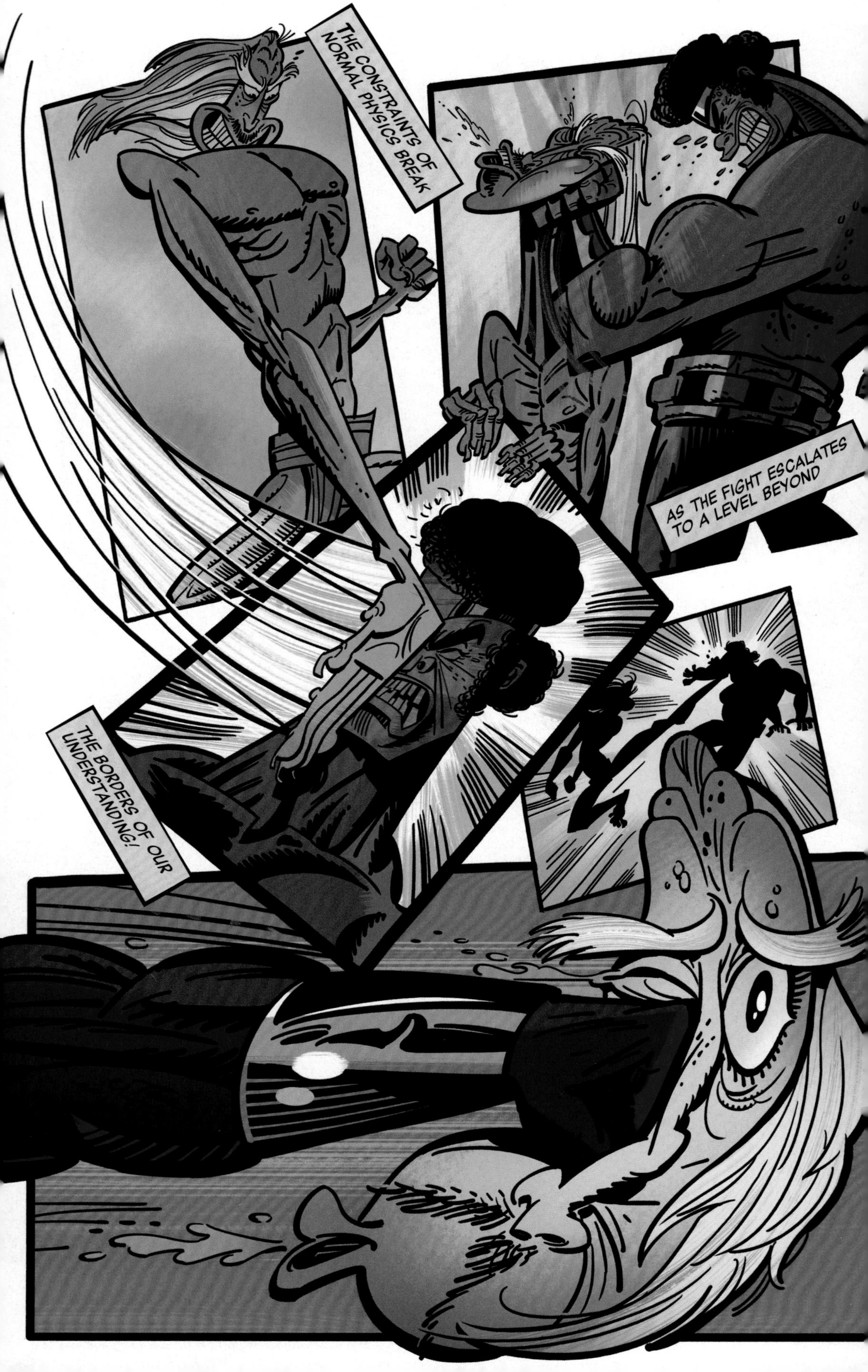
THE CONSTRAINTS OF NORMAL PHYSICS BREAK
AS THE FIGHT ESCALATES TO A LEVEL BEYOND
THE BORDERS OF OUR UNDERSTANDING!

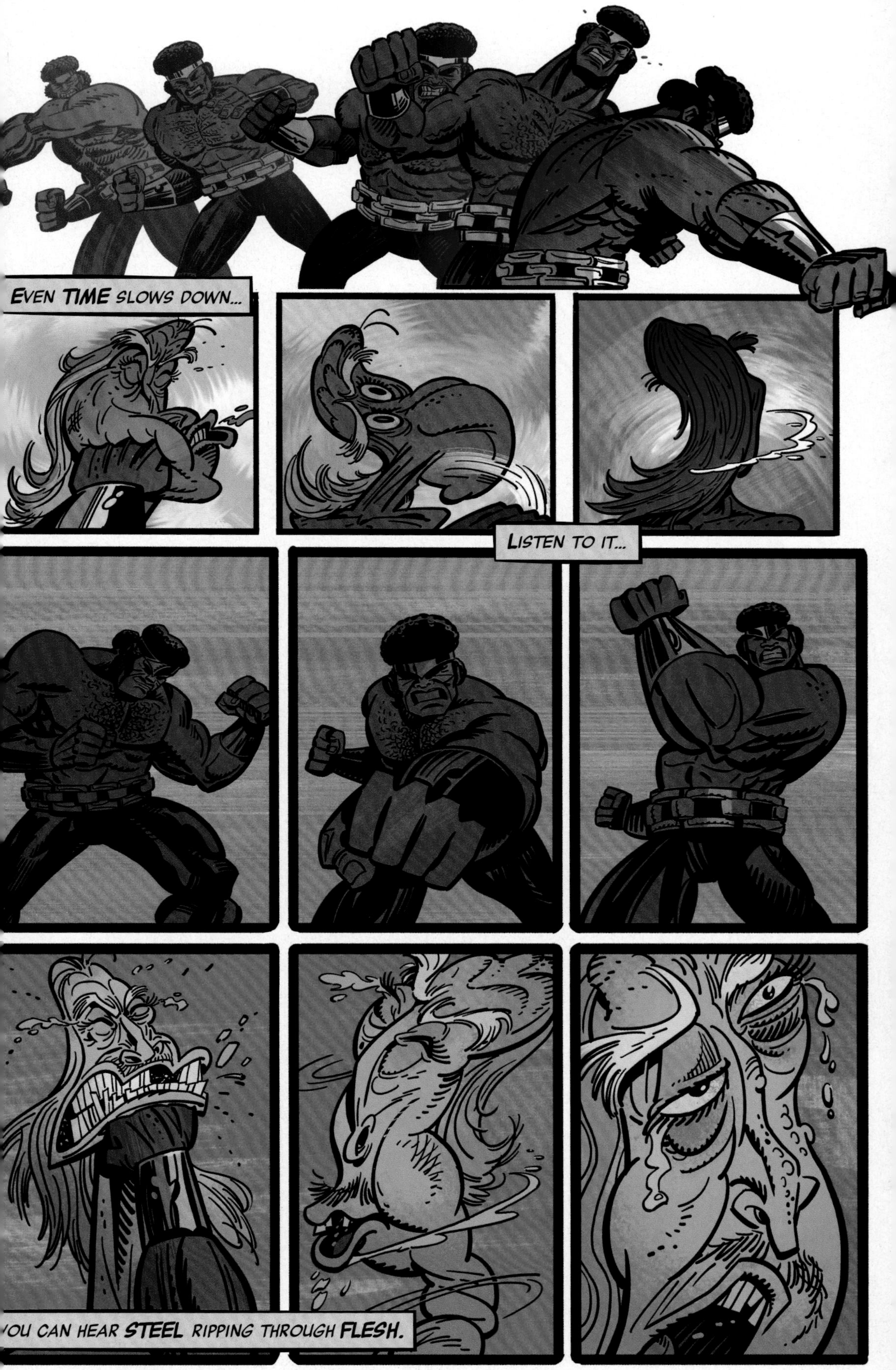
EVEN **TIME** SLOWS DOWN...
LISTEN TO IT...
YOU CAN HEAR **STEEL** RIPPING THROUGH **FLESH**.

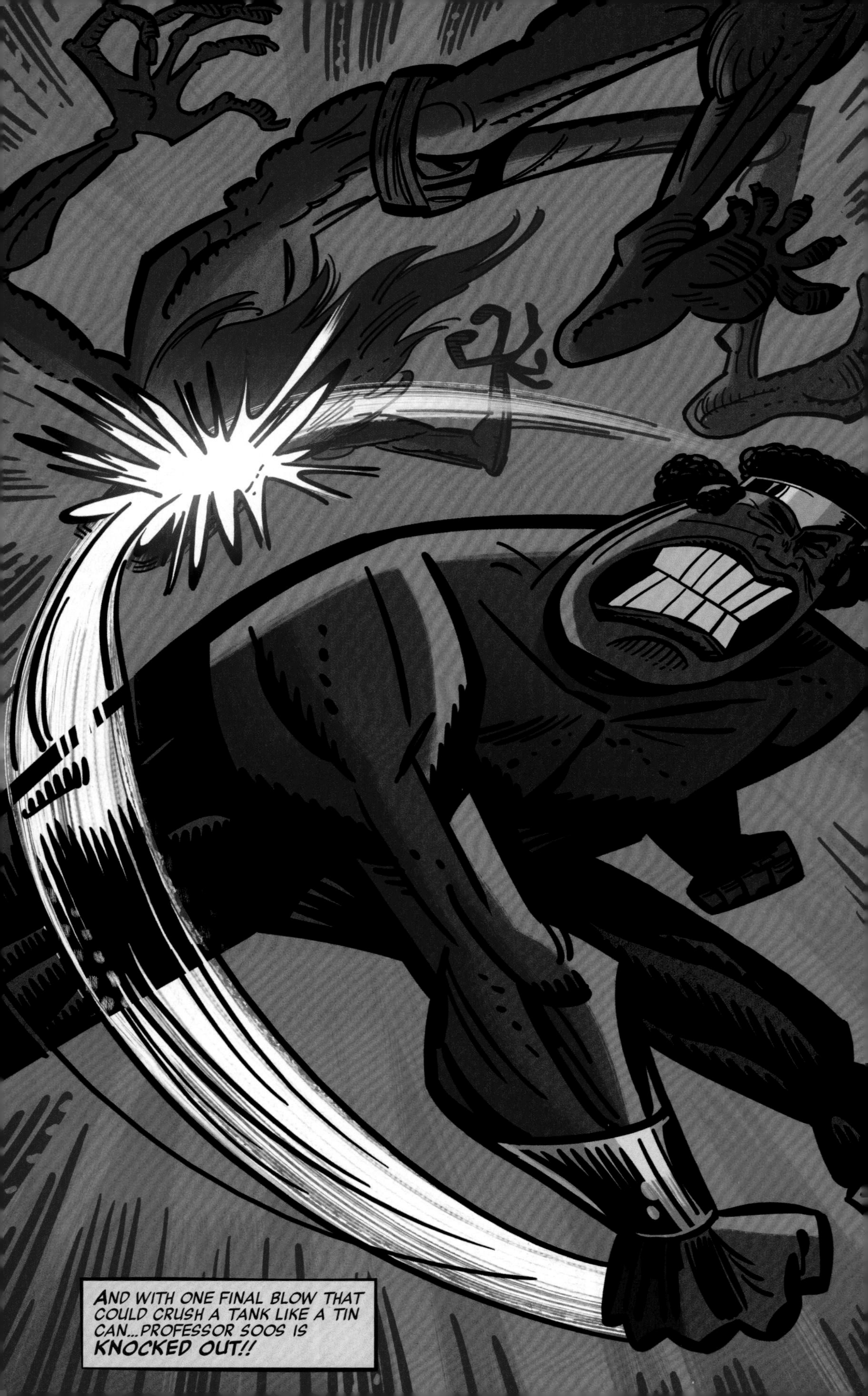
AND WITH ONE FINAL BLOW THAT COULD CRUSH A TANK LIKE A TIN CAN...PROFESSOR SOOS IS **KNOCKED OUT!!**

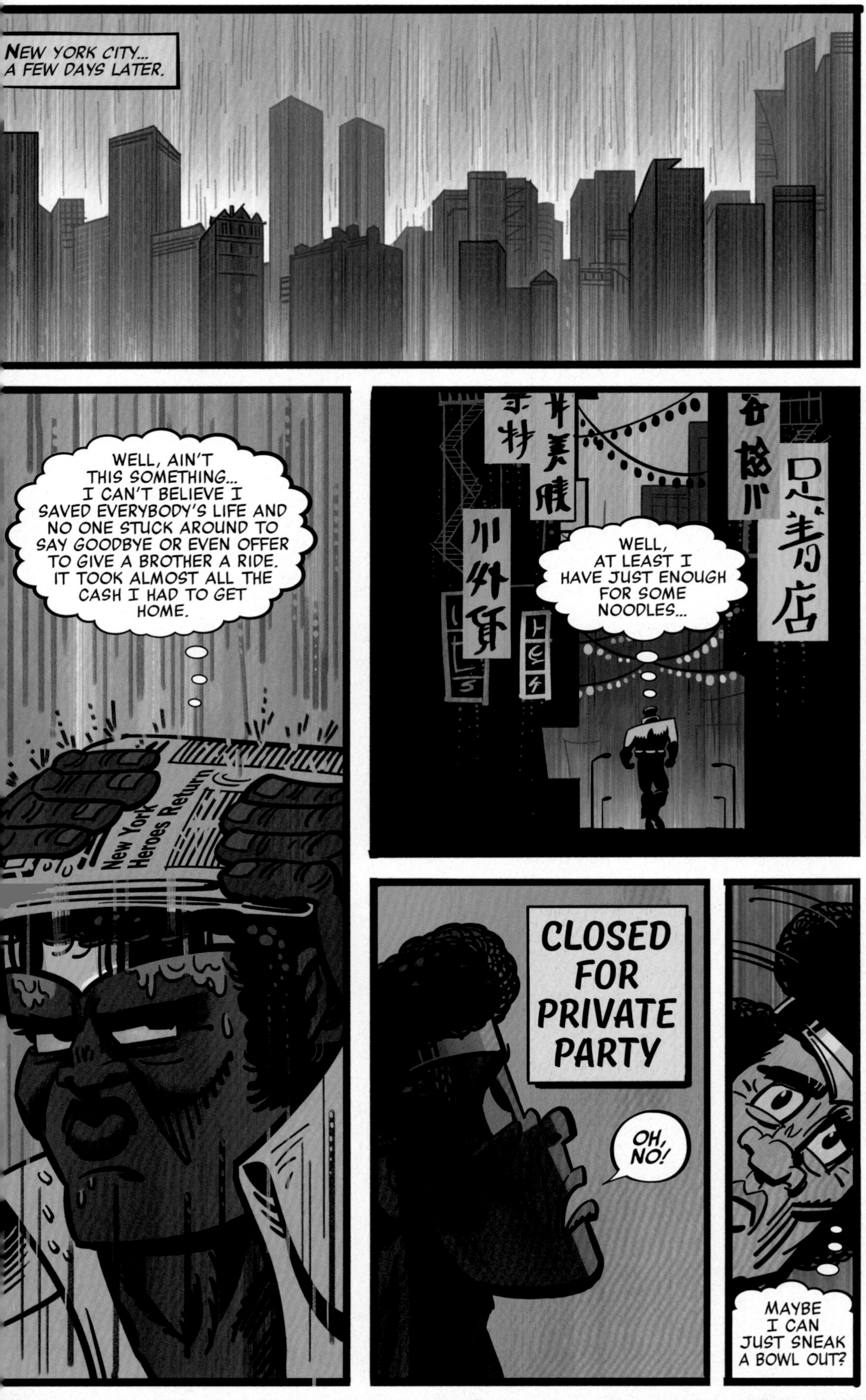
NEW YORK CITY... A FEW DAYS LATER.
WELL, AIN'T THIS SOMETHING... I CAN'T BELIEVE I SAVED EVERYBODY'S LIFE AND NO ONE STUCK AROUND TO SAY GOODBYE OR EVEN OFFER TO GIVE A BROTHER A RIDE. IT TOOK ALMOST ALL THE CASH I HAD TO GET HOME.
New York Heroes Return
WELL, AT LEAST I HAVE JUST ENOUGH FOR SOME NOODLES...
CLOSED FOR PRIVATE PARTY
OH, NO!
MAYBE I CAN JUST SNEAK A BOWL OUT?

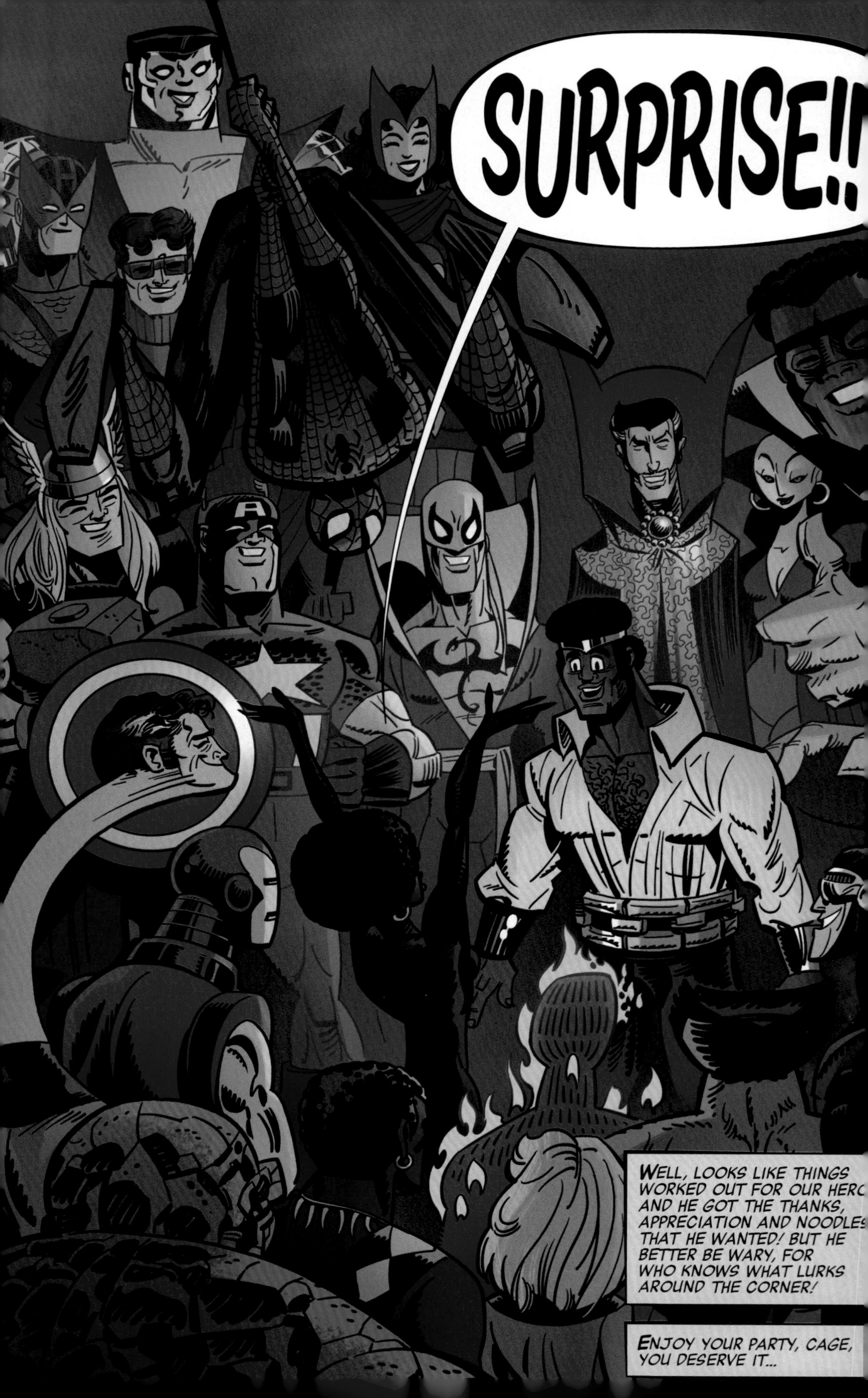
SURPRISE!!
WELL, LOOKS LIKE THINGS WORKED OUT FOR OUR HERO AND HE GOT THE THANKS, APPRECIATION AND NOODLES THAT HE WANTED! BUT HE BETTER BE WARY, FOR WHO KNOWS WHAT LURKS AROUND THE CORNER!
ENJOY YOUR PARTY, CAGE, YOU DESERVE IT...

LOOK OUT, WORLD, HERE HE COMES — AND BULLETS WON'T STOP HIM! PRESENTING THE FIRST APPEARANCE OF LUKE CAGE, HERO FOR HIRE!

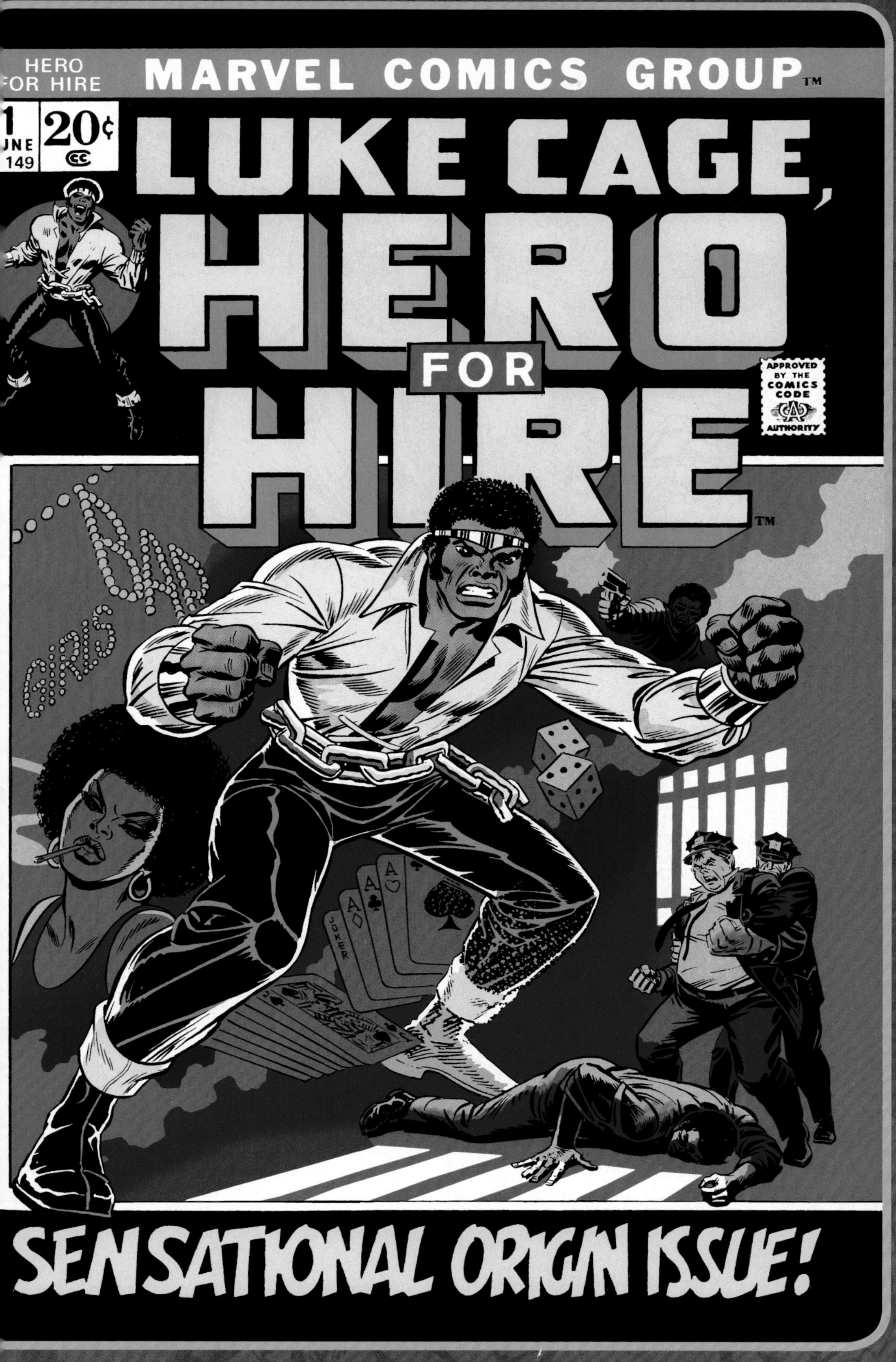

HERO FOR HIRE
MARVEL COMICS GROUP
1
JUNE
149
20¢
LUKE CAGE, HERO FOR HIRE
APPROVED BY THE COMICS CODE AUTHORITY
GIRLS BAR
JOKER
SENSATIONAL ORIGIN ISSUE!

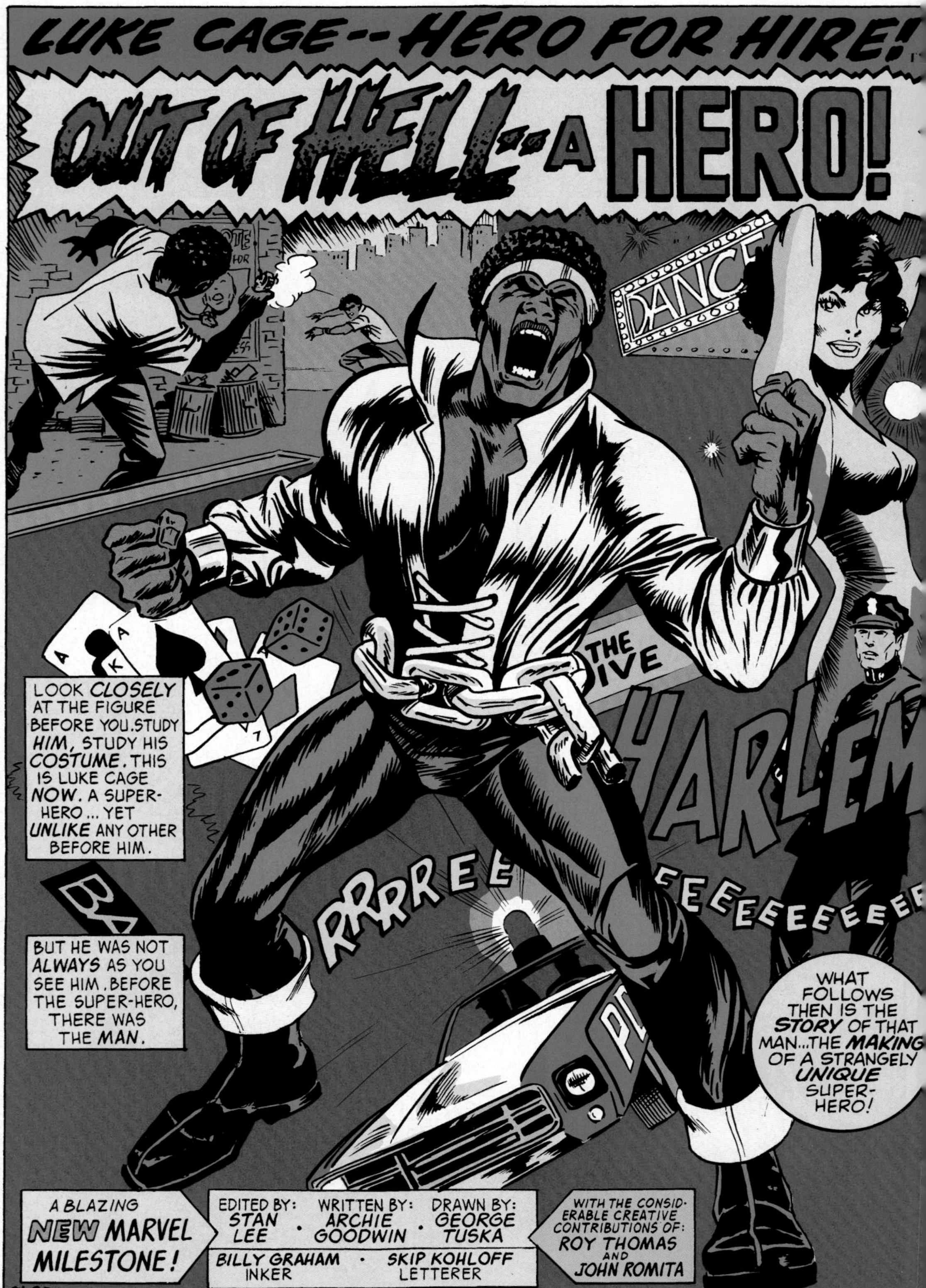
LUKE CAGE--HERO FOR HIRE!
OUT OF HELL--A HERO!
DANCE
THE IVE
HARLEM
LOOK CLOSELY AT THE FIGURE BEFORE YOU. STUDY HIM, STUDY HIS COSTUME. THIS IS LUKE CAGE NOW. A SUPER-HERO... YET UNLIKE ANY OTHER BEFORE HIM.
RRRREEE EEEEEEEEEEEE
BUT HE WAS NOT ALWAYS AS YOU SEE HIM. BEFORE THE SUPER-HERO, THERE WAS THE MAN.
WHAT FOLLOWS THEN IS THE STORY OF THAT MAN...THE MAKING OF A STRANGELY UNIQUE SUPER-HERO!
A BLAZING NEW MARVEL MILESTONE!
EDITED BY: STAN LEE · WRITTEN BY: ARCHIE GOODWIN · DRAWN BY: GEORGE TUSKA
BILLY GRAHAM INKER · SKIP KOHLOFF LETTERER
WITH THE CONSIDERABLE CREATIVE CONTRIBUTIONS OF: ROY THOMAS AND JOHN ROMITA
8632

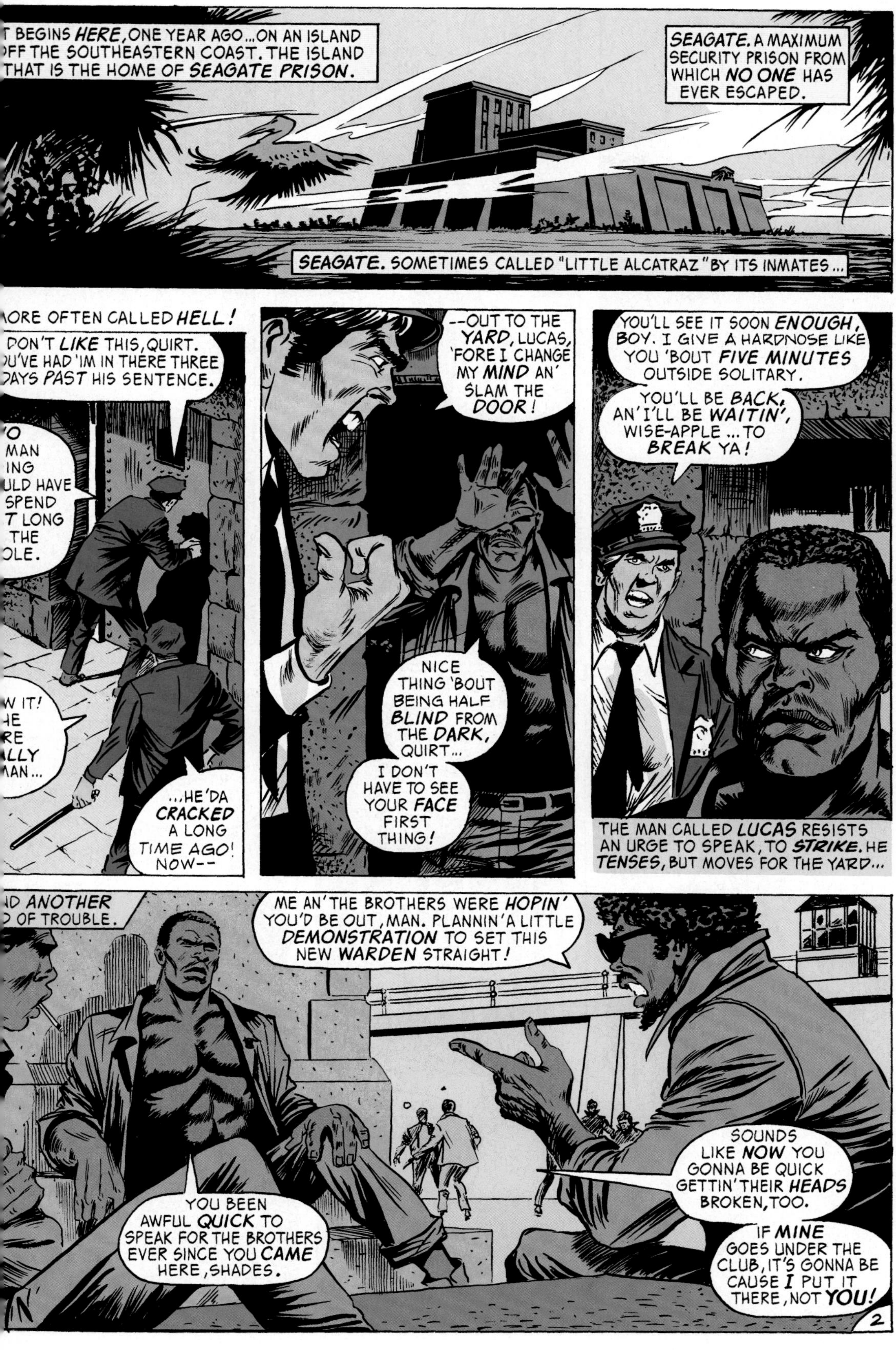
T BEGINS HERE, ONE YEAR AGO... ON AN ISLAND
FF THE SOUTHEASTERN COAST. THE ISLAND
THAT IS THE HOME OF SEAGATE PRISON.
SEAGATE. A MAXIMUM SECURITY PRISON FROM WHICH NO ONE HAS EVER ESCAPED.
SEAGATE. SOMETIMES CALLED "LITTLE ALCATRAZ" BY ITS INMATES...
ORE OFTEN CALLED HELL!
DON'T LIKE THIS, QUIRT. U'VE HAD 'IM IN THERE THREE DAYS PAST HIS SENTENCE.
MAN ING ULD HAVE SPEND T LONG THE OLE.
W IT! HE RE LLY AN...
...HE'DA CRACKED A LONG TIME AGO! NOW--
--OUT TO THE YARD, LUCAS, 'FORE I CHANGE MY MIND AN' SLAM THE DOOR!
NICE THING 'BOUT BEING HALF BLIND FROM THE DARK, QUIRT...
I DON'T HAVE TO SEE YOUR FACE FIRST THING!
YOU'LL SEE IT SOON ENOUGH, BOY. I GIVE A HARDNOSE LIKE YOU 'BOUT FIVE MINUTES OUTSIDE SOLITARY.
YOU'LL BE BACK, AN' I'LL BE WAITIN', WISE-APPLE ... TO BREAK YA!
THE MAN CALLED LUCAS RESISTS AN URGE TO SPEAK, TO STRIKE. HE TENSES, BUT MOVES FOR THE YARD...
D ANOTHER OF TROUBLE.
ME AN' THE BROTHERS WERE HOPIN' YOU'D BE OUT, MAN. PLANNIN' A LITTLE DEMONSTRATION TO SET THIS NEW WARDEN STRAIGHT!
YOU BEEN AWFUL QUICK TO SPEAK FOR THE BROTHERS EVER SINCE YOU CAME HERE, SHADES.
SOUNDS LIKE NOW YOU GONNA BE QUICK GETTIN' THEIR HEADS BROKEN, TOO.
IF MINE GOES UNDER THE CLUB, IT'S GONNA BE CAUSE I PUT IT THERE, NOT YOU!

LOTTA DUDES IN THIS DUMP THINK YOU'RE **SOMETHING**, LUCAS! SHADES NEEDS **YOU** IN TO GET **THEM** WITH US.

MEBBE YOU NEED A LITTLE **SURGERY** TO CUT SOME'A THAT **TOM** AWAY FROM YOUR **SOUL**.

NOW HOW YOU GONNA DO **THAT**, COMANCHE--

--WITH YOUR **CUTTIN'** HAND ALL TIED UP CATCHIN' **TEETH**?

**SHADES** BABY, YOU DON'T HANDLE TH' **DEMONSTRA**- ANY BETTE YOU PICK **SIDEMEN**

--YOU'RE GONNA NEE MORE THA FANCY **SUN- GLASSES** T HIDE BEHIN

NOW STEP **ASIDE**, JIVE- MOUTH!

IF I NEED A **GROUP**, SHADES, **I'LL DO** THE **ORGANIZIN'**.

BUT I DON'T NEED **ANYBODY** OR **ANYTHING**--

--'CEPT **OUT** OF THIS HELLHOLE! AN' BEST CHANCE OF DOIN' **THAT**... IS ON MY **OWN**!

**THERE**, CAP'N RACKHAM!

IT'S ALL THE **EXCUSE** WE NEED TO REALLY **COME DOWN** ON THAT UPPITY--

DON'T GO PUTTIN' **PERSONAL** PLEASURE AHEAD'A **DUTY**, QUIRT. THERE'S **OTHER** POSSIBILITIES.

GET THAT BOY TO MY **OFFICE** ...BUT DO IT **NICE**, HEAR?

AND...

BAD THING, THAT BUSINESS IN THE **YARD**, LUCAS... 'SPECIALLY FOR A MAN WITH **YOUR** RECORD.

'COURSE, WE GOT US KINDA AN **INTERESTIN'** SITUATION HERE --

WHAT WITH THIS NEW **WARDE** COMIN' SHORTLY--

--AN' THAT BUNCH'A **MILITANT** LOOKIN' TO CAUSE **TROUBLE**.

...LIKE **YOU**--WITH NO [NE] FOR THEM SMART-[TALKIN'] **PUNKS**--COULD DO [YOUR]SELF SOME **GOOD.**

[WE] HAVE TO HELP [YOU] LEARN **WHAT** THAT [WITCH] IS UP TO, AN' [WHE]N THEY PLAN TO [MAKE] THEIR **MOVE.**

AN' MAYBE DO **YOU** SOME GOOD WITH THAT NEW **WARDEN,** HUH?

PUBLIC RELATIONS AIN'T MY BAG, CAP'N.

NEITHER IS **INFORMIN'!**

GO **SLOW** WITH THAT HIGH HORSE, BOY. LONER LIKE YOU NEEDS **ANY** BREAK HE CAN **GET.**

WATTA YOU SAY?

YOU SCRATCH **MY** BACK, BOY ...AN' I SCRATCH YOURS.

SORRY, CAP'N, I DON'T [TH]INK **ANYTHING** COULD MAKE [ME] ITCH **THAT** MUCH.

BUT TO BE **SURE,** MAYBE I'LL JUST **SKIP** SHAKIN' YOUR **HAND** WHEN I LEAVE!

**WHAT?! WHY, YOU DIRTY--**

**QUIRT! GET 'IM OUT OF HERE--**

--AN' STRAIGHT BACK INTO THE **HOLE!**

YOU **CALLED** IT, CAP'N!

[CO]ULDN'T **WAIT** TO MOUTH [YO]UR WAY **BACK** TO ME, COULD [YA,] WISE-APPLE?

[OK]AY... [I]T'S [N]O!

YOU ALWAYS **TALK** 'BOUT **BREAKIN'** THAT PUNK, QUIRT.

**THIS** TIME... **DO IT!**

ANY WAY IT TAKES!

...YOU **HEARD** CAP'N RACKHAM UPSTAIRS, MISTER.

WELL, I'M JUST TOO GOOD A MAN TO **DISAPPOINT** 'IM ...

4

...SO WE'RE GONNA **START** WITH A LITTLE **HOMECOMIN'** PARTY!

QUIRT, ARE YOU **NUTS?** NO MATTER **WHAT** THE CAPTAIN SAID--

YOU **CAN'T** TREAT A PRISONER LIKE **THAT!**

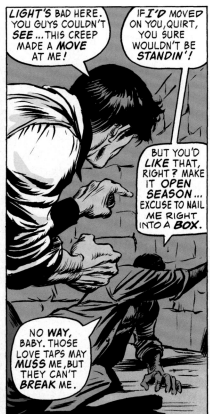

**LIGHT'S** BAD HERE. YOU GUYS COULDN'T **SEE**...THIS CREEP MADE A **MOVE** AT ME!

IF **I'D** MOVED ON YOU, QUIRT, YOU SURE WOULDN'T BE **STANDIN'!**

BUT YOU'D **LIKE** THAT, RIGHT? MAKE IT **OPEN SEASON**... EXCUSE TO NAIL ME RIGHT INTO A **BOX.**

NO **WAY,** BABY. THOSE LOVE TAPS MAY **MUSS** ME, BUT THEY CAN'T **BREAK** ME.

WHY **YOU**--!! SEE **THAT?** STIR-CRAZY PUNK'S TRYIN' IT **AGAIN!**

QUIRT! FOR **CRIPES** SAKE--!

BUT IT **CONTINUES**...

THE UGLY **SOUND** ECHOS THROUGH THE CELL BLOCK... A FLAT, MOIST SOUND OF **FLESH** BEING STRUCK...

...AGAIN AND **AGAIN!** A SOUND TO DRIVE ALL LISTENING INTO A **FRENZY.**

**STOP** IT, YA GUTLESS **BULLS!**

YOU **KNOW** THE MAN CAN'T FIGHT BACK 'GAINST A **GUARD!**

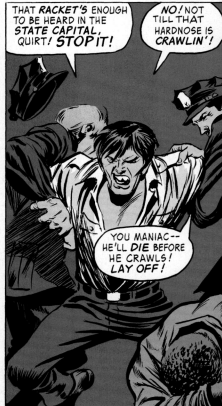

THAT **RACKET'S** ENOUGH TO BE HEARD IN THE **STATE CAPITAL,** QUIRT! **STOP IT!**

**NO!** NOT TILL THAT **HARDNOSE** IS **CRAWLIN'!**

YOU MANIAC-- HE'LL **DIE** BEFORE HE CRAWLS! LAY OFF!

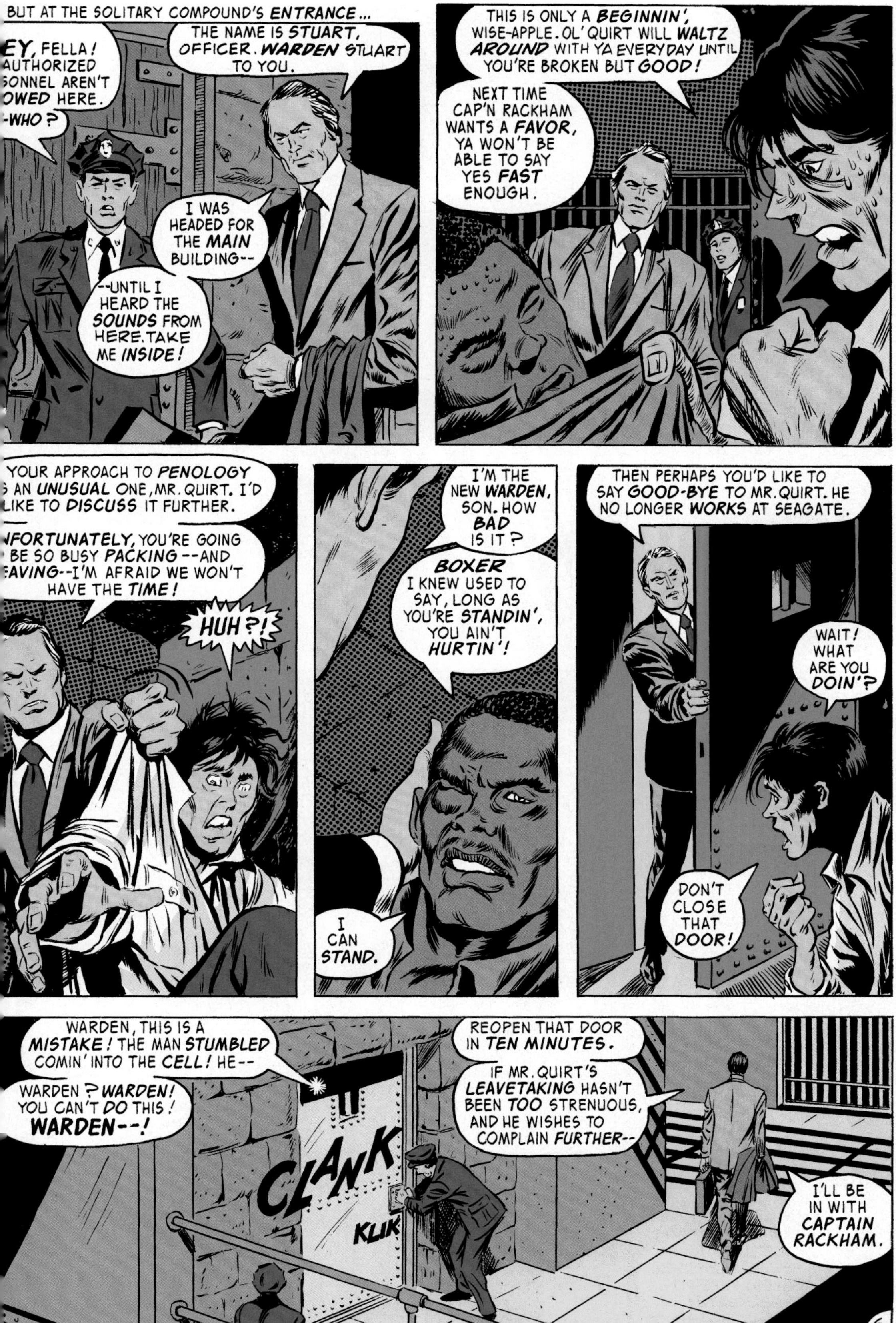
BUT AT THE SOLITARY COMPOUND'S ENTRANCE...
EY, FELLA! AUTHORIZED SONNEL AREN'T OWED HERE. -WHO?
THE NAME IS STUART, OFFICER. WARDEN STUART TO YOU.
I WAS HEADED FOR THE MAIN BUILDING--
--UNTIL I HEARD THE SOUNDS FROM HERE. TAKE ME INSIDE!
THIS IS ONLY A BEGINNIN', WISE-APPLE. OL' QUIRT WILL WALTZ AROUND WITH YA EVERYDAY UNTIL YOU'RE BROKEN BUT GOOD!
NEXT TIME CAP'N RACKHAM WANTS A FAVOR, YA WON'T BE ABLE TO SAY YES FAST ENOUGH.
YOUR APPROACH TO PENOLOGY S AN UNUSUAL ONE, MR. QUIRT. I'D LIKE TO DISCUSS IT FURTHER.
NFORTUNATELY, YOU'RE GOING BE SO BUSY PACKING--AND EAVING--I'M AFRAID WE WON'T HAVE THE TIME!
HUH?!
I'M THE NEW WARDEN, SON. HOW BAD IS IT?
BOXER I KNEW USED TO SAY, LONG AS YOU'RE STANDIN', YOU AIN'T HURTIN'!
I CAN STAND.
THEN PERHAPS YOU'D LIKE TO SAY GOOD-BYE TO MR. QUIRT. HE NO LONGER WORKS AT SEAGATE.
WAIT! WHAT ARE YOU DOIN'?
DON'T CLOSE THAT DOOR!
WARDEN, THIS IS A MISTAKE! THE MAN STUMBLED COMIN' INTO THE CELL! HE--
WARDEN? WARDEN! YOU CAN'T DO THIS! WARDEN--!
CLANK
KLIK
REOPEN THAT DOOR IN TEN MINUTES.
IF MR. QUIRT'S LEAVETAKING HASN'T BEEN TOO STRENUOUS, AND HE WISHES TO COMPLAIN FURTHER--
I'LL BE IN WITH CAPTAIN RACKHAM.
6

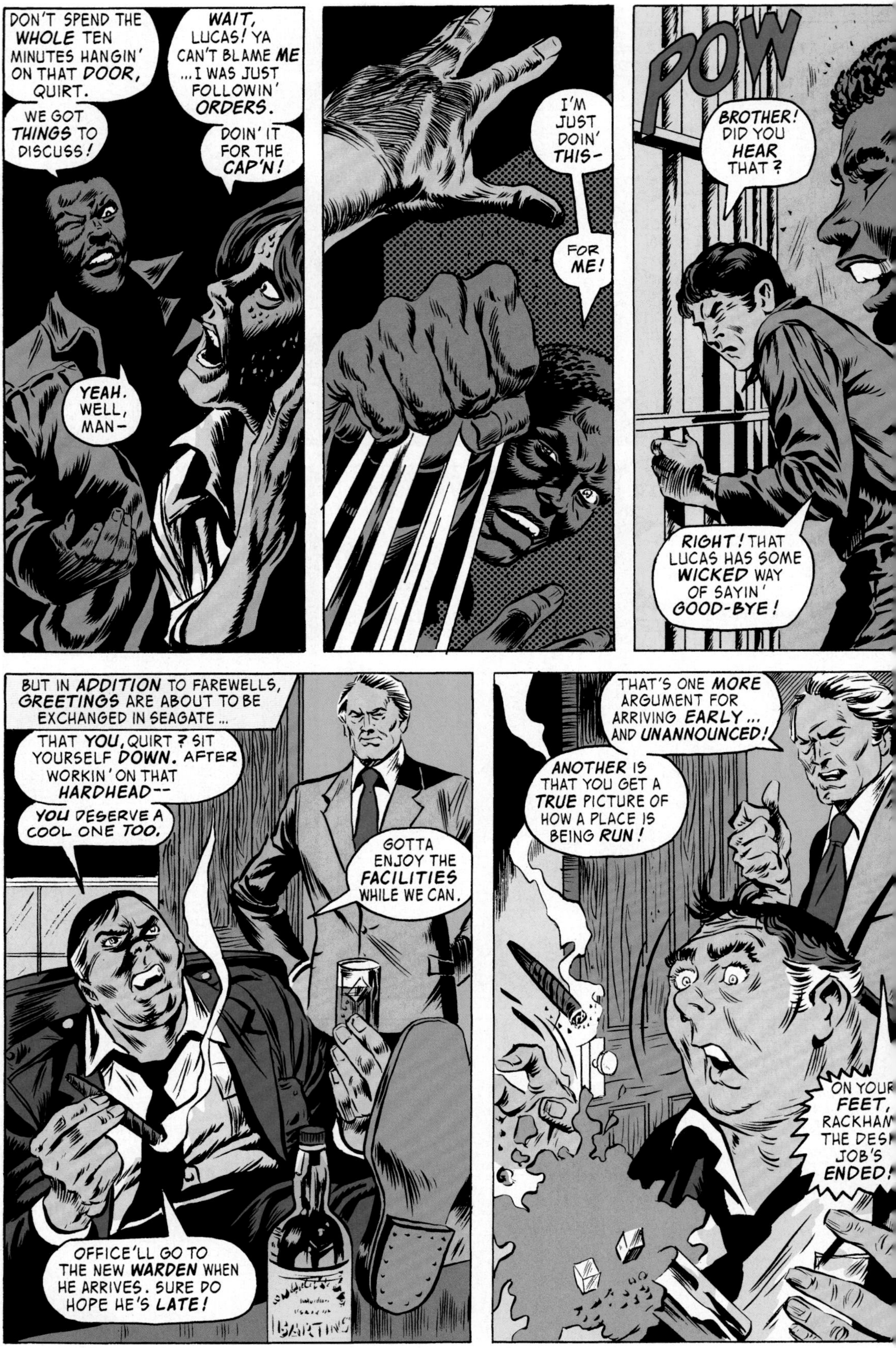

DON'T SPEND THE WHOLE TEN MINUTES HANGIN' ON THAT DOOR, QUIRT.
WE GOT THINGS TO DISCUSS!
WAIT, LUCAS! YA CAN'T BLAME ME ...I WAS JUST FOLLOWIN' ORDERS.
DOIN' IT FOR THE CAP'N!
YEAH. WELL, MAN--
I'M JUST DOIN' THIS-
FOR ME!
POW
BROTHER! DID YOU HEAR THAT?
RIGHT! THAT LUCAS HAS SOME WICKED WAY OF SAYIN' GOOD-BYE!
BUT IN ADDITION TO FAREWELLS, GREETINGS ARE ABOUT TO BE EXCHANGED IN SEAGATE ...
THAT YOU, QUIRT? SIT YOURSELF DOWN. AFTER WORKIN' ON THAT HARDHEAD--
YOU DESERVE A COOL ONE TOO.
GOTTA ENJOY THE FACILITIES WHILE WE CAN.
OFFICE'LL GO TO THE NEW WARDEN WHEN HE ARRIVES. SURE DO HOPE HE'S LATE!
THAT'S ONE MORE ARGUMENT FOR ARRIVING EARLY ... AND UNANNOUNCED!
ANOTHER IS THAT YOU GET A TRUE PICTURE OF HOW A PLACE IS BEING RUN!
ON YOUR FEET, RACKHAM THE DESK JOB'S ENDED!

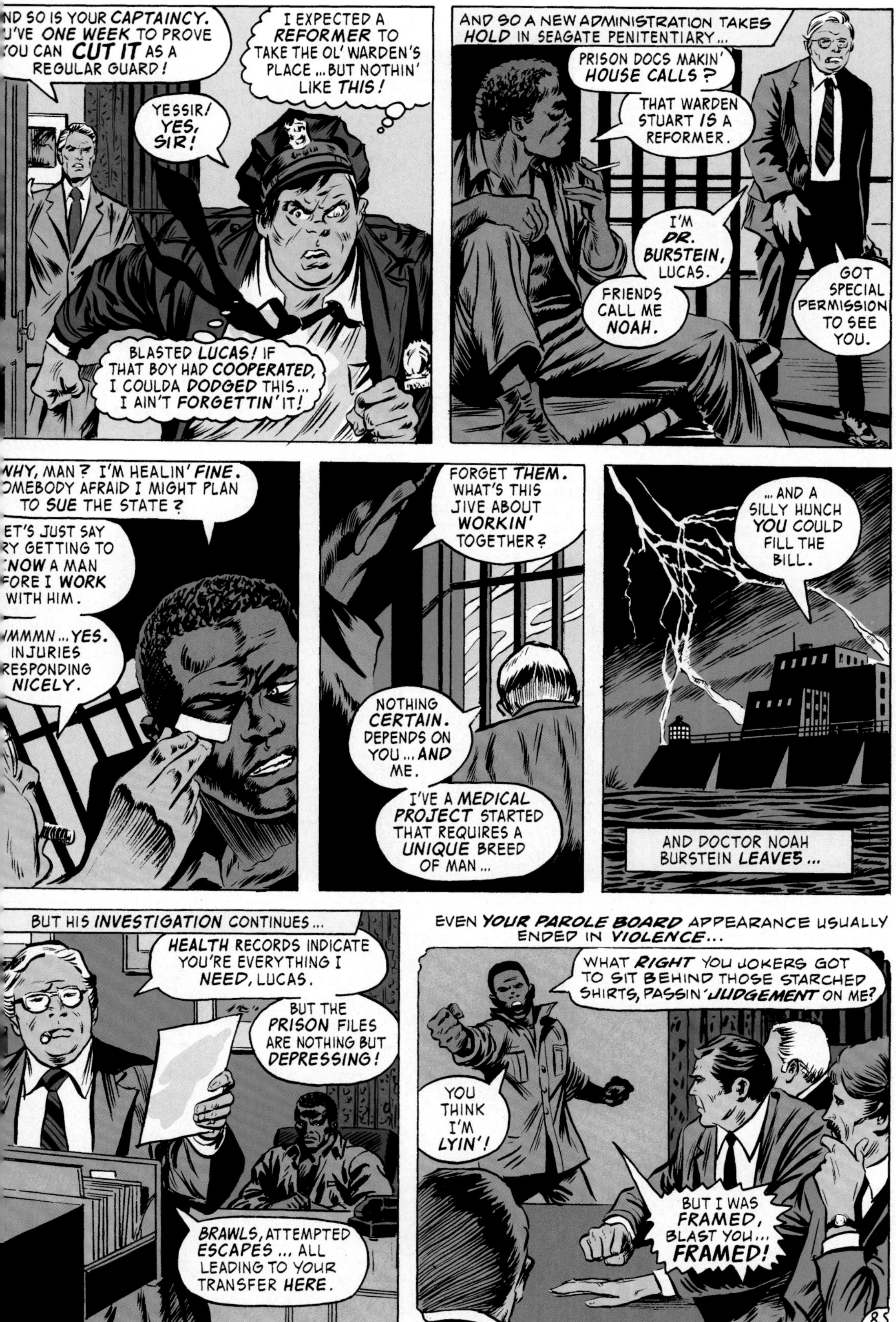
ND SO IS YOUR CAPTAINCY. U'VE ONE WEEK TO PROVE YOU CAN CUT IT AS A REGULAR GUARD!
I EXPECTED A REFORMER TO TAKE THE OL' WARDEN'S PLACE ... BUT NOTHIN' LIKE THIS!
YESSIR! YES, SIR!
BLASTED LUCAS! IF THAT BOY HAD COOPERATED, I COULDA DODGED THIS ... I AIN'T FORGETTIN' IT!
AND SO A NEW ADMINISTRATION TAKES HOLD IN SEAGATE PENITENTIARY ...
PRISON DOCS MAKIN' HOUSE CALLS?
THAT WARDEN STUART IS A REFORMER.
I'M DR. BURSTEIN, LUCAS.
FRIENDS CALL ME NOAH.
GOT SPECIAL PERMISSION TO SEE YOU.
WHY, MAN? I'M HEALIN' FINE. OMEBODY AFRAID I MIGHT PLAN TO SUE THE STATE?
ET'S JUST SAY RY GETTING TO NOW A MAN FORE I WORK WITH HIM.
MMMN ... YES. INJURIES RESPONDING NICELY.
FORGET THEM. WHAT'S THIS JIVE ABOUT WORKIN' TOGETHER?
NOTHING CERTAIN. DEPENDS ON YOU ... AND ME.
I'VE A MEDICAL PROJECT STARTED THAT REQUIRES A UNIQUE BREED OF MAN ...
... AND A SILLY HUNCH YOU COULD FILL THE BILL.
AND DOCTOR NOAH BURSTEIN LEAVES ...
BUT HIS INVESTIGATION CONTINUES ...
HEALTH RECORDS INDICATE YOU'RE EVERYTHING I NEED, LUCAS.
BUT THE PRISON FILES ARE NOTHING BUT DEPRESSING!
BRAWLS, ATTEMPTED ESCAPES ... ALL LEADING TO YOUR TRANSFER HERE.
EVEN YOUR PAROLE BOARD APPEARANCE USUALLY ENDED IN VIOLENCE ...
WHAT RIGHT YOU JOKERS GOT TO SIT BEHIND THOSE STARCHED SHIRTS, PASSIN' JUDGEMENT ON ME?
YOU THINK I'M LYIN'!
BUT I WAS FRAMED, BLAST YOU ... FRAMED!
8.

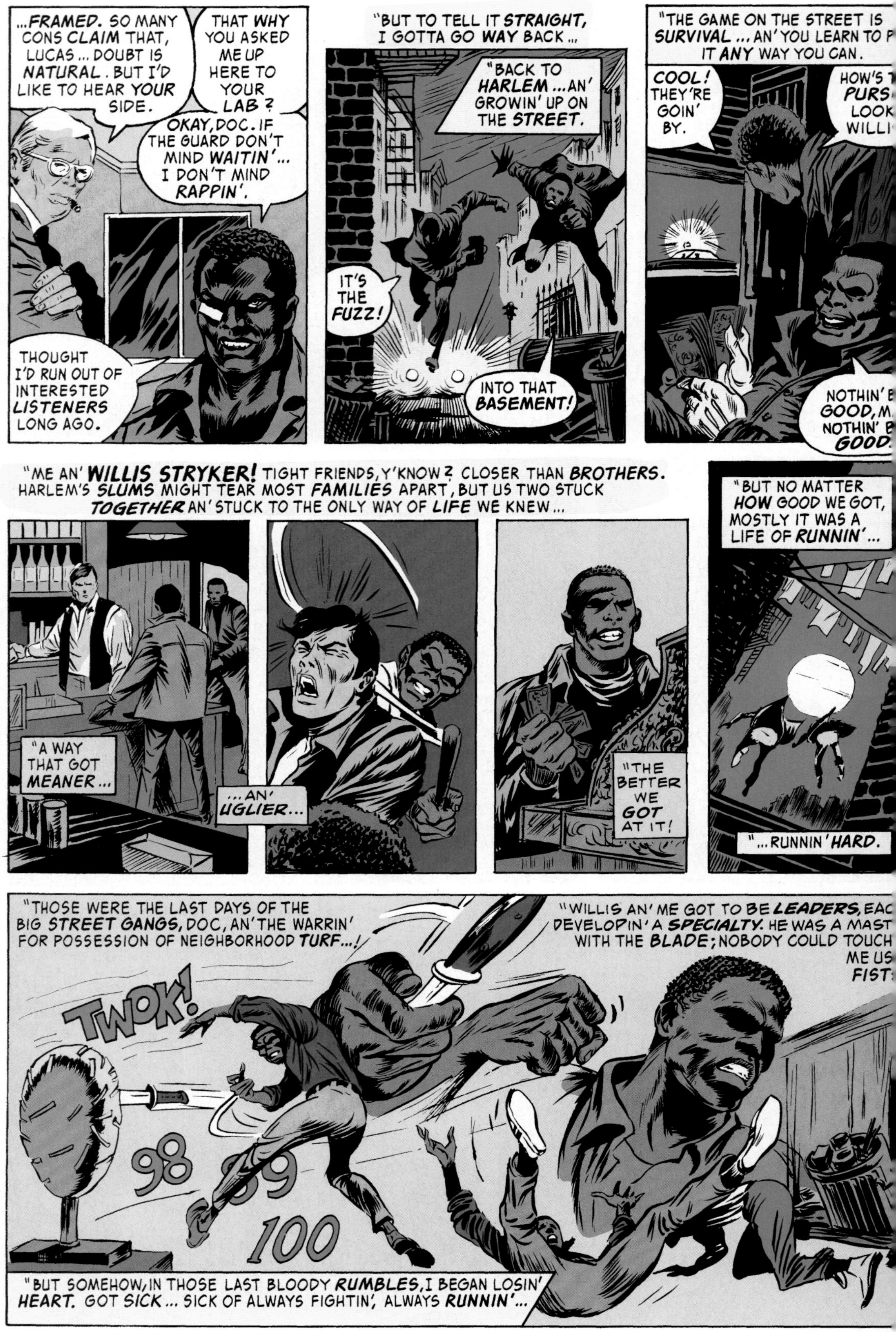
...FRAMED. SO MANY CONS CLAIM THAT, LUCAS ... DOUBT IS NATURAL. BUT I'D LIKE TO HEAR YOUR SIDE.
THAT WHY YOU ASKED ME UP HERE TO YOUR LAB?
OKAY, DOC. IF THE GUARD DON'T MIND WAITIN'... I DON'T MIND RAPPIN'.
THOUGHT I'D RUN OUT OF INTERESTED LISTENERS LONG AGO.
"BUT TO TELL IT STRAIGHT, I GOTTA GO WAY BACK...
"BACK TO HARLEM ... AN' GROWIN' UP ON THE STREET.
IT'S THE FUZZ!
INTO THAT BASEMENT!
"THE GAME ON THE STREET IS SURVIVAL ... AN' YOU LEARN TO P
IT ANY WAY YOU CAN.
COOL! THEY'RE GOIN' BY.
HOW'S T
PURS
LOOK
WILLI
NOTHIN' B
GOOD, M
NOTHIN' B
GOOD.
"ME AN' WILLIS STRYKER! TIGHT FRIENDS, Y'KNOW? CLOSER THAN BROTHERS. HARLEM'S SLUMS MIGHT TEAR MOST FAMILIES APART, BUT US TWO STUCK TOGETHER AN' STUCK TO THE ONLY WAY OF LIFE WE KNEW...
"A WAY THAT GOT MEANER...
...AN' UGLIER...
"THE BETTER WE GOT AT IT!
"BUT NO MATTER HOW GOOD WE GOT, MOSTLY IT WAS A LIFE OF RUNNIN'...
"...RUNNIN' HARD.
"THOSE WERE THE LAST DAYS OF THE BIG STREET GANGS, DOC, AN' THE WARRIN' FOR POSSESSION OF NEIGHBORHOOD TURF...!
"WILLIS AN' ME GOT TO BE LEADERS, EAC
DEVELOPIN' A SPECIALTY. HE WAS A MAST
WITH THE BLADE; NOBODY COULD TOUCH
ME US
FIST
TWOK!
98
99
100
"BUT SOMEHOW, IN THOSE LAST BLOODY RUMBLES, I BEGAN LOSIN' HEART. GOT SICK ... SICK OF ALWAYS FIGHTIN', ALWAYS RUNNIN'...

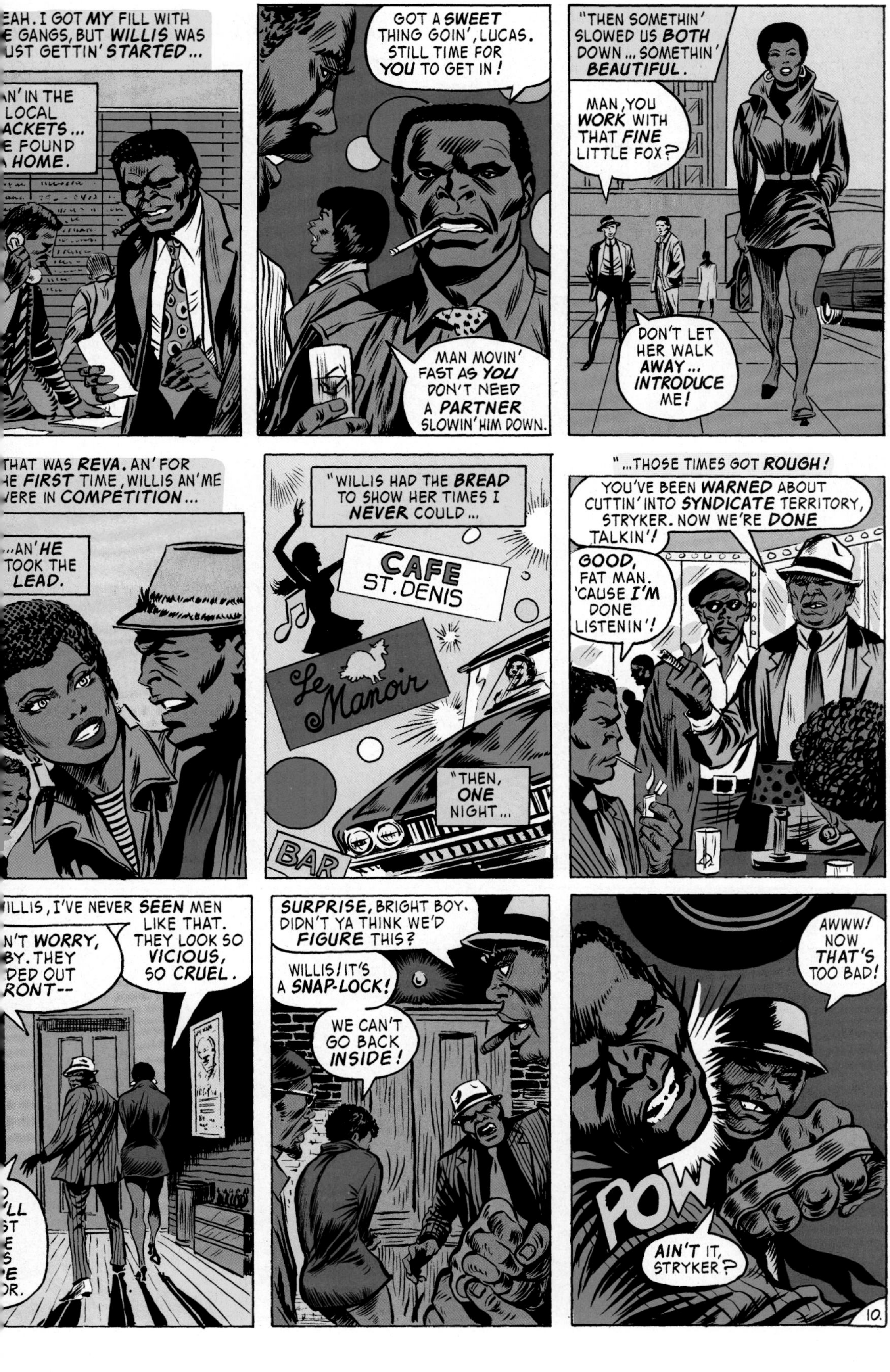
EAH. I GOT MY FILL WITH
E GANGS, BUT WILLIS WAS
UST GETTIN' STARTED...
N' IN THE LOCAL ACKETS... E FOUND HOME.
GOT A SWEET THING GOIN', LUCAS. STILL TIME FOR YOU TO GET IN!
MAN MOVIN' FAST AS YOU DON'T NEED A PARTNER SLOWIN' HIM DOWN.
"THEN SOMETHIN' SLOWED US BOTH DOWN... SOMETHIN' BEAUTIFUL.
MAN, YOU WORK WITH THAT FINE LITTLE FOX?
DON'T LET HER WALK AWAY... INTRODUCE ME!
THAT WAS REVA. AN' FOR
HE FIRST TIME, WILLIS AN' ME
VERE IN COMPETITION...
...AN' HE TOOK THE LEAD.
"WILLIS HAD THE BREAD TO SHOW HER TIMES I NEVER COULD...
CAFE ST. DENIS
Le Manoir
BAR
"THEN, ONE NIGHT...
"...THOSE TIMES GOT ROUGH!
YOU'VE BEEN WARNED ABOUT CUTTIN' INTO SYNDICATE TERRITORY, STRYKER. NOW WE'RE DONE TALKIN'!
GOOD, FAT MAN. 'CAUSE I'M DONE LISTENIN'!
WILLIS, I'VE NEVER SEEN MEN LIKE THAT. THEY LOOK SO VICIOUS, SO CRUEL.
N'T WORRY, BY. THEY DED OUT RONT--
SURPRISE, BRIGHT BOY. DIDN'T YA THINK WE'D FIGURE THIS?
WILLIS! IT'S A SNAP-LOCK!
WE CAN'T GO BACK INSIDE!
AWWW! NOW THAT'S TOO BAD!
POW
AIN'T IT, STRYKER?
10.

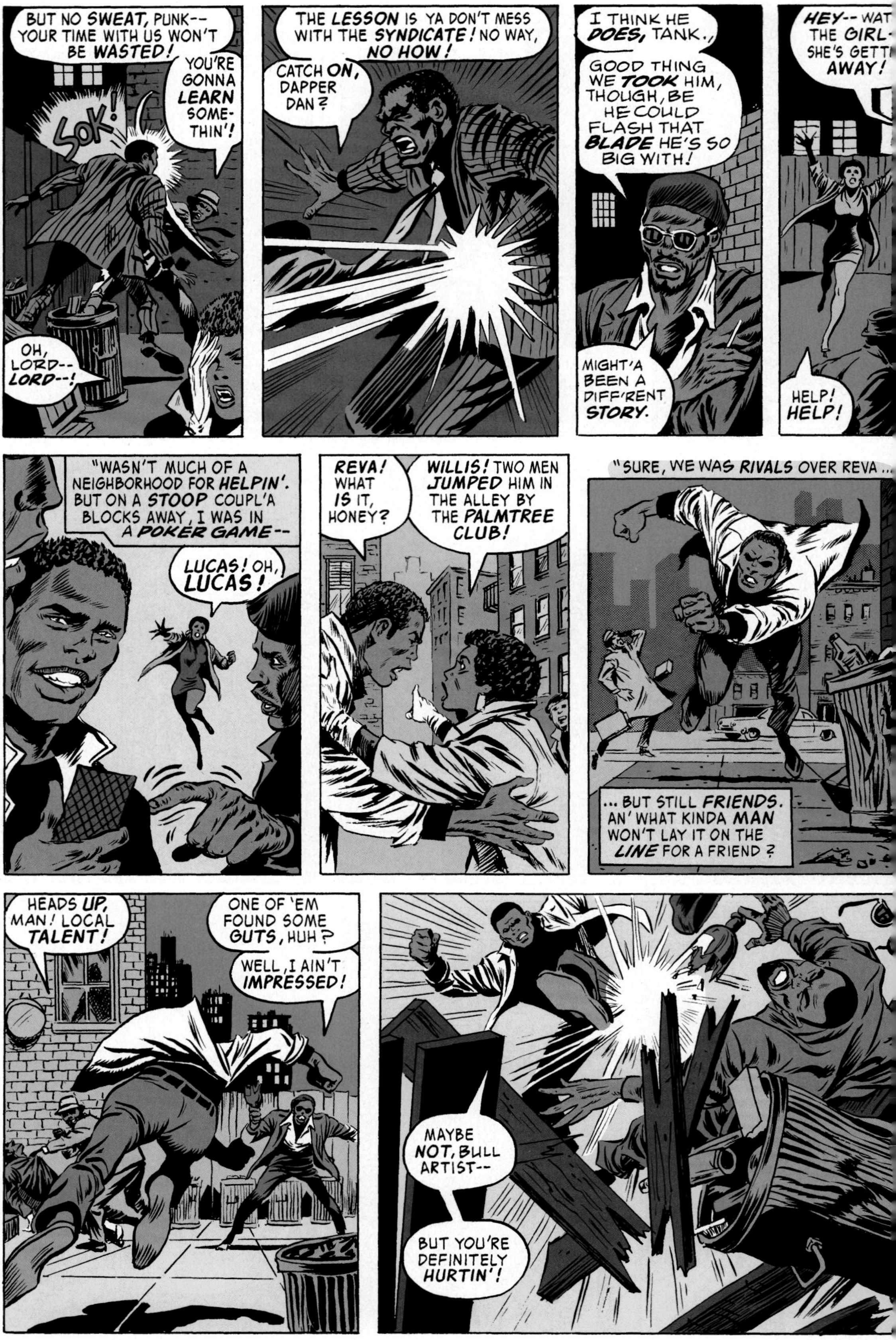
BUT NO SWEAT, PUNK-- YOUR TIME WITH US WON'T BE WASTED!
YOU'RE GONNA LEARN SOME-THIN'!
SOK!
OH, LORD-- LORD--!
THE LESSON IS YA DON'T MESS WITH THE SYNDICATE! NO WAY, NO HOW!
CATCH ON, DAPPER DAN?
I THINK HE DOES, TANK.,
GOOD THING WE TOOK HIM, THOUGH, BE HE COULD FLASH THAT BLADE HE'S SO BIG WITH!
MIGHT'A BEEN A DIFF'RENT STORY.
HEY-- WAT THE GIRL-- SHE'S GETT AWAY!
HELP! HELP!
"WASN'T MUCH OF A NEIGHBORHOOD FOR HELPIN'. BUT ON A STOOP COUPL'A BLOCKS AWAY, I WAS IN A POKER GAME--
LUCAS! OH, LUCAS!
REVA! WHAT IS IT, HONEY?
WILLIS! TWO MEN JUMPED HIM IN THE ALLEY BY THE PALMTREE CLUB!
"SURE, WE WAS RIVALS OVER REVA...
...BUT STILL FRIENDS. AN' WHAT KINDA MAN WON'T LAY IT ON THE LINE FOR A FRIEND?
HEADS UP, MAN! LOCAL TALENT!
ONE OF 'EM FOUND SOME GUTS, HUH?
WELL, I AIN'T IMPRESSED!
MAYBE NOT, BULL ARTIST--
BUT YOU'RE DEFINITELY HURTIN'!

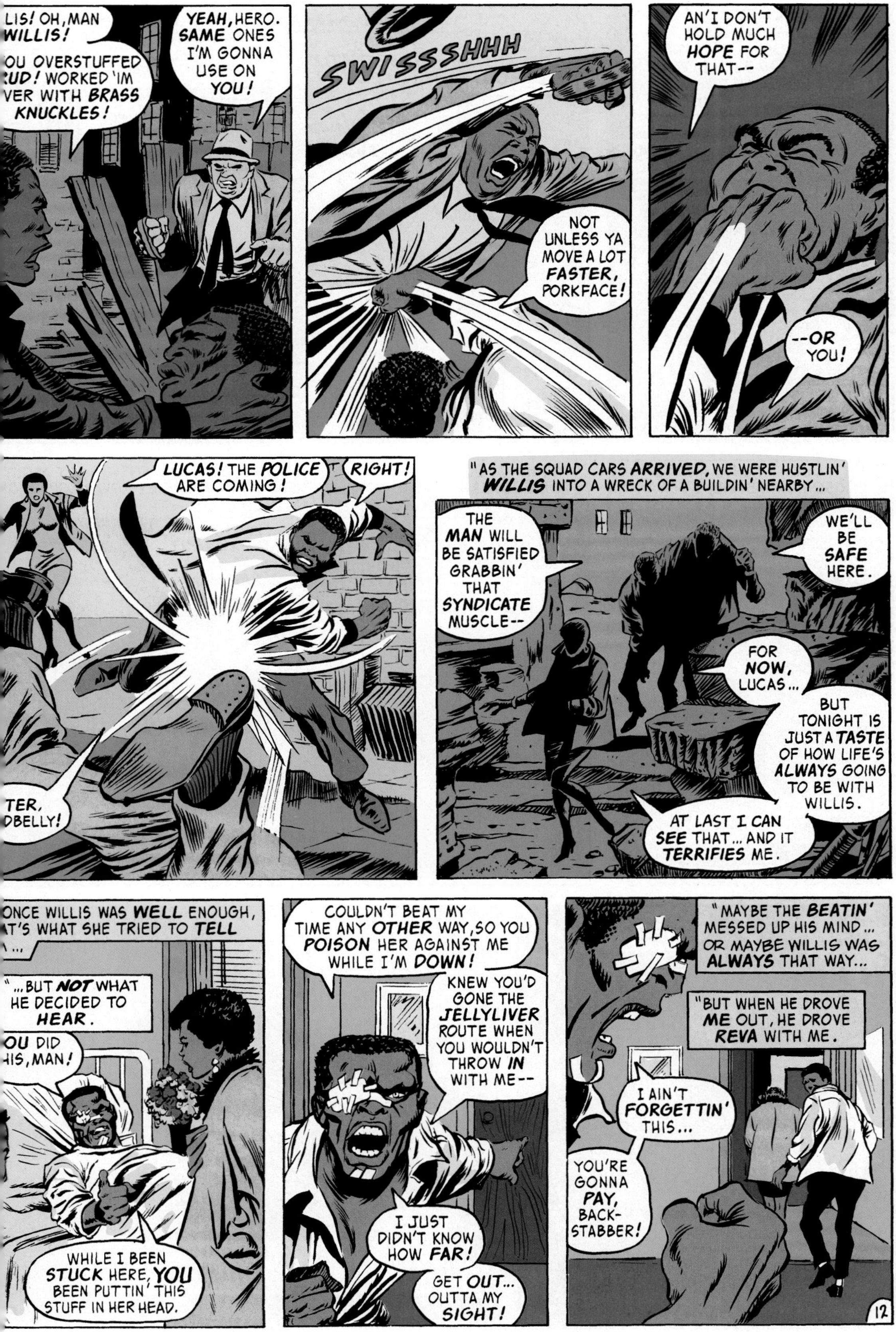
LIS! OH, MAN WILLIS!
OU OVERSTUFFED RUD! WORKED 'IM VER WITH BRASS KNUCKLES!
YEAH, HERO. SAME ONES I'M GONNA USE ON YOU!
SWISSSHHH
NOT UNLESS YA MOVE A LOT FASTER, PORKFACE!
AN' I DON'T HOLD MUCH HOPE FOR THAT--
--OR YOU!
LUCAS! THE POLICE ARE COMING!
RIGHT!
TER, DBELLY!
"AS THE SQUAD CARS ARRIVED, WE WERE HUSTLIN' WILLIS INTO A WRECK OF A BUILDIN' NEARBY...
THE MAN WILL BE SATISFIED GRABBIN' THAT SYNDICATE MUSCLE--
WE'LL BE SAFE HERE.
FOR NOW, LUCAS...
BUT TONIGHT IS JUST A TASTE OF HOW LIFE'S ALWAYS GOING TO BE WITH WILLIS.
AT LAST I CAN SEE THAT... AND IT TERRIFIES ME.
ONCE WILLIS WAS WELL ENOUGH, T'S WHAT SHE TRIED TO TELL ...
"...BUT NOT WHAT HE DECIDED TO HEAR.
OU DID HIS, MAN!
WHILE I BEEN STUCK HERE, YOU BEEN PUTTIN' THIS STUFF IN HER HEAD.
COULDN'T BEAT MY TIME ANY OTHER WAY, SO YOU POISON HER AGAINST ME WHILE I'M DOWN!
KNEW YOU'D GONE THE JELLYLIVER ROUTE WHEN YOU WOULDN'T THROW IN WITH ME--
I JUST DIDN'T KNOW HOW FAR!
GET OUT... OUTTA MY SIGHT!
"MAYBE THE BEATIN' MESSED UP HIS MIND... OR MAYBE WILLIS WAS ALWAYS THAT WAY...
"BUT WHEN HE DROVE ME OUT, HE DROVE REVA WITH ME.
I AIN'T FORGETTIN' THIS...
YOU'RE GONNA PAY, BACK-STABBER!
12

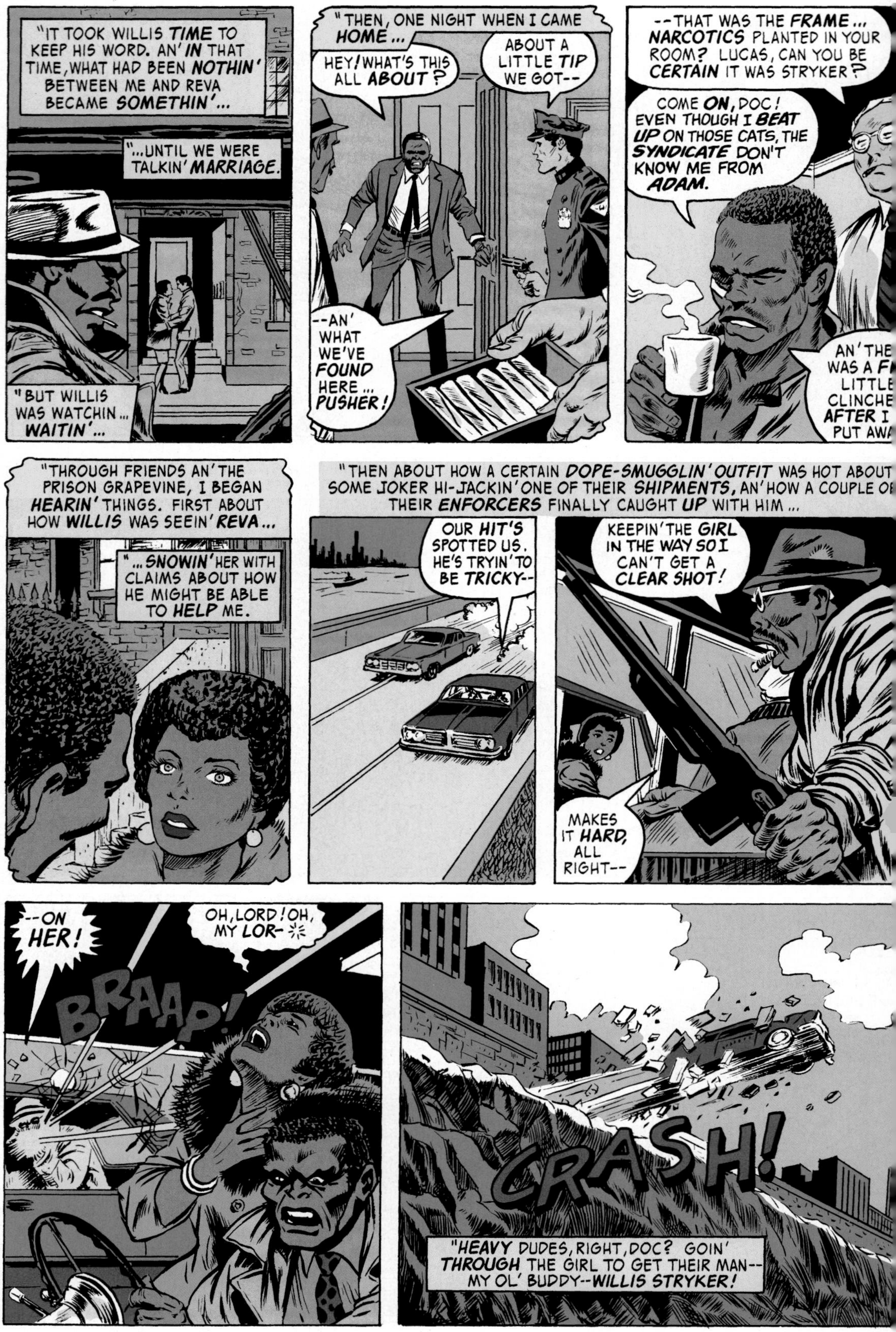
"IT TOOK WILLIS TIME TO KEEP HIS WORD. AN' IN THAT TIME, WHAT HAD BEEN NOTHIN' BETWEEN ME AND REVA BECAME SOMETHIN'...
"...UNTIL WE WERE TALKIN' MARRIAGE.
"BUT WILLIS WAS WATCHIN... WAITIN'...
"THEN, ONE NIGHT WHEN I CAME HOME...
HEY! WHAT'S THIS ALL ABOUT?
ABOUT A LITTLE TIP WE GOT--
--AN' WHAT WE'VE FOUND HERE... PUSHER!
--THAT WAS THE FRAME... NARCOTICS PLANTED IN YOUR ROOM? LUCAS, CAN YOU BE CERTAIN IT WAS STRYKER?
COME ON, DOC! EVEN THOUGH I BEAT UP ON THOSE CATS, THE SYNDICATE DON'T KNOW ME FROM ADAM.
AN' THE WAS A F LITTLE CLINCHE AFTER I PUT AWA
"THROUGH FRIENDS AN' THE PRISON GRAPEVINE, I BEGAN HEARIN' THINGS. FIRST ABOUT HOW WILLIS WAS SEEIN' REVA...
"...SNOWIN' HER WITH CLAIMS ABOUT HOW HE MIGHT BE ABLE TO HELP ME.
"THEN ABOUT HOW A CERTAIN DOPE-SMUGGLIN' OUTFIT WAS HOT ABOUT SOME JOKER HI-JACKIN' ONE OF THEIR SHIPMENTS, AN' HOW A COUPLE OF THEIR ENFORCERS FINALLY CAUGHT UP WITH HIM...
OUR HIT'S SPOTTED US. HE'S TRYIN' TO BE TRICKY--
KEEPIN' THE GIRL IN THE WAY SO I CAN'T GET A CLEAR SHOT!
MAKES IT HARD, ALL RIGHT--
--ON HER!
OH, LORD! OH, MY LOR-
BRAAAP!
CRASH!
"HEAVY DUDES, RIGHT, DOC? GOIN' THROUGH THE GIRL TO GET THEIR MAN-- MY OL' BUDDY--WILLIS STRYKER!

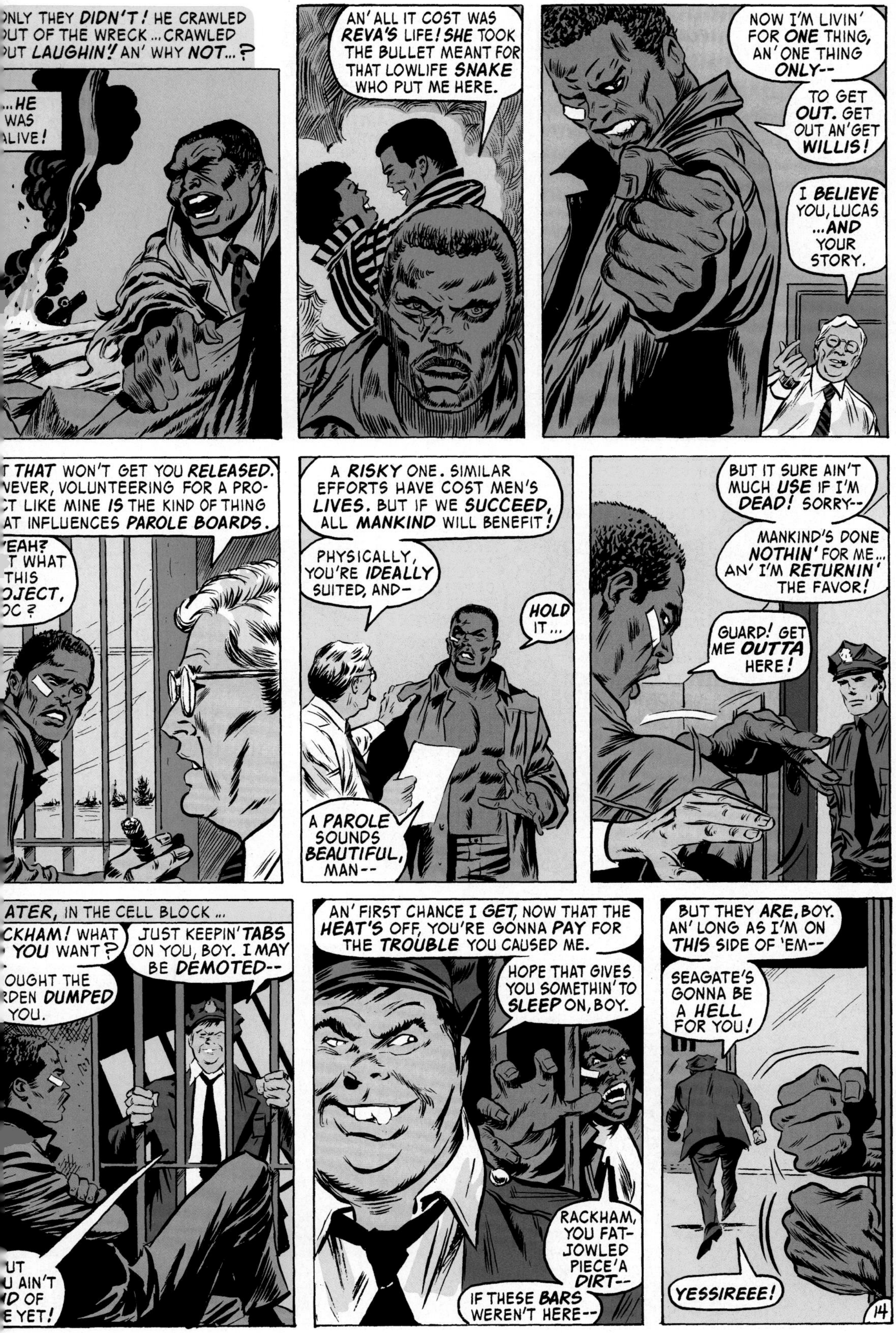

ONLY THEY DIDN'T! HE CRAWLED OUT OF THE WRECK... CRAWLED OUT LAUGHIN'! AN' WHY NOT...?
...HE WAS ALIVE!
AN' ALL IT COST WAS REVA'S LIFE! SHE TOOK THE BULLET MEANT FOR THAT LOWLIFE SNAKE WHO PUT ME HERE.
NOW I'M LIVIN' FOR ONE THING, AN' ONE THING ONLY--
TO GET OUT. GET OUT AN' GET WILLIS!
I BELIEVE YOU, LUCAS ...AND YOUR STORY.
T THAT WON'T GET YOU RELEASED. WEVER, VOLUNTEERING FOR A PRO- CT LIKE MINE IS THE KIND OF THING AT INFLUENCES PAROLE BOARDS.
YEAH? T WHAT THIS OJECT, OC?
A RISKY ONE. SIMILAR EFFORTS HAVE COST MEN'S LIVES. BUT IF WE SUCCEED, ALL MANKIND WILL BENEFIT!
PHYSICALLY, YOU'RE IDEALLY SUITED, AND-
HOLD IT...
A PAROLE SOUNDS BEAUTIFUL, MAN--
BUT IT SURE AIN'T MUCH USE IF I'M DEAD! SORRY--
MANKIND'S DONE NOTHIN' FOR ME... AN' I'M RETURNIN' THE FAVOR!
GUARD! GET ME OUTTA HERE!
ATER, IN THE CELL BLOCK...
CKHAM! WHAT YOU WANT?
JUST KEEPIN' TABS ON YOU, BOY. I MAY BE DEMOTED--
OUGHT THE RDEN DUMPED YOU.
UT U AIN'T D OF E YET!
AN' FIRST CHANCE I GET, NOW THAT THE HEAT'S OFF, YOU'RE GONNA PAY FOR THE TROUBLE YOU CAUSED ME.
HOPE THAT GIVES YOU SOMETHIN' TO SLEEP ON, BOY.
RACKHAM, YOU FAT-JOWLED PIECE'A DIRT--
IF THESE BARS WEREN'T HERE--
BUT THEY ARE, BOY. AN' LONG AS I'M ON THIS SIDE OF 'EM--
SEAGATE'S GONNA BE A HELL FOR YOU!
YESSIREEE!
14

MOTHER OF--! IS THIS HOW IT'S GONNA BE? CAGED LIKE AN ANIMAL--

AN' SOME MEAN-MINDED FOOL LIKE RACKHAM PLAYIN' KEEPER?!

I'M SICK OF IT!

SICK TO DEATH! GONNA BUST OUT OF HERE, EVEN IF IT KILLS M--

WAIT! AN ESCAPE COULD DO THAT CERTAIN. IF I'M LAYIN' MY LIFE ON THE LINE--

IT OUGHTA BE WHERE THE ODDS ARE NOT IN MY FAVOR!

GUARD, GUAR[D] GET DOC BURSTEIN! TELL HE'S HIS GU[INEA] PIG AF[TER] ALL

KLA[NK] CLAN[K]

AND NEXT DAY, IN A SELDOM-USED SECTION OF THE PRISON...

MAN DESERVES HIS PAROLE JUST FOR WALKIN' IN HERE, DOC.

LOOKS LIKE STRICTLY MAD SCIENTIST TERRITORY-- INCLUDIN' A BATHTUB FOR FRANKENSTEIN'S MONSTER!

THE EQUIPMENT WAS MADE BY STARK INDUSTRIES, LUCAS--

AS PART OF A RESEARCH GRANT GIVEN ME.

IT'S AN ELECTRO-BIOCHEMICAL SYSTEM FOR STIMULATING HUMAN CELL REGENERATION.

IF SUCCESSFUL, IT COULD COUNTER THE DAMAGES OF ALMOST ANY DISEASE--PERHAPS EVEN AGING.

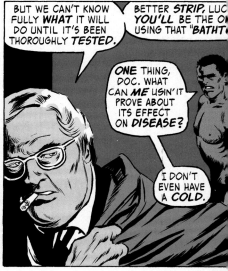

BUT WE CAN'T KNOW FULLY WHAT IT WILL DO UNTIL IT'S BEEN THOROUGHLY TESTED.

BETTER STRIP, LUC[AS] YOU'LL BE THE O[NE] USING THAT "BATHT[UB]"

ONE THING, DOC. WHAT CAN ME USIN' IT PROVE ABOUT ITS EFFECT ON DISEASE?

I DON'T EVEN HAVE A COLD.

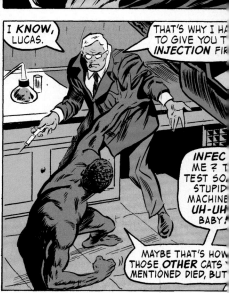

I KNOW, LUCAS.

THAT'S WHY I HA[VE] TO GIVE YOU T[HIS] INJECTION FIR[ST]

INFEC[T] ME ? T[O] TEST SO[ME] STUPID MACHINE UH-UH[,] BABY!

MAYBE THAT'S HOW THOSE OTHER CATS [I] MENTIONED DIED, BUT

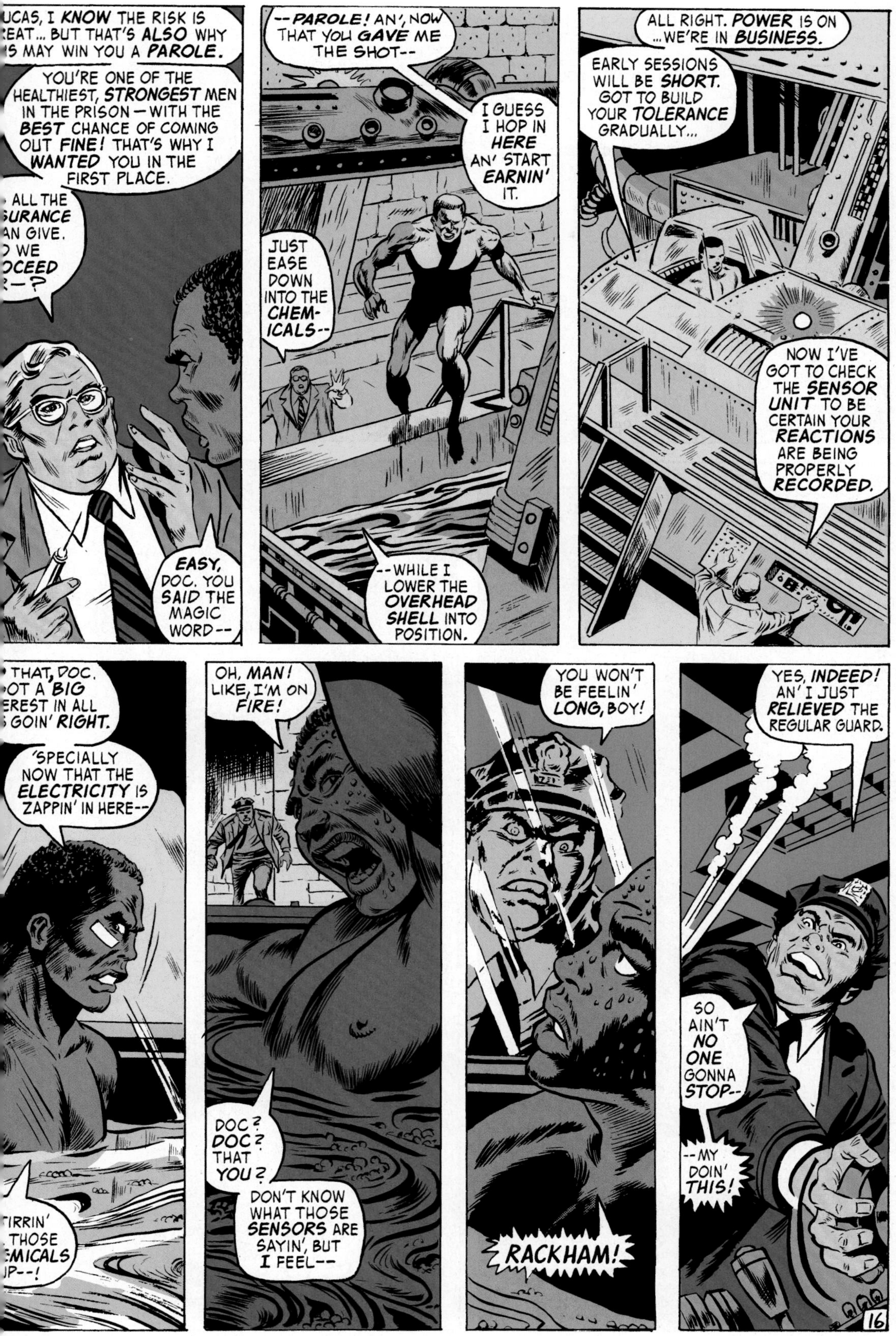
UCAS, I KNOW THE RISK IS
EAT... BUT THAT'S ALSO WHY
S MAY WIN YOU A PAROLE.
YOU'RE ONE OF THE HEALTHIEST, STRONGEST MEN IN THE PRISON — WITH THE BEST CHANCE OF COMING OUT FINE! THAT'S WHY I WANTED YOU IN THE FIRST PLACE.
ALL THE SURANCE AN GIVE. O WE OCEED —?
EASY, DOC. YOU SAID THE MAGIC WORD--
--PAROLE! AN', NOW THAT YOU GAVE ME THE SHOT--
I GUESS I HOP IN HERE AN' START EARNIN' IT.
JUST EASE DOWN INTO THE CHEMICALS--
--WHILE I LOWER THE OVERHEAD SHELL INTO POSITION.
ALL RIGHT. POWER IS ON ...WE'RE IN BUSINESS.
EARLY SESSIONS WILL BE SHORT. GOT TO BUILD YOUR TOLERANCE GRADUALLY...
NOW I'VE GOT TO CHECK THE SENSOR UNIT TO BE CERTAIN YOUR REACTIONS ARE BEING PROPERLY RECORDED.
THAT, DOC. OT A BIG EREST IN ALL GOIN' RIGHT.
'SPECIALLY NOW THAT THE ELECTRICITY IS ZAPPIN' IN HERE--
TIRRIN' THOSE EMICALS UP--!
OH, MAN! LIKE, I'M ON FIRE!
DOC? DOC? THAT YOU?
DON'T KNOW WHAT THOSE SENSORS ARE SAYIN', BUT I FEEL--
YOU WON'T BE FEELIN' LONG, BOY!
RACKHAM!
YES, INDEED! AN' I JUST RELIEVED THE REGULAR GUARD.
SO AIN'T NO ONE GONNA STOP--
--MY DOIN' THIS!
16

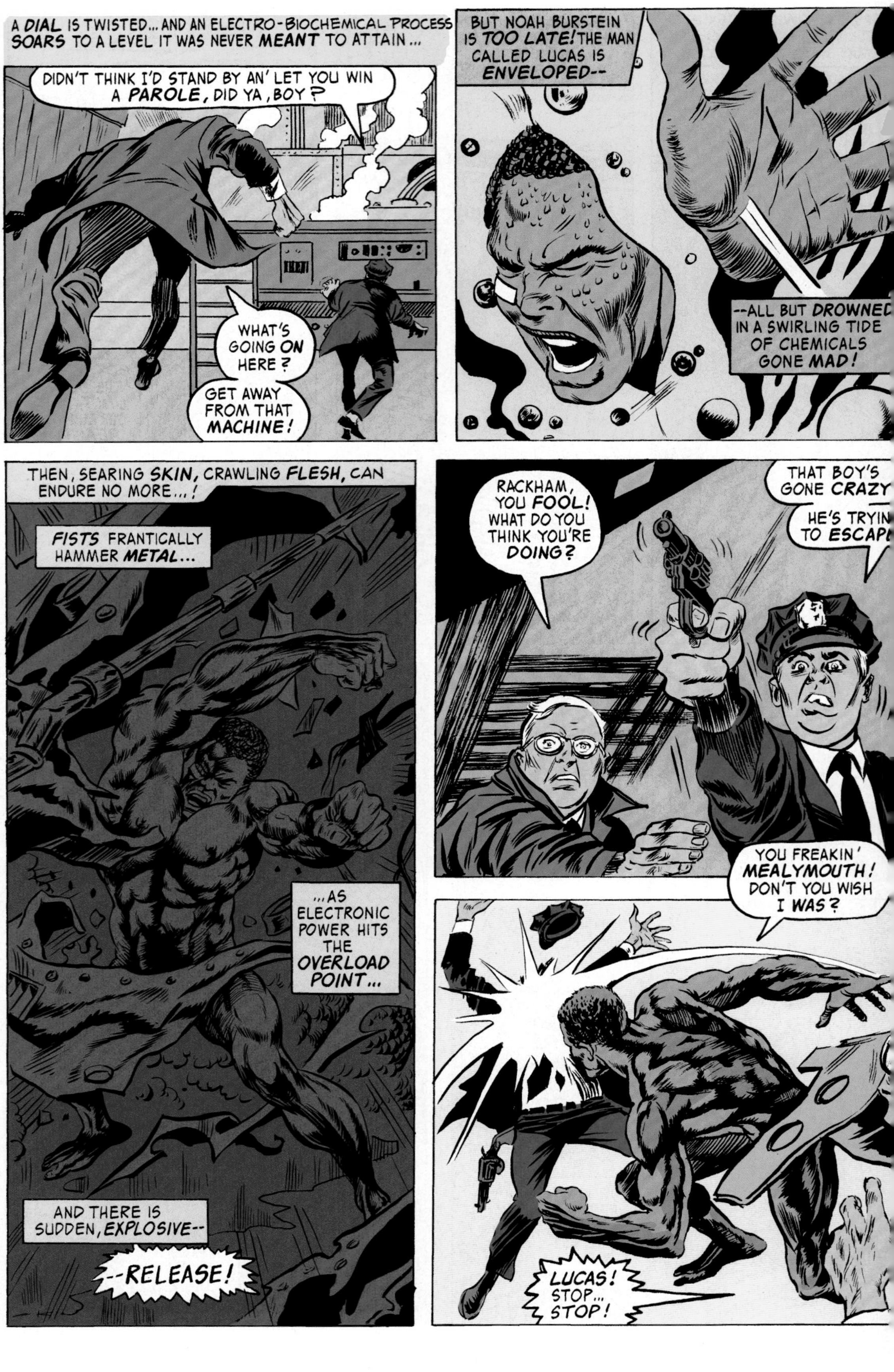
A DIAL IS TWISTED... AND AN ELECTRO-BIOCHEMICAL PROCESS SOARS TO A LEVEL IT WAS NEVER MEANT TO ATTAIN...
DIDN'T THINK I'D STAND BY AN' LET YOU WIN A PAROLE, DID YA, BOY?
WHAT'S GOING ON HERE?
GET AWAY FROM THAT MACHINE!
BUT NOAH BURSTEIN IS TOO LATE! THE MAN CALLED LUCAS IS ENVELOPED--
--ALL BUT DROWNED IN A SWIRLING TIDE OF CHEMICALS GONE MAD!
THEN, SEARING SKIN, CRAWLING FLESH, CAN ENDURE NO MORE...!
FISTS FRANTICALLY HAMMER METAL...
...AS ELECTRONIC POWER HITS THE OVERLOAD POINT...
AND THERE IS SUDDEN, EXPLOSIVE--
--RELEASE!
RACKHAM, YOU FOOL! WHAT DO YOU THINK YOU'RE DOING?
THAT BOY'S GONE CRAZY
HE'S TRYIN TO ESCAP
YOU FREAKIN' MEALYMOUTH! DON'T YOU WISH I WAS?
LUCAS! STOP... STOP!

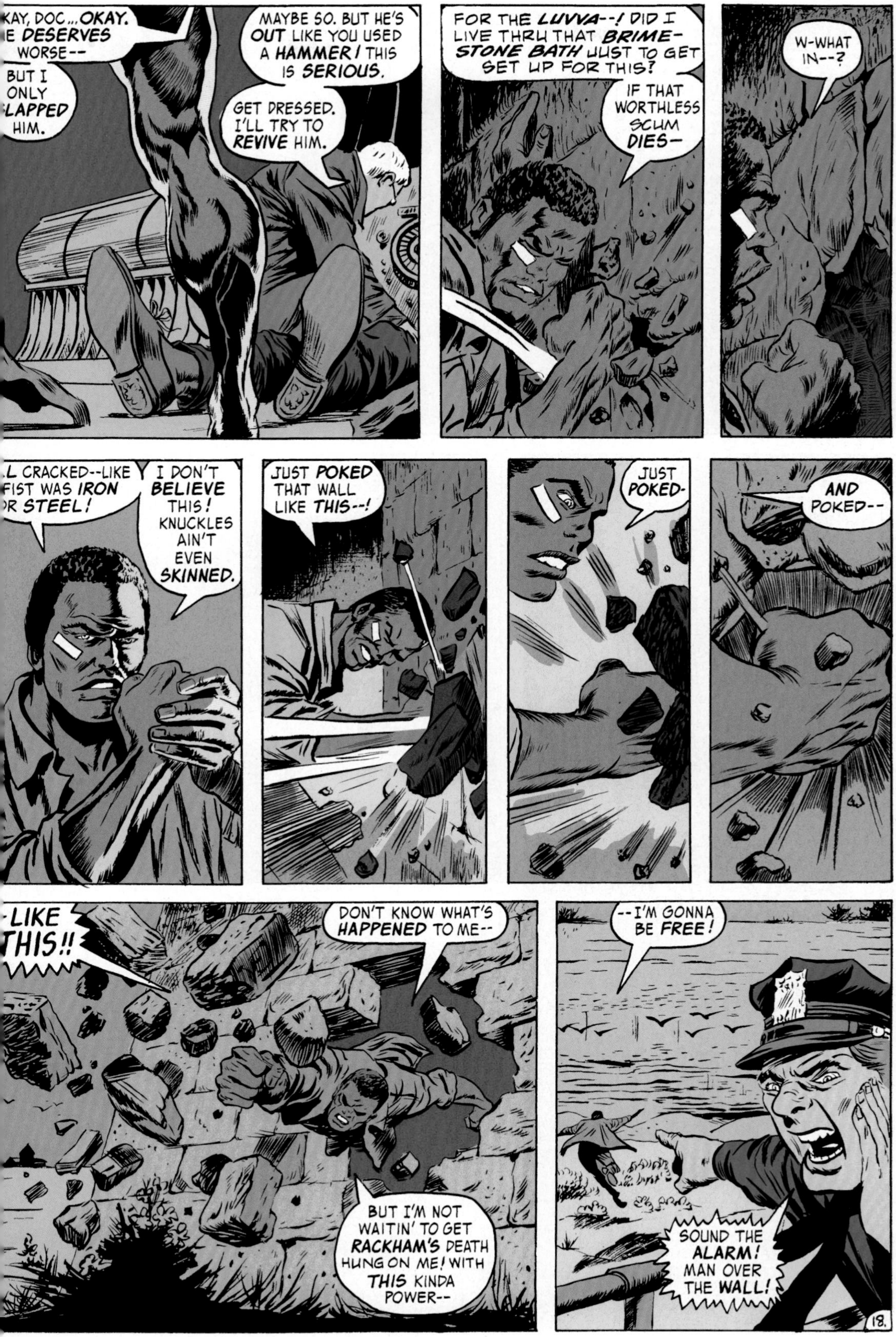
KAY, DOC...OKAY. E DESERVES WORSE--
BUT I ONLY LAPPED HIM.
MAYBE SO. BUT HE'S OUT LIKE YOU USED A HAMMER! THIS IS SERIOUS.
GET DRESSED. I'LL TRY TO REVIVE HIM.
FOR THE LUVVA--! DID I LIVE THRU THAT BRIME-STONE BATH JUST TO GET SET UP FOR THIS?
IF THAT WORTHLESS SCUM DIES--
W-WHAT IN--?
.L CRACKED--LIKE FIST WAS IRON OR STEEL!
I DON'T BELIEVE THIS! KNUCKLES AIN'T EVEN SKINNED.
JUST POKED THAT WALL LIKE THIS--!
JUST POKED-
AND POKED--
-LIKE THIS!!
DON'T KNOW WHAT'S HAPPENED TO ME--
BUT I'M NOT WAITIN' TO GET RACKHAM'S DEATH HUNG ON ME! WITH THIS KINDA POWER--
--I'M GONNA BE FREE!
SOUND THE ALARM! MAN OVER THE WALL!
18.

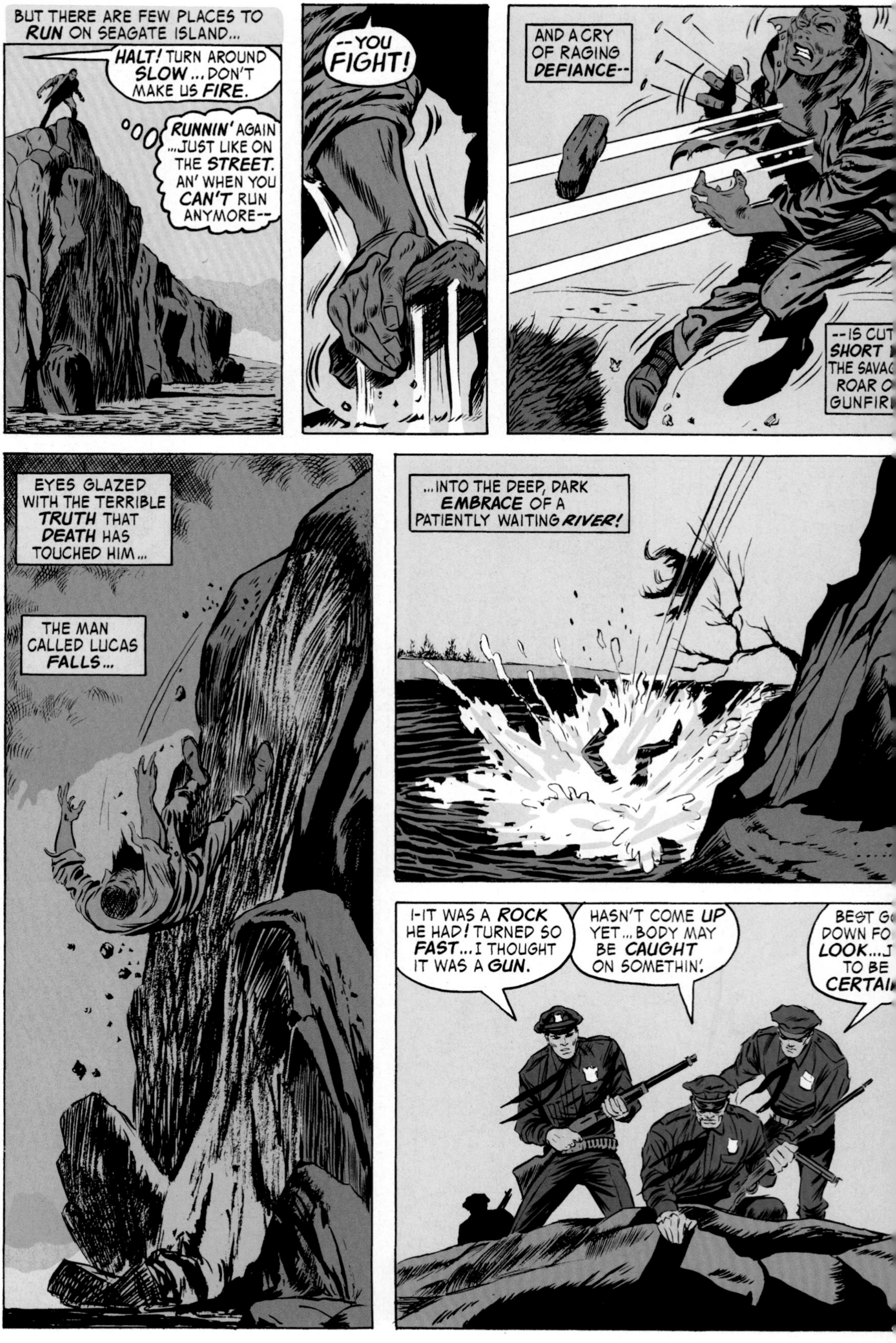
BUT THERE ARE FEW PLACES TO RUN ON SEAGATE ISLAND...
HALT! TURN AROUND SLOW... DON'T MAKE US FIRE.
RUNNIN' AGAIN ...JUST LIKE ON THE STREET. AN' WHEN YOU CAN'T RUN ANYMORE--
--YOU FIGHT!
AND A CRY OF RAGING DEFIANCE--
--IS CUT SHORT THE SAVAG ROAR O GUNFIR
EYES GLAZED WITH THE TERRIBLE TRUTH THAT DEATH HAS TOUCHED HIM...
THE MAN CALLED LUCAS FALLS...
...INTO THE DEEP, DARK EMBRACE OF A PATIENTLY WAITING RIVER!
I-IT WAS A ROCK HE HAD! TURNED SO FAST... I THOUGHT IT WAS A GUN.
HASN'T COME UP YET... BODY MAY BE CAUGHT ON SOMETHIN'.
BEST G DOWN FO LOOK... TO BE CERTAI

...ONLY **YARDS** FROM WHERE THE GUARDS PEER, STRONG [CU]RRENTS THRUST A **FORM**, LAZURUS-LIKE, TO THE SURFACE.

[T]HOUGHT I [WA]S **DEAD**...! [FEL]T THOSE [BU]LLETS [HI]T ME!

[BUT] THERE'S [ONL]Y THESE [BRU]ISES!

MY WHOLE **BODY'S** JUST LIKE MY **FISTS**...**HARD**! HARD AS **STEEL**!

DOC'S MACHINE WORKED ON MY **BODY'S CELLS** ALL RIGHT... CHANGED 'EM SO I AIN'T **HUMAN** ANYMORE!

LOOK AT THIS **SHIRT**... CAUGHT ON THE BRANCH WHEN HE **FELL**.

TIDE MAY HAVE CARRIED OFF HIS **BODY**, BUT ALL THOSE **HOLES** ANSWER ANY QUESTION 'BOUT HIS BEIN' **ALIVE**!

THERE'S **ONE** FILE--

--THEY CAN MARK **CLOSED**!

[IS] **THIS** WHAT IT COMES TO, [YE]AH BURSTEIN? YOU START [OU]T TO **SAVE** MANKIND--

[AN]D END UP WITH [ON]E MAN DRIVEN [T]O HIS **DEATH**.

[WHE]RE[V]ER YOU [A]RE, [LUC]AS... [SOR]RY.

EVERYONE'S **GIVIN'** UP! WON'T BE LONG TILL **DARK**.

IF I CAN **COOL** IT TILL **THEN**--

AND, WITH **NIGHTFALL**...

A **BOAT**! MAN, YOU'RE GONNA **MAKE** IT...

THEY MUST FEEL **CERTAIN** I'M DEAD, OR ELSE THIS'D **NEVER** BE HERE!

THE MAN CALLED LUCAS MOVES IN DARKNESS TO THE **MAINLAND**...

...AND HERE BEGINS LONG **MONTHS** OF WORKING HIS WAY **NORTH**.

NO SMALL TASK FOR A MAN OFFICIALLY **DEAD**. A MAN WITHOUT MODERN SOCIETY'S CARDS OF **IDENTITY**...

A MAN FOREVER SET **APART** FROM OTHERS BY FANTASTIC CHEMISTRY GONE BERSERK. A MAN SUSTAINED SOLELY BY A DRIVING NEED FOR ...**REVENGE**!

20

NEW YORK! BACK LIKE YOU ALWAYS *DREAMED* IT, MAN--

ONLY YOU'RE A WALKIN' *SIDESHOW* WITH POWER YOU DON'T *USE*, FOR FEAR OF DRAWIN' *ATTENTION*--

--AN' NEAR *BUSTED* 'CAUSE YOU CAN'T RISK A REGULAR *JOB* EITHER!

BUT TO FIND *WILLIS* IS GONNA TAKE *BREAD* AN'--

HEY! WHAT'RE THEY *SERVIN'* IN THERE SENDS YOU *FLYIN'* OUT LIKE THAT?

YA STUPID, FLEABITTEN *BUM*--

I'M SERVIN' *THIS* TO ANYBODY IN MY *WAY!*

BAM!

YEAH, BABY? WELL, HERE'S YOUR *TIP!*

FELLA, I CAN'T THANK YOU *ENOUGH*... THAT WAS OUR DAY'S *TAKE* HE HAD!

YOU DODGED THAT *SHOT* AN' NAILED HIM LIKE A REAL *SUPER-HERO!*

NOT MANY PEOPLE *NOWADAYS* WOULD TAKE A CHANCE LIKE *THAT*--

AND I WANT TO SHOW MY *GRATITUDE!*

AND... THE DUDE AT THAT DINER WAS *ALL RIGHT* NOT ONLY GAVE ME A *CASH REWARD*--

--BUT AN *IDEA* HOW TO TURN WHAT I GOT *GOIN'* FOR ME INTO A *LIVIN'!*

AN' TH' *COSTUM* SHOPS PLACE STAR

MOD FLAI

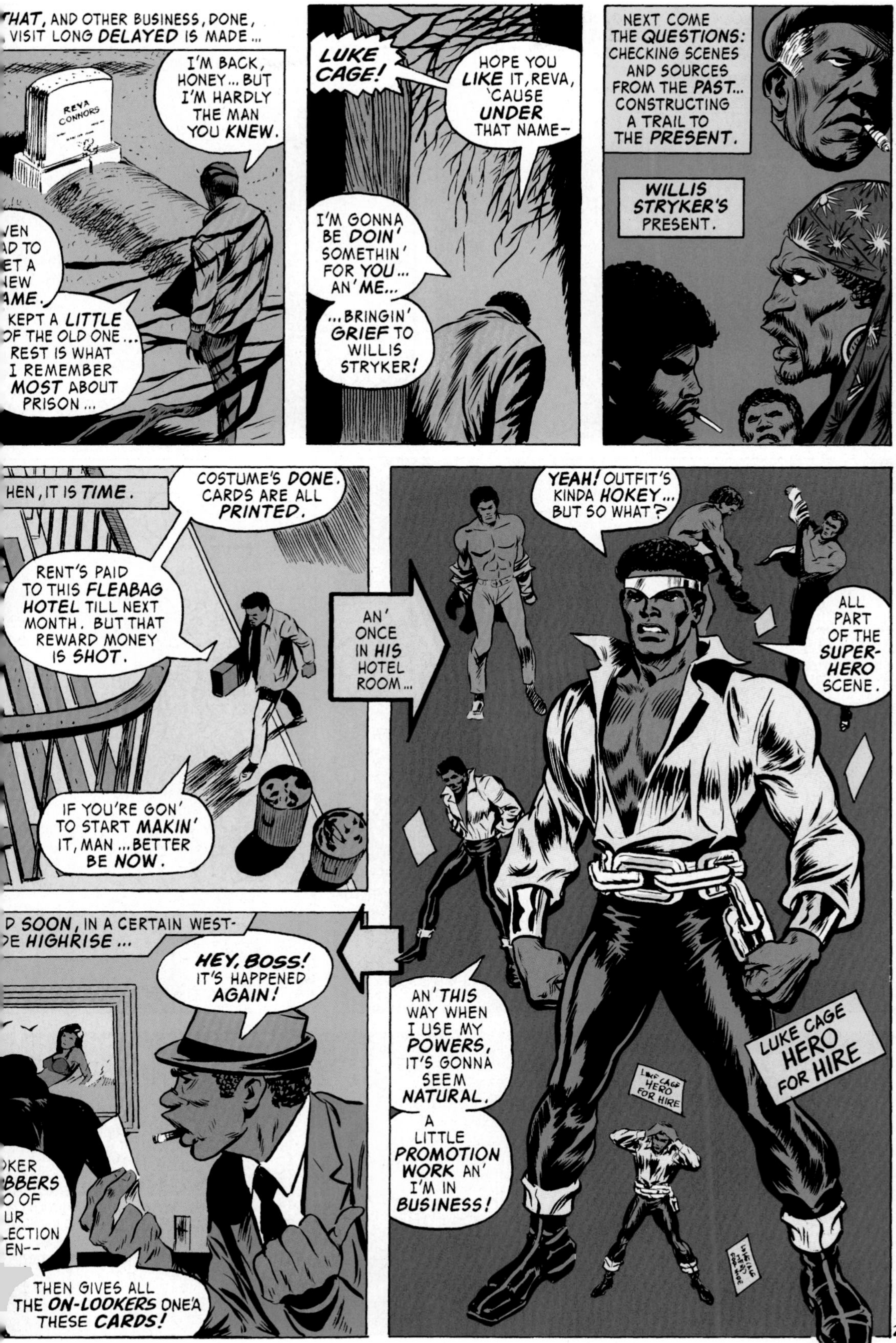
THAT, AND OTHER BUSINESS, DONE, VISIT LONG DELAYED IS MADE...
REVA CONNORS
I'M BACK, HONEY... BUT I'M HARDLY THE MAN YOU KNEW.
VEN AD TO ET A NEW AME.
KEPT A LITTLE OF THE OLD ONE... REST IS WHAT I REMEMBER MOST ABOUT PRISON...
LUKE CAGE!
HOPE YOU LIKE IT, REVA, 'CAUSE UNDER THAT NAME–
I'M GONNA BE DOIN' SOMETHIN' FOR YOU... AN' ME...
...BRINGIN' GRIEF TO WILLIS STRYKER!
NEXT COME THE QUESTIONS: CHECKING SCENES AND SOURCES FROM THE PAST... CONSTRUCTING A TRAIL TO THE PRESENT.
WILLIS STRYKER'S PRESENT.
HEN, IT IS TIME.
COSTUME'S DONE. CARDS ARE ALL PRINTED.
RENT'S PAID TO THIS FLEABAG HOTEL TILL NEXT MONTH. BUT THAT REWARD MONEY IS SHOT.
IF YOU'RE GON' TO START MAKIN' IT, MAN... BETTER BE NOW.
AN' ONCE IN HIS HOTEL ROOM...
YEAH! OUTFIT'S KINDA HOKEY... BUT SO WHAT?
ALL PART OF THE SUPER-HERO SCENE.
AN' THIS WAY WHEN I USE MY POWERS, IT'S GONNA SEEM NATURAL.
A LITTLE PROMOTION WORK AN' I'M IN BUSINESS!
LUKE CAGE HERO FOR HIRE
LUKE CAGE HERO FOR HIRE
D SOON, IN A CERTAIN WEST-DE HIGHRISE...
HEY, BOSS! IT'S HAPPENED AGAIN!
OKER BBERS O OF UR LECTION EN--
THEN GIVES ALL THE ON-LOOKERS ONE'A THESE CARDS!

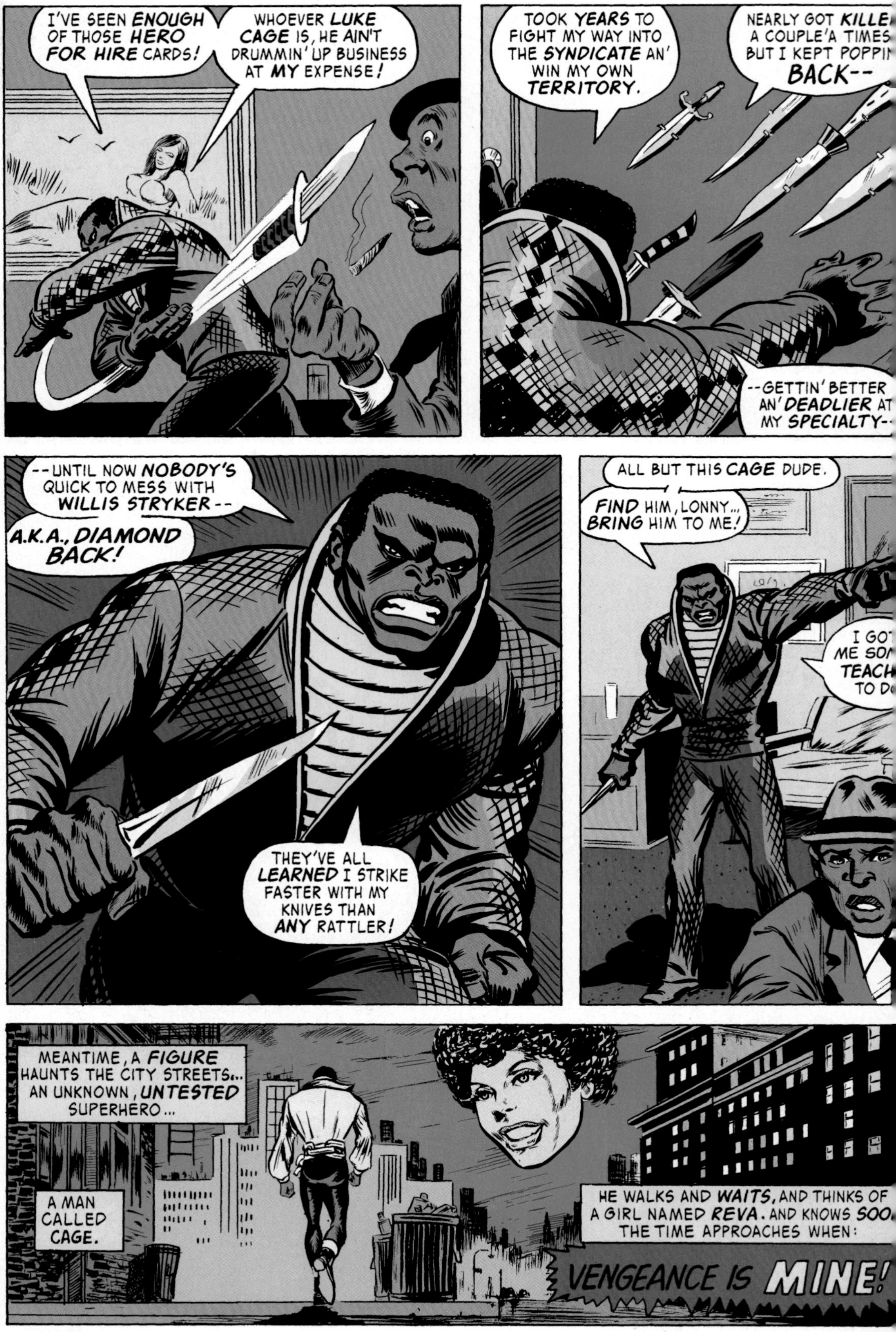
I'VE SEEN ENOUGH OF THOSE HERO FOR HIRE CARDS!
WHOEVER LUKE CAGE IS, HE AIN'T DRUMMIN' UP BUSINESS AT MY EXPENSE!
TOOK YEARS TO FIGHT MY WAY INTO THE SYNDICATE AN' WIN MY OWN TERRITORY.
NEARLY GOT KILLE A COUPLE'A TIMES BUT I KEPT POPPI BACK--
--GETTIN' BETTER AN' DEADLIER AT MY SPECIALTY--
--UNTIL NOW NOBODY'S QUICK TO MESS WITH WILLIS STRYKER--
A.K.A., DIAMOND BACK!
THEY'VE ALL LEARNED I STRIKE FASTER WITH MY KNIVES THAN ANY RATTLER!
ALL BUT THIS CAGE DUDE.
FIND HIM, LONNY... BRING HIM TO ME!
I GOT ME SO TEACH TO D
MEANTIME, A FIGURE HAUNTS THE CITY STREETS... AN UNKNOWN, UNTESTED SUPERHERO...
A MAN CALLED CAGE.
HE WALKS AND WAITS, AND THINKS OF A GIRL NAMED REVA. AND KNOWS SOO THE TIME APPROACHES WHEN:
VENGEANCE IS MINE!